The Making of a Manager

Guidelines to His Selection and Promotion

Felix M. Lopez

American Management Association, Inc.

18170

International standard book number: 0-8144-5220-5
Library of Congress catalog card number: 77-119383

FIRST PRINTING

To Virginia and Flix

Preface

THIS book focuses exclusively on one subject, the manager. It deals with such considerations as what he is, what he does, and where he does it; how he is identified, chosen, promoted, motivated, and rewarded. I found that this ambitious undertaking could be managed successfully only by writing for a specific reader, by adopting a particular orientation, and by treating the subject matter selectively.

The reader I chose to address is the organization chief executive. As I wrote, I imagined that I was fortunate enough to sequester a president in his office for a whole afternoon, canceling his appointments, cutting off his phone, and locking his in-basket in his desk. Of course, it was a little dark in my imaginary room, so that I was not quite sure whether he was the head of a business corporation, a government agency, a university, or a hospital. It really didn't matter because, whichever he was, he would have a deep concern for picking effective subordinate executives. And what I would have to say would be of interest to him.

This choice of reader dictated the style and format of my presentation. It meant that I would have to cover certain material that would be quite familiar to personnel managers and management-development directors. At the same time, since I was addressing a president, I would have to try not to treat the subject too superficially nor to talk down to him. It also meant eschewing the customary documentation, footnotes, and journal references that are considered essential by social scientists. But just to show that I still retain respect for scholarly traditions, I would include some references that seemed particularly useful to the presentation. Because it appeared to me to be so basic yet so frequently omitted, I would also attempt to present a theoretical framework within which to develop the personnel system recommended later.

This book is oriented quite plainly toward the future, toward the last 30 years of this century. It is not, therefore, a compendium of present and past managerial selection practices. They are described and analyzed only in sufficient detail to underscore their good points and to expose their deficiencies. The result is neither a textbook nor a manual. It is rather a treatise that challenges many of the traditional notions of organizational and managerial behavior. The ideas presented, however, are not the outpourings of an armchair philosopher. They are based on practice and research in one organization over a 20-year period during which I had the opportunity to track young managers throughout their careers, to assess them at periodic intervals, to make promotion decisions about them, to note their successes and their failures, and to try to fathom all the puzzles, the enigmas, and the surprises I encountered along the way. They are based also on my observations over the past ten years of many other organizations and of many other managers from all kinds of enterprises.

The results of these studies are noted in this book for the first time, simply because, as an active practitioner, I have not had the time to put them in the form required by academic journals. But I am also mindful of the fact that the proof of the pudding is still in the eating. The theories and the models I describe are currently being put to the test in a major research endeavor involving the assessment of the personalities and the roles of the 500 key operating managers of one major American corporation.

For proper elucidation it was also necessary to treat the subject matter in perspective. Excursions were required, therefore, into personality, role, and organization theory; in addition, I had to review such current notions as management by objectives, participative management, and organization development. And, above all, I was forced to expound my own views of the decision-making process. To some, these excursions will undoubtedly appear to be needless digressions. But, since these ideas have important implications for managerial selection and promotion, they had to be considered.

It was possible to make the task manageable by a rigorous definition of the book's subject. This book is about managers. It is not about engineers, accountants, bankers, merchants, manufacturers, or salesmen. It is not about high-talent personnel, leaders, problem solvers, or policy makers. It deals simply with the men who fill the managerial roles in an organization, who, like aircraft pilots, are charged with the responsibility of bringing it from one point to another on schedule and according to plan.

The presentation is designed to be neither definitive nor dogmatic. It is intended to stimulate those responsible for selecting managers to take a good hard look at the ways they are now doing it and to suggest new approaches that may enable the organization to adapt to the social, economic, political, and technological changes that are occurring so rapidly in the postindustrial society.

Finally, I would like to acknowledge the help I have received in writing this book. Specifically, I would like to thank Dr. John Holland, of the Center for Study of Social Organization of Schools at Johns Hopkins University, for permitting me to draw heavily upon his theories of vocational choice in Chapters 2 and 5; Mr. V. Jon Bentz, director of Psychological Services, Sears, Roebuck and Co., for permission to quote him in Chapter 2 and to describe his research in Chapter 5; the Systems Development Corporation for permission to use material taken from its excellent publication, the *SDC Magazine,* in Chapter 5; and the Kaiser Aluminum & Chemical Corporation for use of material from its publication, *The Dynamics of Change,* in Chapter 1. I would also like to thank Mrs. Marilyn Grindley for typing the manuscript. And, last but not least, I would like to express my appreciation to those thousands of managers who have, from time to time, patiently spent their valuable hours completing tests, questionnaires, and inventories to help me in my career-long study of how managers are made.

—FELIX M. LOPEZ

Contents

No great thing is created suddenly, any more than a bunch of grapes or a fig. If you tell me that you desire a fig, I answer you that there must be time. Let it first blossom, then bear fruit, then ripen.—EPICTETUS, *Discourses,* CHAPTER 15

PART ONE

Theories, Models, and Facts

1

The Managerial Crisis

THE worth of a good manager is almost incalculable. For centuries it was the custom of the Moslem Ismaili sect to bestow annually upon its hereditary ruler a treasure in gold and jewels that matched his weight. This primitive but realistic practice might well be emulated by the members of most modern social institutions. But, even if they did, it would hardly be enough. Good managers are worth more than their weight in gold. Men with the ability and the courage to plan, organize, and decide the affairs of an enterprise are its very life force.

This assertion is not just a pious platitude; it is a hard financial fact. A newspaper advertisement by a large Wall Street firm assured its readers not long ago that its analysts view a company's management as *the* dominant element in the evaluation of the growth potential of the company's stock. The advertisement also noted that "unfortunately, sizing up management is one of the most complex tasks that analysts and investors have to face."

Managers make or break an enterprise. We are told by economists that two-thirds of America's top corporations at the beginning of this century are no longer in business today; that the average life of a corporation is about seven years; and that, on the basis of current trends, over 50 percent of today's top firms will pass into oblivion via merger, take-over, or bankruptcy in the next quarter-century. The facts seem to confirm this gloomy prophecy. Eighty of the top 500 corporations listed by *Fortune* magazine in

1962 were part of or controlled by other corporations just five years later. And the process seems to be accelerating. Thirty of the companies in *Fortune's* 1968 listing did not appear in the 1969 listing at all.

In business, a corporation's life expectancy can be directly traced to the general level of its managerial competence. In government, education, health administration, and the church, however, the relationship is not nearly as direct nor as obvious. But the effect is the same. Each year an unknown but substantial portion of public and private organizations achieve results— sales volume, profits, client services, cost effectiveness, budget performance— markedly below optimal. These institutions and their investors, taxpayers, and customers pay a high price represented by the difference between what is actually realized and what could have been realized by more effective management.

Managerial incompetence is a frequently overlooked but very real inflationary pressure. When the housewife complains about the rising cost of meat and groceries, of shoes and sewing thread, she doesn't realize that the higher prices are due, in part, to the inability of the food and retailing firms to attract and retain capable managers. But the retailing industry is not the only enterprise suffering from a lack of managerial talent. For good managers are not only valuable, they are also very scarce. And the whole world, in one way or another, is in the grip of a managerial crisis.

A crisis signifies a period of instability, a stage in a sequence of events at which future events are determined. It is in the nature of a living organism to encounter crises as it develops, grows, and finally dies. Humans pass through them repeatedly on their journey from infancy to old age; churches and business corporations are continually caught up in them; nations feel their intensity in depression, war, and revolution; and even whole civilizations must confront them. The way the crisis is met represents the difference between renewed growth and steady decay of the organism.

The Managerial Society

The managerial crisis is only one phase of a universal crisis that extends throughout every level and every dimension of modern society. The unavailability of competent men to make organizational decisions represents a crisis in the survival and growth, not just of individual organizations, but of whole societies. This is so because the rapid changes in technology, politics, and social status have created a society of organizations, no one of which is all-powerful and all-pervasive but each of which has an important and unique purpose for the society. And, like every society, a society of organizations creates its own elite group, the managers. Thus it is quite proper to call the times we live in the Managerial Society.

Historians classify periods of human history by their dominant social movements. The period from the fall of Rome to the printing of the Gutenberg Bible is known as the Dark Ages; the period immediately following the Protestant Reformation has been termed the Age of Enlightenment; and that marked by the emergence of such political and social philosophers as Voltaire, Hume, and Locke, the Age of Reason.

The period following the close of World War II has been termed by some the Age of the Managerial Revolution and by others the Twentieth Century Capitalist Revolution. These designations stress the fact that there is something new and different in the world, a brand of capitalism that has pervaded the whole society and has created a social system in which managers play a key role. This new society has introduced the Age of the Manager into an era of radical change in a world that is polarized politically and economically and depends for its viability on the strength and the health of its major institutions. To understand the full dimensions of the managerial crisis, it is necessary to examine each of these notions in more depth.

The Age of the Manager

The Age of the Manager, which, as Peter Drucker points out,[1] is also an age of discontinuity, is marked by the preeminence of the manager as the shaper of its values and the mover of its social forces. The Age of the Manager has sprung up from a capitalistic system that is distinctly different from the classical form deplored by nineteenth-century economists and socialists. This new capitalism is the work of a highly specialized managerial group selected and rewarded primarily for its competence. The motivations of these men differ markedly from those of the owner-manager of the classical capitalistic system.

While the Managerial Society is by no means confined to the United States, it exists here in its most sophisticated form. It is characterized by a central core, perhaps 500 to 600 firms, government agencies, and educational institutions, surrounded by thousands of smaller enterprises that com-

---

[1] Peter F. Drucker, *The Age of Discontinuity* (New York: Harper & Row, 1968).

pare with them neither in size, organization, technology, nor capitalization. Within each of the large organizations can be found a nucleus of decision makers who run the corporation. The emergence of the men that form this nucleus as the dominant force in a rapidly changing and highly technical society, enjoying a status not shared by any other elite group in history, is what has been termed the Managerial Revolution. Almost without realizing it, the nation has become so wholly dependent upon these men that its very status as a world power and its ability to deal with internal economic and social problems rest on their continuing competency.

What has brought about this dramatic new order? The answer is simply *change*—change stemming first of all from the technological innovations that have shifted the nation into a knowledge economy and that require parallel changes in organizational forms and administrative systems. The Managerial Society represents the convergence of not one but three revolutions—technological, social, and economic—creating a new social system that well might transform the world or destroy it. The emerging system certainly creates a situation by which one or a few nations—United States, Japan, Sweden, West Germany—threaten to outstrip the rest in standard of living and affluency. The Managerial Society, however, did not emerge like earlier ages after a long, slow process of transition; it exploded into the twentieth century in an era of radical change.

The Era of Radical Change

In 1967, as part of the observance of its twentieth anniversary, the Kaiser Aluminum & Chemical Corporation undertook an examination of what may well happen to the world in the next 20 years; an examination that combined many fields of thought: industrial, financial, social, biological, psychological, philosophical, political, moral, and ethical. The results were published in six issues of its corporate magazine and distributed to the company's friends in business, finance, government, education, and the press.

The national response to this issue was so great that a major publishing house decided to publish the six issues of the magazine in a single hardbound book for general distribution.[2] *The Dynamics of Change,* as it was called, suggests that the world of 1986 will be almost totally different in climate and texture from the world we live in today, as different as our

---

[2] Don Fabun, *The Dynamics of Change* (Englewood Cliffs, N.J.: Prentice-Hall, 1967).

world is from the world of the Civil War. The book sums up this change in the words of archaeologist Kurt Marek: "We in the twentieth century are concluding an era of mankind five thousand years in length; we open our eyes like prehistoric men; we see a world totally new."

Today's newspaper portrays a way of life that is radically different from that of 1947 when the Managerial Society was born. Then people were concerned with the problems of housing shortages, the scarcity of automobiles, and postwar unemployment. Such ideas as television, jet engines, nuclear fission, computer technology, black power, and systems analysis were barely known and their significance was recognized only by an elite few. Today, life is filled with miracles that we regard as commonplace: men walking on the moon, organ transplants, satellite television, and huge jet transports carrying hundreds of people thousands of miles in a few hours.

But the rate of change, fast as it has been, is scheduled to increase sharply. Like the pitchman at the country fair, scientists assure us that we haven't seen anything yet. Recent projections by the Hudson Institute's Kahn and Weiner include as likely events by the year 2000 such phenomena as major reductions in hereditary and congenital defects, some control over weather and climate, human hibernation for extensive periods, and the capability of choosing the sex of unborn children.[3]

In terms of human progress, however, the technological explosion has not been all that glorious. It has raised gnawing doubts about the accelerated nuclear proliferation, the invasion of privacy, excessive government or private power over individuals, interference with natural systems to such an extent as to threaten the possibility of continued life on this planet—issues that are much too complex, too comprehensive, and too important to be left to mere mortals. For the technological revolution has brought with it problems that are causing dramatic upheavals in social and political realms. The population explosion is one of the most serious.

Twenty-five percent of all the people who ever lived are alive today. It took nearly 8 million years for the earth's human population to reach the figure of 10 million souls. In the following 10,000 years, the figure grew to one billion; in the next hundred, to 2 billion; in the following 50 years it will reach 4 billion, which will bring us only to the year 1975. By 1980, we are told, the city of New Delhi at present rates will contain something around 35 million people. There is nothing in human experience, no technique of the past, that can guide us in the solution of the problems raised

---

[3] Herman Kahn and Anthony J. Weiner, *The Year 2000* (New York: Macmillan, 1967), p. 51.

by this kind of population density. With all our managerial know-how, we cannot now administer American cities of more than one or two million people.

Technology and population explosions have caused a similar reaction in the knowledge field. Peter Drucker points out that we have now changed from an economy of goods to a knowledge economy.[4] Ninety percent of all the scientists who ever lived are living today. The amount of technical information available doubles every ten years; the number of technical journals doubles every 15 years. In 1955, those industries that distribute ideas and information accounted for one-quarter of the gross national product. In the late 1970s, we are informed, these industries will account for one-half of the total national output. Yet, 4,000 or 5,000 years after the introduction of the written word, more than one-third of adult mankind still remains illiterate. In the decade of the 1960s the number of illiterates in the world rose by almost 60 million to a total of about 800 million people.

Most educated people have been exposed to this litany of change so often that it has become monotonous. Most managers and professionals, however, continue to operate on the assumption that their world is relatively static; that, at best, the way to chart the future is to make straight-line projections of past and present trends. They waste their energy trying to recreate the past or at least to preserve the status quo. Such tactics simply will not work, and as a consequence the organizations involved are continually unready to meet the future when it arrives. There is a need, therefore, to face squarely the reality of change because it is the only stable event in this precarious world.

Nowhere is a strategy for the future needed more in a Managerial Society than in the selection and development of managers. The design of such a strategy must begin by examining the forces of change that affect managerial performance, by trying to understand how they originated and where they seem to be taking us. Only in this way can we guide and control these forces and cushion ourselves and our companies against what is referred to as "future shock."

A Polarized World

A global look at the world we live in will reveal two startling phenomena. First, it is quite apparent that in terms of material and economic resources the nations of the world are subdivided into the developed and the under-

[4] Peter F. Drucker, op. cit., p. 263.

developed or, in plainer terms, into the rich and the poor. Although the rich nations constitute less than a third of the total human population, they produce and consume more than two-thirds of the world's goods—and, what is more, their output is increasing rapidly. But, even among the rich nations, the ratio of population to production is uneven. Ninety percent of the world's industrial output is concentrated in areas inhabited by people of European origin, and the leading producer in this group is the United States of America.

This economic gap threatens to yawn wider and wider, creating political tensions and international conflicts that will continue to threaten the peace and stability of the world until the gap is closed.

The second major phenomenon is the correlation between industrial development and managerial talent. Although the economic gap can be traced to such other gaps as capital supply, technology, and education, it always boils down to a managerial gap. Able managers are required to release the energy pent up in a social system and to channel it into productive paths that lead to profitable outputs. No matter how much capital and technical know-how may be available, the enterprise will come to a dismal ending without effective management.

One of the harsh realities of the Managerial Society is the stark and shocking inequality in the production and consumption of goods among the world's people. This inequality, which has existed for well over a century, is increasing so rapidly that two-thirds of the world's population is caught up in a Malthusian trap where the population growth equals or exceeds productive growth. Consequently, even if the developing countries were to increase their per capita income ten times faster than the developed countries, the technological gap would still widen.

The importance of managerial talent can be underscored by the experience of the richest industrial country in the world, the United States. This relative newcomer to the ranks of the world's great powers, a nation whose religion, philosophy, science, and law have all been borrowed from other nations, whose traditions, culture, and civilization date back only 200 years or so, whose people represent only 6 percent of the world's population, and whose boundaries enclose only 7 percent of the earth's land surface is by any test the most powerful and the richest nation in the world. Its pre-eminence rests on the simple fact that its output equals a third of the total production of all the other countries and is two and one-half times larger than that of its closest competitor, the Soviet Union, and twice that of all European industry combined.

But what is more significant is the realization that this overwhelming lead is expected to increase. The French economist J.-J. Servan-Schreiber predicts that, by 1980 or thereabouts, the world's third greatest industrial power just after the United States and the Soviet Union will be the American corporation in Europe.[5] And Kahn and Weiner predict that by the year 2000 America will become a postindustrial society; that is, a mass-consumption society whose gross national income per capita will exceed $10,000 per year.[6] In the case of India, on the other hand, they predict for the same year a per capita GNP of $270—a figure that puts this country in the preindustrial category and a stage not much superior to that experienced by man 5,000 years ago.

At this point, an extraordinary event will have occurred in terms of world history. Within a single generation the array of the world's nations will have changed from differences in degree of development and economic affluence to differences in kind. The world of the postindustrial societies, the United States, Japan, Canada, Sweden, France, and West Germany, will be totally unlike that of the rest of the world's people. World Bank President Robert McNamara has stated that this difference in kind rather than degree is no mere gap; it is a seismic fissure driving deep into the earth's crust.

There is a natural tendency to view the disparity between American affluence and world poverty as essentially an economic and a technological gap. But other more astute observers recognize it for what it really is—a managerial gap. The astonishing rise of American capitalism, power, and productivity is due to a combination of circumstances that have given the country a worldwide lead in the development of managerial talent and administrative science. The key to its success lies in its management, in the group of men who form the guiding intelligence of the organization, who possess the specialized knowledge, talent, or experience to direct the affairs of the enterprise. Management constitutes the act of combining diverse patterns of human behavior into a unified, coordinated pattern of organizational behavior. And the behavior of organizations must be coordinated with that of the other institutions in the society if that society is to prosper.

A Society of Organizations

While it is true to say that each person behaves in a way best guaranteed to satisfy his own needs, it is simply not the whole truth. On closer exam-

---

[5] J.-J. Servan-Schreiber, *The American Challenge* (New York: Atheneum House, Inc., 1968).
[6] Kahn and Weiner, op. cit., p. 119.

ination it becomes apparent that each person's behavior is organized into patterns that follow closely certain norms prescribed by the groups to which he belongs—families, clubs, and work units. These standards are, in turn, strongly influenced by larger and more complex social clusters called *institutions*—corporations, government agencies, schools, and churches. In their turn, the norms of the larger social groupings are influenced by macro-institutions referred to as *societies*. Thus the individual, strongly influenced by groups, institutions, and society, does for the most part what he is expected to do.

But the direction of influence between larger and smaller units is two-way. The individual contributes to his group norms, and smaller groups influence larger groups.

In this way, the character of a society is shaped by the organizations of which it is composed, and it in turn shapes them. A dynamic, viable society is one that is made up of a number of dynamic, viable institutions, which, while differing in purpose and function, operate in concert to achieve the common good of the whole society. As John Gardner so aptly pointed out, "A society is only as healthy as its institutions; if they are growing, it grows; if they are decaying, it decays." [7]

While there are many forces that contribute to organizational health, the essential force is its ability to attract and to hold a sufficient number of people capable of and interested in achieving its purposes. Self-evident as it may be, this fact is often overlooked. Equally overlooked is the notion that membership in any organization in a free society must necessarily be voluntary. The organization's ultimate success and, hence, that of the society in which it operates is bound by the extent to which its members accept and internalize the purposes of the organization and of society. This commitment to the common purpose cannot be secured by force; it has to be earned by sound administration.

The organization binds its members to its purposes so that they accept them as their own and commit freely their personal energies and resources to their fulfillment through the *administrative process*. This process represents man's highest form of behavior and, as such, has been the subject of intense study since the dawn of civilized history. Putting a man on the moon was a triumph more of administration than of technology. One of the basic problems today is that our mastery of the administrative process lags far behind our technological achievements.

[7] John W. Gardner, *Self-Renewal—The Individual and The Innovative Society* (New York: Harper & Row, 1963).

Up until recently, the administrative process has been understood by reference to military, ecclesiastical, and agricultural models of organization. In this view, it was considered to be simply the problem of exercising authority. Today, the administrative process is considered from the standpoint of systems theory, which among other ideas includes the notion of multiple causation and multiple effects. Systems analysis frees us from the older and more comforting idea of single cause-and-effect relationships in administration. Managers tend to cling to the latter notion because they like to believe that they understand things as they occur. By systems analysis managers can free themselves from the dangers of oversimplification, and at the same time they can make complexity more manageable.

In the systems view the organization becomes a cooperative system of people tied together by an external purpose and an internal pattern of communications and relationships. Always required to adapt to outside economic and social forces, the organization strives to maintain order among its internal members. Since the more stability internally the less ability to adapt externally, maintaining a delicate balance between the two environments proves to be a rather ticklish venture. If an organization fails to adapt to its outside environment, like the dinosaurs it will pass into extinction—a fate that, as we have already noted, has befallen a surprisingly high percentage of twentieth-century business corporations. If it fails to maintain sufficient internal stability, it will, like many nations and empires, disintegrate in continual conflict and dissension.

The fine tuning of the organization is the job of the men at its controls, the managers. More than any other task, it is their job to keep the organization running, exchanging inputs and outputs with the environment in which it functions. Without a sufficient supply of managers to run its institutions capably, a society will putter along at a bare subsistence level, its individual members going their separate and unproductive ways. Managers are indeed vital; if they are available in ample numbers, a Managerial Society and a rich nation flourish; if they are absent, a preindustrial society and a poor nation result.

The Managerial Gap

The world's supply of capable managers is shockingly low. Even in the richest nations there are barely enough. Harvard Professor James Q. Wilson, as he was quoted in the 1968 United States Civil Service Commission annual report, sums the situation up most succinctly: "Talent is scarcer than money. Some things literally cannot be done—or cannot be done well—because there is no one available to do them who knows how. The supply of able, experienced executives is not increasing nearly as fast as the number of problems being addressed by public policy." This scarcity is what we have referred to as *the managerial gap.*

The more astute observers have noted that American preeminence does not lie in scientific and technological expertise because most basic discoveries were made in European laboratories. The American contribution lies in the art of organization, of finding practical applications for the discoveries, developing, producing, and marketing them. Take, for example, the computer, which promises to revolutionize man's ability to communicate, to process information, and to solve problems. The first computer, requiring only 1,500 tubes, was invented by German scientists and put into operation in Berlin in 1941. The first American computer, requiring 18,000 tubes, was put into operation in 1946 at a time when both Germany and Britain led the world in computer technology. Yet, today, 80 percent of all European computers are controlled by American corporations, which, at the same time, control 95 percent of the market for the integrated circuits that are crucial to the coming generation of computers.

The difference lies in management, a process in which the whole world lags behind the Americans. For managers are not born, nor can they be developed overnight. If a society is to provide a steady supply of competent managers, it must overhaul its long-accepted traditions and cultural patterns and perhaps even realign its social structure. The American society has for over a hundred years wagered much more on human knowledge and growth than it wastes on gadgets or upon time-honored traditions. This wager forms the heart of America's lead in the managerial sciences.

The Worldwide Shortage of Managers

There is now a worldwide shortage of managerial talent whose practical effect is an inhibition of company development and national growth. For reasons which differ by geographical location, this shortage is likely to last for a very long time. While it is probable that it has existed throughout man's history, the complex and urgent problems of a radically changing society make it now more urgent than ever. It is a situation that is placing strains not only on business corporations and government agencies but upon educational, religious, and other social institutions.

It is not practical here to document a country-by-country analysis of the managerial gap. Its European characteristics are quite different from those it displays in the United States or in Brazil or Ghana, and the problems of an American manufacturing corporation differ markedly from those of an American university. In the interests of space, we shall confine ourselves to a review of the dimensions of the problem in American industry and in the developing countries. To some extent these represent opposite ends of the worldwide spectrum, and all other problems lie somewhere in between them.

Managerial Gaps in American Business

Three factors account for the current American dearth of capable managers: the rapid expansion of business, technological and social changes, and the depression of the 1930s.

The rapid expansion of business. Since the end of World War II, American business has pursued a path of nearly unbroken expansion. During the years between 1961 and 1969, for example, the number of firms with over $500 million in sales increased by nearly 50 percent. During that same period, the sales of all corporations increased 40 percent. This rapid business expansion was the result of the ability of the workforce to expand.

During this period, the workforce grew from 57 million to nearly 74 million workers, the largest increase coming in the white collar qualifications. This expansion occurred, however, as a result of an influx of women into the labor market. The demands of the military, the rapid increase in college enrollment, the development of earlier retirement ages, and a shrinking work week and year absorbed nearly all of the extra manpower supplied by the male population.

Since business expansion depends to a large extent on the supply of managerial talent, which comes mainly from the male population, a corporation's ability to expand may be severely curtailed by a lack of managers. According to federal statistics, a growth in the managerial classifications has not accompanied the growth in the labor force. While the precise number of managers is difficult to estimate because of classification problems, this category has remained at the 10 percent level of the total labor force for the past 20 years. If we leave out the number of small-business proprietors enumerated in this category, it is probable that the ratio of managers to workers has actually declined. Thus we are forced to conclude that fewer managers are running larger and larger enterprises, a situation which, even with automation, is highly questionable.

Technological and social changes. While business has grown, it has also become extremely complex. The number of professional and technical employees has increased 200 percent since 1947. Whole new industries—television, computer science, pharmaceuticals, and chemicals—have sprung up. Rapid social changes have also occurred. The average worker is far better educated and more highly skilled than his 1947 counterpart. Thus the manager of today has to be a college graduate and pretty well trained technically.

One study of the hundred largest U.S. corporations showed that between 1955 and 1965 the average number of corporate offices rose by 28 percent. This rapid increase during a single decade was due in large measure to industry's growing complexity. Added to the managerial roster were such functions as personnel, engineering, systems, foreign activities, and research and development.

The proverbial notion that the road to managerial success lies through birth or marriage into a wealthy family is now obsolete. And the equally compelling legend that the successful business executive is a man of little schooling who overcame his academic shortcomings through hard work and ability is also folklore. The Horatio Alger story of the orphaned newsboy rising to become a business tycoon enjoyed its popularity in the days when the top business posts remained largely in the hands of the rich and the well born. But the real triumph of an open society has been achieved in the past 15 years in the Managerial Society.

In 1950 about 36 percent of the nation's big-business executives were identified as the sons of wealthy families; in the current generation of business managers only 11 percent come from such a background. Even more conclusive is the fact that two-thirds of the business managers at the turn of the century had fathers who were heads of the same corporation or were independent businessmen, whereas fewer than half the present managers at the summit fit into this category.

At the same time, there has been a remarkable shift toward technological-scientific training in the educational backgrounds of those who run the nation's business and industry. At present, some 40 percent of the big-business executives have a technical education with degrees in engineering or the natural sciences. Other studies have indicated the remarkable fact that 75 percent of today's American managers have at least a college degree and a third have advanced degrees.

But the technological and social changes that have occurred in American economy during the rise of the Managerial Society have not only required much more highly trained managers, they have created intense competition for these same men from other sectors of the economy: from the government, from education, and from the nonprofit areas. In the decade between 1954 and 1964, the number of employees in the executive classes of the federal government jumped 58 percent. The result is an unprecedented demand for managers that is likely to continue unabated for the next three decades.

If we assume that the shortage has been met in the same way as in technical fields, it is probable that a substantial number of managerial positions are filled by people not fully qualified—or that the positions have been diluted by the inclusion of duties incompatible with those of a manager. Since this latter strategy is most commonly employed, it is possible to assert that many managers are managers in name only.

What lies immediately ahead? Will there be a break in the drought? The answer is no.

The depression of the 1930s. Aside from the prospects of increased expansion and even more radical technological and social changes, the irreversible fact of the 1930 depression will play a major role in the supply of managerial talent for the next ten years.

It is now a well-known fact that the severe economic setback of the 1930s shrank the American birthrate substantially. This dip in the manpower supply constitutes a permanent fault in the population profile, for each succeeding decade, which will only disappear by the year 2000. In the 1970s the dip occurs in the 36-to-44-year-old group, the prime age group for managers. In 1950 this age group constituted 14 percent of the population; in 1970 it will represent 11 percent and in 1975 10 percent. In the last-named year, there will actually be 800,000 fewer males in the 35-to-44-year age group than there were in 1965. During this same period, the labor force is expected to grow from 73 to 90 million workers.

Another development in the 1930 economic wasteland has also had a telling effect on the managerial supply. Most firms did little or no hiring during this decade. This recruitment and development inactivity was extended about another five years by World War II when American men were absorbed by the millions into the military forces. A 15- to 20-year hiatus (including the early postwar years) in the supply of managerial talent was thereby created.

During the 1970s the number of executive replacements at the highest levels will be sharply reduced because those who would normally be ready simply were never developed. The resulting picture, then, appears to be something like this. The technological expansion in the next five years will require 50 percent more managers than American industry now possesses. Fifty percent of the present managers will have to be replaced during this same period. The competition from other sources in the economy is likely to intensify. The requirements for competence in managerial jobs will grow stiffer than ever before, and the supply will decline except in the youngest age groups.

THE MANAGERIAL GAP IN THE DEVELOPING COUNTRIES

Just as they provide the dimensions of the American managerial crisis, rapid growth, increasing complexity and diversity, and demographic realities have created managerial shortages in the developing countries. However, the picture here is far different and decidedly grimmer. Lack of industry and capital are most frequently cited as the important reasons for this situation. But it is hard to say whether they are causes or effects. The generally low level of educational development in the poor countries is probably the major cause.

The wealth of a nation depends in the final analysis upon the productive skills and the educational levels of its people. In the advanced countries, for example, the number of persons with 12 years' education or its equivalent exceeds 100 per 1,000 inhabitants. In the developing countries, on the other hand, only one person in a thousand may have 12 or more years of education. And each year millions pass beyond school age without having learned to read or write. In general, says Princeton's manpower expert Professor Frederick Harbison, there is a positive correlation between a country's human-resources development and its national income per capita.

Most economists agree that the most important factors today in creating economic expansion are education and technological innovation rather than growth in invested capital or labor-force expansion. In the developed countries, the rate of accumulation of high-level manpower exceeds both the growth rate of the total labor force and gross national product. In the United States, for example, 43 percent of the population between the ages of 20 and 24 is enrolled in a college or university; in Europe the percentages range from 7 to 16. In the developing countries, the figure is less than one percent.

Consequently, the growing gap between the developing and the developed countries is due primarily to a paucity of education (particularly higher education) among the population of the developing country and its inability or unwillingness to invest in its people. But this is not the only reason.

For the most part, newly emerging countries have been tradition-bound in their economic, social, and political policies and practices. Domestic enterprises tend to be family-owned, and those that are foreign-owned are usually managed by expatriates. Thus highly trained people are employed in jobs beneath their skill merely because that is all there is for them to do. Or talented young people tend to migrate to more promising areas. This situation provides little incentive to the children of all but a few families to seek higher levels of education.

The experiences of these poorer societies are really nothing more than extreme cases of what can be observed in other areas of the world and even in certain sections of the highly developed countries. Industries such as retailing, trucking, railroading, and the building trades, to name only a few, have been notably deficient in recruiting and developing educated young managers. Now they find themselves in the precarious position of attempting to compete in a highly dynamic and largely technological market with managers who possess only experience gained in a past that is no more.

Organizations grow strong only in proportion to the number of skilled managers they can attract and hold, and societies prosper in direct proportion to the number of healthy, striving institutions they embrace within their boundaries. Only in this way can the latent energy and the creative potential of a people be fully released.

The fact that only a small proportion of the world's societies has even partially realized the enormous potential of the human brain and spirit is due primarily to the inability of the unorganized majority to produce capable managers from their teeming millions. And, even within the affluent minority, many hard problems threaten the economic positions its members now enjoy, problems that in one way or another can be traced back to a failure to provide the kind of management required. This failure is attributable to an inaccurate, ambiguous, and even erroneous notion.

How Managers Are Made

Historically, good managers have always been hard to come by; and, despite the advances in technology and the social sciences, their numbers relative to the population are not likely to increase over the next third of a century. The reason is quite simple. Effective managers are neither born, as the Europeans somehow continue to insist, nor are they developed, as most American corporations have found to their chagrin. Like a fine sherry, they are the product of a long and meticulous cultivation and aging process. To produce a great fino or amontillado, one must start first with the high-quality Palomino grape and then bring the wine to a point of excellence and perfection through the mysterious *solera* process by which the older and finer wines educate and improve the younger ones. As in the solera process, good managers are first carefully selected and then developed in a way that only occasionally is achieved without planned direction. But this is not how it is being done today for the most part.

PRESENT-DAY PRACTICES

The idea of a managerial crisis is certainly not new. Throughout history, every institutional head becomes aware of it at some point in his tenure of office, however painful it is to contemplate and however much he tries to repress it. What is new in America, at least, is not its widespread recognition but the elaborate and expensive attention being paid to ways of coping with it. There is, for one thing, an extensive literature on management and the principles of organization. For another, hundreds of millions of dollars are being spent annually in the United States by private and public corporations to develop men designated as managers. And the national government has made available large sums for the expansion of the college and university system.

However laudable these efforts have been, they have constituted little more than random attempts to deal with the problem. So far it has been somewhat like the blind leading the blind. Organizations are now spending large sums of money to teach *men* who may or may not have the potential to learn what they are being taught—that is, *skills* that may or may not be effective for use in *positions* about which the teachers know very little.

Despite this observation, relatively little formal attention has been directed to the heart of the problem, the selection of managers, because this problem is really as old as man himself. As with nearly every old and unresolved problem, numerous habits, customs, and superstitions have accumulated in all the world's cultures that are accepted as incontestable solutions. History reveals a wide and varied assortment of managerial selection practices ranging from physical force, heredity, divine intervention, and lotteries to seniority, ordination, election, and competitive examination. In one culture or another, at one point in time or another, each of these methods has been granted a nearly sacramental status that makes it almost blasphemous to question.

To suggest, for example, that there might be a more effective way to select a president of the United States than the Electoral College marks one as a progressive thinker, but even to hint that there might be a more efficient way than popular election would mark one as a revolutionist. Yet most historians are willing to call only three or four of our thirty-seven presidents "great" and to consider only five or six above average. The rest have been consigned to categories ranging from mediocre to poor.

Private industry has done no better, if the truth were really acknowledged. Many of the changes in the executive suite noted daily in the business section of the newspaper are little more than awkward attempts to rectify the selection mistakes that no one is willing to admit have been made. These errors occur simply from failure to understand the process by which human ability is identified and nurtured.

THE CULTIVATION OF TALENT

Romantic fiction is full of stories of the great painter who was suddenly discovered or of the magnificent concert singer who was found in the five-and-ten-cent store. And indeed the mass of people who lead lives of quiet desperation are probably sustained by such fantasies.

But reality is quite different. Genuine talent is a product of unusual ability, a very positive attitude toward its expression, and long years of development. And precisely because the combination of these three elements occurs so infrequently in a single person, high talent is rare. Most top managers readily understand the fictional quality of instant success. Nevertheless, they continue to live by it. An experienced engineer or physician or educator is suddenly projected into a managerial role in a laboratory, a hospital, or a university and expected to perform it superbly overnight.

Whether the supply of managerial talent can be increased depends upon two assumptions. The first assumption concerns its potential in the general population. If we assume that there are many more people who possess managerial ability than are presently developed, then the task for society is to seek out those with the potential and give them the necessary opportunities to develop it.

The second assumption has to do with how valuable society considers certain talents. Since its resources are limited, society must establish its priorities and determine which human talents it needs to develop. Skill at ballet dancing, for example, is admittedly an extraordinary talent giving pleasure and beauty to many, but there is no pressing urgency to turn the population into a nation of ballet dancers. Society must be convinced that managerial talent is well worth developing.

This is an important point. The development of talent in a society or an organization usually follows no master plan. In fact, it has progressed historically in a rather haphazard fashion, creating imbalances that have tended to impede or accelerate organization growth. Manpower planning on a national or even on an international scale has emerged today as a social necessity. Although it still is only in its infancy, enough work has been done already to suggest a basic model to underlie the selection and the development of managers.

A Managerial Selection Model

The complex, precedent-bound, and often unevaluated managerial selection and development programs of most employers are actually dysfunctional in yielding a high-talent managerial group. This situation stems from incorrect assumptions about the nature of the human skills and attitudes required to perform the functions of the managerial role and the capabilities of the procedures used to assess these skills. Inadequate or incomplete understanding of these variables leads to managerial selection and development policies and practices that produce management teams characterized by inferior talent, less than adequate work habits, and early obsolescence.

Up until recently, most American employers in both the public and private sectors have developed selection practices that were based on notions of economy, convenience, and acceptability. The evidence is now accumulating in impressive degrees to demonstrate that such programs at best yield only short-run advantages that are more than offset by long-range liabilities.

Most research efforts in managerial selection in the United States have been quite limited in their results because they have focused solely upon direct relationships between selection instruments and specific criterion variables. The most recent work, however, strongly suggests that a more dynamic and realistic model of the selection process is necessary. In this model, successful job performance is viewed as the dynamic outcome of the transactions that occur among three major variables:

1. *Personality.* This variable includes the physical, intellectual, emotional, moral, and motivational characteristics of the person performing the job.

2. *Role*. This variable includes the duties and the requirements of the position created to achieve the organization's goals and objectives.
3. *Milieu*. This variable includes the structure, management style, values, and rewards of the organization in which the job is performed.

The transaction that occurs among these three variables determines the characteristics of such end-result variables as job performance and job satisfaction. Consequently, an effective program of selecting managers and upgrading them must be based upon a dynamic model that includes careful consideration of each of them.

This conclusion leads to one final consideration. We have mentioned how systems theory states that, to remain viable, an organization must remain open to its environment. The operation of a managerial selection system, therefore, must also be viewed in terms of its relationships to its external environment. Thus what is happening in the larger society has a profound effect upon managerial selection processes requiring continual changes in personality, in role, and in milieu. A comprehensive, realistic selection system has to be adaptable to the ever changing demands of the organization's internal and external environment. Failure to adapt completely or quickly enough leads to the effects noted earlier in this chapter: to mergers, to acquisitions, to bankruptcies, and to failure.

To sum up, then: If it is to pass through the managerial crisis, management must recruit and select many more managers than it is currently doing. To accomplish this, however, will require that it know a lot more about managers than it does today. Management needs to know, first of all, what manner of men managers are, what they are required to do, and where they are to do it. And this is precisely what we shall discuss in the next five chapters.

2

The Human Side
of the Manager

Nowhere is the managerial crisis more apparent than in the attitudes of young people toward business. As far as youth is concerned, says noted economist Dr. Pierre A. Rinfret, American industry has a terrible credibility gap. Speaking recently to a staff meeting of the executive recruiting firm Ward Howell and Associates, he noted that when the time comes to pick a career the bright young college graduate is scared off by what happened to those who preceded him into the business world. Too many managements, Dr. Rinfret said, are simply afraid of mavericks. Why, he continued, does anyone have to conform if he has imagination and guts?

Too harsh an indictment? Not according to V. Jon Bentz, chief psychologist for Sears, Roebuck & Co. A few years ago, Sears thoroughly overhauled its campus recruiting program to attract and to hire more top college graduates. Like many U.S. corporations, Sears' expansion plans require as many high-caliber managers as it can develop as soon as possible. The aim is to reduce the 10- to 12-year apprenticeship store managers heretofore have served to two or three years. "In our assessment program," Bentz declared, "we are trying to identify the top 10 percent and then push them as far and as fast as they can go."

Yet, in spite of the overall success of the new program in its early stages, Sears still is losing some of the best of the top 10 percent. Why? Sears doesn't know! But it is determined to find out and to correct the problem even if, says Bentz, *"we* have to adjust to *them!"*

Adjusting to them? That apparently is the name of the game in the next 20 years not only for industry but for every other institution in the post-industrial society. It is no longer a case of fitting a round peg in a round hole. If the peg is square, then the hole will have to be reshaped. Management development is out; organization development is in.

All of which makes such good common sense that it is surprising it has been overlooked so long. Managers, like all other workers, are first of all human beings. And human beings possess certain unchangeable properties around which every system has to be built. The NASA engineers planning man's ventures into space had to start with the astronaut and then build every detail of the Mercury, Gemini, and Apollo programs around him. Yet, for the past 75 years, managers have been developing and running organizational systems that require people somehow to adapt to them.

In formulating an approach to the selection and the promotion of managers, we must first examine the human side of the manager to find out what makes him tick. This will not be an easy task. We will be confronted immediately with the question civilized man has been trying to answer for thousands of years: What *is* man? He has found that answering this question is like exploring a tropical forest. All about him are brilliant flowers, exotic sounds, and strange fragrances that excite his imagination. But there are also tangled underbrush, clinging vines, and treacherous quicksand to trap and engulf him.

The answers to the riddle of human personality are part of our heritage. Hippocrates, Plato, and Aristotle laid down principles of personality that underlie the traditions and values of modern society. In the intervening years, many other scholars such as Aquinas, Locke, Spinoza, Comte, and Machiavelli have added to the store of wisdom concerning man's nature. However, it was not until the twentieth century, when the study of human behavior was uprooted from its parental homestead, philosophy, and placed in a foster home, the physical sciences, that a rigorous, data-bound methodology was developed. It is from under this scientific umbrella that most of the current theories and findings have emerged, but they haven't really solved the problem.

Despite the breathtaking advances in chemistry, physiology, neurology, electronics, and the computer sciences, modern society does not yet possess an anatomy of the human personality that even approaches that of the human body. It is not even close to such a model, and none of the major theoretical systems offers more than the bare outlines of one. As we enter the last three decades of the twentieth century, man still remains a mystery to himself.

Another problem in the study of human behavior is the fact that nearly every educated person possesses his own personality system, complete with theoretical concepts, technical vocabulary, and practical applications. And if he has taken Psychology I he is prone to use in his conversation such terms as "introvert," "Freudian slip," and "erotic fixation" without any clear idea of the theoretical systems from which they were derived. He does not realize that his "system" resembles a Mulligan's stew more than a clear bouillon. Even the way he uses the word "personality" itself is imprecise. An attractive actress *has* personality; a front-page figure *is* a personality; a delinquent youth is a *maladjusted* personality; and personality *tests* are an invasion of his privacy. Thus broadly construed, the word conveys little information, and its interpretation depends upon the context in which it is used.

Yet managers have no alternative but to develop and apply a theory of the human personality. That is the only way they can manage; and, whether they realize it or not, they have been doing this for many years. Managers used to believe that people were motivated to work by the need for economic security. Then, shortly after World War II, management thinking shifted to the notion that people worked to obtain social gratification. Judging by results, neither theory was very useful.

It is no wonder, then, that many managers throw up their hands in dismay at the idea of developing a sensible strategy concerning the utilization of their human resources. The result of this despair has been an inconsistent and superficial approach to manpower utilization that takes its toll in corporate productivity and morale. Even in the more progressive companies, human-resources policies have been rather contradictory. Policies that affect the managerial group assume that human beings are free, responsible, and autonomous people; others, which concern the development of incentive programs, treat people as though they were instinct-bound brute animals; and still others, affecting plant operations, consider people to be no more than machines.

This is hardly management's fault. It really reflects the present state of the behavioral sciences. Managers are largely unaware that there are, at present, over 16 major and conflicting theories of personality. Some are highly technical and unknown outside of the academy. Others have found their way not only into the popular vocabulary but into the managerial world. We must explore these theories in more detail to provide a cognitive map for our own journey into psychological space.

A new interdisciplinary approach, loosely termed the "behavioral sciences," has produced fruitful and useful models of human behavior in system activities. Behavioral scientists, most of whom are psychologists, draw upon three basic theoretical systems. Each system is based on the values and the thought processes of the tradition from which it sprang.

In the first category are the behavioristic systems whose roots dig deeply into biology and physics. Adherents of this approach, utilizing a biophysical, mechanical model of human behavior, adopt the position that man's behavior is determined by a lifelong conditioning process. To them, man is a machine—a sensitive and flexible machine whose behavior is controlled by an elaborate but explainable switching network in his brain.

Behaviorists are naturally concerned with such ideas as reinforcement and association, and most of their postulates are based on animal experiments. Management has utilized the fruit of their work in developing incentive programs, in designing man-machine relationships, and particularly in teaching skills through programmed learning.

At the other end of the theoretical spectrum stands a group of systems whose origins can be traced to the ideas of Sigmund Freud and whose theoretical position is based on the observation of disturbed people in clinical settings. The psychoanalytic school has been a potent intellectual force in the twentieth century that has added to man's knowledge by discovering the unconscious forces that shape his behavior. Medically and clinically oriented, psychoanalytic theorists see man as an emotional animal, the product of the interaction of his conscious and subconscious forces.

Because psychoanalytical rhetoric is so strongly intuitive and mentalistic, it is dismissed by behaviorists as rooted in primitive animism and, therefore, having no meaning. But its ideas have gained wide acceptance in management circles—much wider than appears on the surface. Modern advertising and marketing techniques have borrowed heavily from psychoanalytic theory. Four times a year at the Menninger Foundation of Topeka, Kansas, a blue-ribbon panel of top managers meets to discuss industrial emotional problems from the viewpoint of psychoanalytic theory. And a distinguished professor at the Harvard Business School, Harry Levinson, employs a strongly psychoanalytic framework for his theory of managerial motivation.[1]

But the system that is having the heaviest impact upon modern management thinking is that devised by social psychologists who stand midway between the behaviorists and the psychoanalysts. This group asserts that any explanation of the personality must take into account the powerful influences

[1] See, for example, Harry Levinson, *The Exceptional Executive* (Cambridge, Mass.: Harvard University Press, 1968).

of his environment. Man to these theorists is primarily a social being, the product of his class and his culture. In actual fact, they assert, man is neither a machine nor a biological organism responding to his latent animal instincts. He is, on the contrary, a functionally autonomous being; a free, intelligent, and responsible person who behaves in a pattern formed by the people with whom he lives, works, and eventually dies.

In the past ten years, American industry has been trying hard to apply social-psychological ideas to its activities. The managerial grid, sensitivity training, democratic styles of leadership, and participative management represent practical applications of social and/or psychological theories. We shall return to these ideas in much more detail later. Suffice it to say now that these varying approaches to personality theory have formed the foundation of the behavioral sciences that now are underpinning current organizational philosophy and techniques. By adopting an eclectic approach, we can construct a useful model of human behavior if we are willing to make two important concessions: First, we must leave to the philosophers the search for an explanation of the why of human behavior and focus simply on the what; that is, on what we can observe. Second, we must recognize that current scientific paradigms and particularly the language of mathematical physics are not adequate to analyze and to interpret human nature.

This approach may lack the impartial, dispassionate observation and analysis that are the hallmarks of science. But, on the other hand, as Kenneth Boulding notes, we will be given a tremendous assist in this effort by the fact that we do have an inside track in studying human nature precisely because we are, in effect, studying ourselves.

The Human Personality

If we look beneath the diverse vocabularies of the three major theoretical systems, we will note a surprising degree of consensus on the central aspects of human behavior. This consensus enables us to develop the main outlines of the human personality. Briefly, we find that man is a system—a *living* system and a *special kind* of living system.

The System Called Life

The planet Earth is unique in that it is the only satellite in the solar system that is populated by objects possessing a quality that biologists call *life*. To put it simply, life is a system of internal stimulations, tensions, or dis-equilibriums called *needs* that move the organism toward activities to satisfy them. The flowers reaching up to the sunlight, the cow grazing in the pasture, and the sculptor chiseling a piece of stone are one in the fact that each is responding to its need.

The result of the satisfaction is not merely pleasure but rather tension reduction, closure, or the return to a state of equilibrium. The force that links the need to the goal is called a *motive*. Thus it is possible to say that all behavior is motivated. The sum total of felt needs, plus goals and motives, provides the main elements of the behavior of all living systems. But even a cursory observation of living systems makes it evident that the satisfaction of needs is not altogether smooth and uninterrupted.

Obstacles have an annoying habit of appearing between needs and goals. Behavior can be viewed, therefore, in terms of simple responses not only to needs but to the blocks that prevent the satisfaction of needs. Thus we have two types of behavior, a simple response to a need called *motivated behavior* and responses to an obstacle in the path of the need-goal sequence called *frustrated behavior*. The two types of responses differ in many important respects.

When an organism encounters a block, the tension is so increased that the organism must find some way to reduce it even though the original need goes largely unsatisfied. This process of tension reduction is called *adjust-ment;* it lends another characteristic to the behavior of living systems. Ad-justment that both reduces the tension and satisfies the need is functional and developmental; adjustment that merely reduces the tension without satisfying the need is dysfunctional because it only leads to further obstacles that sooner or later bring about the total extinction of the organism.

The behavior employed to adjust to blocks is chosen by the organism as a result of its prior experience and learning. There is a delicate balance be-tween under- and overlearning that is necessary for the organism's optimal growth. If it fails to learn how to adjust, it will find survival difficult for lack of an appropriate repertory of responses. A hothouse plant that is placed in the open garden will die in the first frost. On the other hand, if too many and too severe obstacles are encountered in the early stages of its life, the organism will either die or learn a set of responses that are dysfunctional. A plant deprived of adequate sunlight or moisture does not grow to full maturity.

To sum up, then, the behavior of living organisms can be viewed as the actions of a system of interacting subsystems moving through time.

The Need Systems of Human Beings

We are interested in only one of the numerous species of organisms that inhabit this planet: man. While he shares some of the behavioral characteristics of all living, sentient organisms, he possesses characteristics that are unique. Despite the claims that he is no more than a naked ape and that some of his actions can be traced ultimately to instincts common to most animals (such as the territorial imperative), the fact really is that his most distinctive behaviors are different in kind rather than in degree from all other animals.

The most obvious difference between man and the other animals is the way in which he communicates. All humans have the ability to speak, whereas the acquisition of even the barest rudiments of speech is quite beyond the capacities of his cousins the apes, who can only grunt and growl. Noam Chomsky points out that "when we ask what human language is, we find no striking similarity to animal communications systems." [2]

A close inspection of human behavior forces us to conclude that man possesses two separate need systems, one which he shares with the animal world and the other which is distinctly his own. Some needs, such as those for food and water, are inborn; others, like the need for a power lawnmower or a vice-presidency, are learned. The first are called primary needs; the second, secondary or social needs. Nearly always, except in extreme emergencies, human behavior represents a response to a social need. The way a man satisfies his need for food is an expression of his previously having learned what objects he considers appropriate food for him: rice, locusts, or sirloin steak. But social needs always mask a primary need. They are the exterior that forms the hard outer surface of human behavior. It is only when we patiently peel off layer after layer of social needs that we can fathom the primary need underlying most of human behavior.

HUMAN NEEDS

At times, however, no matter how many social layers are peeled off, we are unable to account for a person's behavior in terms of biological needs. How can we explain a man's desire to climb Mount Everest? To fashion a *Pietà*? To nurse a leper colony? Only by accepting the idea that man has primary

---

[2] Noam Chomsky, "Language and the Mind: II," *Columbia Forum*, Vol. XI, No. 3 (1968), p. 23.

needs that are essentially different from his animal needs. We call these distinctive needs *human*.

Psychologists have cataloged a whole host of human needs that can bewilder the layman: need for power, affiliation, achievement, nurturance, aggression, abasement, understanding, and self-actualization. It is easier to understand them if we reduce them to three unique but interdependent needs: to know, to love, and to become.

The need to know. From the first moment of life man thirsts for knowledge about himself and his environment. This "effort after meaning" is quite different from the exploratory and sniffing behavior of other animals. Man abhors ambiguity, confusion, or doubt. He cannot resist the tendency to put meaning into his sensations and to organize them in a systematic, logical pattern. Not to know is frustrating, painful, and beneath his dignity.

Psychologists give many names to this internal drive: the need for intraception, for understanding, for achievement; but it is best described simply as man's need to know. The drive to satisfy it underlies all human progress. Man continually creates mysteries for himself; and, when he solves them, he presses on to larger and more complex enigmas. It is this need that put a man on the moon.

The need to love. Again, from the day he emerges from his mother's womb man yearns for a positive, mutually supportive relationship with other human beings. This need is vastly different from the simple herding behavior of other animals. It is, as Marvin Dunnette says, not just sexual love nor simply the feeling of attraction, affection, or warm attachment to another person. It is something close to the early Christian concept of *agape*, "a sense of the spontaneous giving of the self, the free expression of the self in interaction with others, without calculation of cost or gain to either the giver or the receiver and a deep commitment to the warmth and the humanity of man."[3]

Freud's basic thesis that all mental illness is, at bottom, due to the unconscious distortion of love relationships has never been successfully challenged. At the Menninger Clinic, it has been found that some mental disorders can be cured only by generous doses of "unsolicited love."

Often expressed by psychologists as the need for affiliation, nurturance, succorance, or recognition, love is an active force stemming from the need to have a high regard for others and to know that others have a high regard for oneself. The inability to love properly, which seems to be the prevalent

[3] Marvin D. Dunnette, "People Feeling: Joy, More Joy, and the 'Slough of Despond,' " *Journal of Applied Behavioral Science*, Vol. 5, No. 1 (1969), p. 26.

malady of the Managerial Society, is the root of all anxiety; it is the failure to be a complete human being. And at the heart of genuine love is love for oneself. It is an active striving for the growth and happiness of other persons rooted in one's own capacity to love others because one loves oneself properly.

The need to become. Man also has an irresistible, unquenchable desire for autonomy and for identity. While this need appears superficially to be similar to the drive for self-preservation present in all animals, it is much more than that. It pervades man's whole personality. He is aware, however, dimly and subconsciously of his own dignity and his own potential, of the difference between what he is and what he might be or ought to be. This need underlies the value systems of Western civilization, and responses to its frustration have been the driving forces behind all social revolutions. A man will not be bought or sold; he will not be treated as a commodity, nor will he remain in a state of servility or subjection indefinitely. He will not, because he simply cannot.

In its more overt form, the need to become appears as the drive for autonomy and for equality, but in its more subtle and more profound aspects it is the need for identity and self-actualization.

ANIMAL VS. HUMAN NEEDS

As with animal needs, human needs are usually expressed in a social form. Take the social desire for promotion with which we are concerned in this book. After stripping off its cultural veneer, we see it exposed as the simple need for recognition, for respect, and finally for love.

It appears to be a workable hypothesis, therefore, to assume that human needs are as primary and as innate as animal needs and that they often underly man's social behavior. Awareness of the dynamics of the human need system is basic to the development of an effective system of manpower utilization.

If we assume that men work only to satisfy animal needs, then we can structure our organizational system to satisfy his needs for food, shelter, clothing, and rest. But, if we accept the premise that men work to master their environment, to love and be loved, and ultimately to establish their own identities as free, responsible human beings, then we shall have to do much more than feed and clothe them. We shall have a much larger task of selection, placement, development, and reward. This is so for two reasons.

First, each need system has its own satisfying objects and activities. A biological need is never satisfied by a psychological activity, and vice versa.

We do not have to be told that a starving man will not be filled by reading a cookbook, but it is surprising how many people try to satisfy their need for love by sexual activity and fail.

Second, each need system has a different effect upon the tension that arouses it. Satisfaction of a biological need results in tension reduction. There is a point in eating beyond which we simply can eat no more. But the satisfaction of a psychological need leads to the arousal of tension at a higher level. The more knowledge a person acquires, the greater seems to be his need for it. Wisdom brings with it a deeper appreciation of one's ignorance.

Healthy, mature adults seek to fulfill themselves through the attainment of psychological goals—knowledge, love, and identity. Pathological or sick people try to satisfy their human needs through animal activities, and that is impossible.

Early Developmental Experiences

Life is not so simple, however. For one thing, much of our everyday behavior is aimed at satisfying a host of superficial social needs. For another, behavior is often of a purely defensive character, representing not so much the satisfaction of a need as the avoidance of a real or imagined threat. Both types of behavior are the consequences of early developmental experiences.

Every human being arrives in the world with two distinct sets of needs. But it is a world with a fairly firm conviction as to how these needs may properly be satisfied, and it is a world composed of people with needs of their own. The needs of the newly born child, therefore, impel him to activities to satisfy them; some are rewarded, some are not, and some are punished. Through this process of socialization the very malleable youngster acquires an interpretation of his environment and a pattern of behavior to cope with it. If he is lucky, his behavior will be functional and integrated. If he is not, it will be dysfunctional and he will spend his life in defensive patterns of behavior that are largely self-defeating. As he grows to adulthood, his style of life will continue to bring results that reinforce his earlier interpretation of his world. As a fully grown adult, he will have a pattern of behavior and adjustment so firmly rooted that the likelihood of changes in it is quite remote. Such a pattern of behavior and responses to needs is what constitutes a personality. Its consistency and durability make human assessment possible.

For, by the time a person reaches his adult years, his genetic inheritance and his early experiences have thrust him into a trajectory through life that is as fixed as that of a guided missile. If we know the characteristics of the roles he must play and the life-space through which he must pass, we can plot his course as precisely as the orbit of an astronaut. In assessment, then, the problem is not just the evaluation of the personality but the description of the job the person is to do and the characteristics of the environment in which he must do it. Let us keep this in mind as we continue our examination of the manager's human side.

The Dimensions of the Personality

A person's physical constitution is composed of several subsystems: the central nervous system, the circulatory system, and the digestive system. All these systems interact to form the behavior that satisfies his biological needs. Similarly, the psychological constitution is composed of subsystems: the intellectual system and the motivational system. These subsystems form a complex, interdependent, and dynamic network of personality traits that we call the *human personality*.

The Intellectual System

Common sense and our own experiences inform us that every human being possesses a faculty for organizing and interpreting his sensations and acting upon them, that some people seem to have a greater amount of it than others, that it seems to be distinct from all other human characteristics, and that the degree to which one possesses it has a good deal to do with one's personal effectiveness. This faculty is what we refer to as the *intellectual system*. It includes not only the functions of the intellect itself, such as perceiving, remembering, abstracting, and judging, but all the abilities, skills, and knowledge that go into human activity.

Ability refers to the physical or mental power to perform an act, either now or in the future. If the ability is possessed now, it is usually referred to as a *skill;* if it can be exercised only by special training, it is referred to as an *aptitude*. A person with an unusually fine voice has the ability to *become* a talented singer; without it no amount of training could produce good singing. Thus, the first task in developing talent is to identify ability, either potential or realized.

Ability can be either generalized or special. General ability, which is the capacity to perform a variety of mental or physical tasks, is called *intelligence*. Intelligence, which is essential to the development of talent, appears to be influenced by heredity to a considerable extent, a fact that is too little recognized or appreciated. Just as some people are born athletes, possessing strength, agility, and endurance to perform well in almost any sport, some people are endowed with mental faculties that enable them to perform well in any intellectual activity.

Most people possess a number of special abilities that result from their unique combination of mental and physical abilities. The ability to carry a tune, to draw a picture, to solve a mechanical puzzle, or to learn to type fast—all these are instances of special ability; and the line between heredity and early parental encouragement as sources of special abilities is so fuzzy that it is difficult to say where one begins and the other leaves off. But one thing is sure: Special abilities show up early in life or never.

We can now identify one major key to our problem of making managers—ability. If an ability does not exist at least potentially, it can never emerge as a highly developed skill. Since not everyone possesses general or special abilities in the same degrees, not everyone possesses managerial ability. To determine whether a person does possess it, we must look for signs of it relatively early in his life. For by early adulthood the intellectual system is pretty well formed. There is likely to be a change in only one respect: in the accumulation of information. By the age of 18, therefore, a person is as "smart" as he ever will be.

But the question is, what constitutes "smartness"? What do we really mean by "intelligence"? We are not really sure, but one thing we do know: It is not just the ability to learn, a trait measured by most "intelligence" tests. For centuries the notion prevailed that intelligence was a unitary quality, a global capacity of the individual to act purposefully, to think rationally, and to deal effectively with his environment. However, more recent studies based on advanced statistical designs have exploded this idea and have shown intelligence to be many-faceted. Thus it is quite unsound to make sweeping conclusions about a person's intellectual ability on the basis of a test score that measures only one portion of it.

There have been several attempts to build models of the intellectual system. Two of the most explicit and empirically oriented are those of Raymond Cattell and J. P. Guilford.

Guilford. Guilford organizes the intellect into three major categories—content, operation, and product.[4] *Content* refers to the material or informa-

---

[4] J. P. Guilford, *The Nature of Human Intelligence* (New York: McGraw-Hill, 1967).

tion manipulated by the intellect and is divided into four subcategories: figural, symbolic, semantic, and behavioral. *Operations* refers to the processes involved in manipulating the information and is divided into five subcategories: cognition, memory, divergent production, convergent production, and evaluation. *Product* pertains to the way in which the information occurs and is divided into six subcategories: units, classes, relations, systems, transformations, and implications.

Thus Guilford's model divides the structure of the intellect into three dimensions with 120 cells, each containing a distinctly different factor. It is well to note that this model describes only the capacity of the individual; that is, the basic machinery as it exists in his genes. It is not the only intellectual model developed by psychologists.

Cattell. Cattell's system is less elaborate,[5] but it does not deny the validity of Guilford's model. Cattell refers to Guilford's 120 factors as primary variables that can be grouped under two broad types of intelligence, fluid and crystallized. Crystallized general ability shows up in skills that can be acquired by cultural experience: vocabulary, numerical skills, and even habits of logical reasoning.

Fluid intelligence, while related to crystallized intelligence, is not as amenable to cultural influences. It shows up as the ability to perceive complex relationships in new environments. Most standard measures of intelligence, about which we shall have much more to say in Chapter 10, really only measure crystallized intelligence. Yet for management positions, as we shall also point out, the skills affected most by fluid intelligence are the more critical.

Because of its many-faceted nature, and because of the complex interaction of abilities, skills, and knowledge, we prefer the term "intellectual system" to the word "intelligence." This view of the intellectual system has many implications for the selection of managers, among the most important being the following:

1. The intellectual capacities of human beings are quite varied and complex. It is, therefore, quite misleading to generalize about a person's intelligence on the basis of performance on a single test calling for only a few intellectual skills.
2. Certain abilities, such as verbal fluency, may give a person of average intelligence the appearance of possessing a high order of general intel-

[5] Raymond B. Cattell, "Are I.Q. Tests Intelligent?" in *Readings in Psychology Today* (Del Mar, Calif.: CRM Books, 1969), pp. 336–342.

ligence. The measurement and the evaluation of the intellectual system, therefore, are quite complex and require a good deal of caution and considerable expertise.

3. The intellectual system is a product of a person's heredity and environmental exposure, but early life experiences seem to play a critical role in its emergence as a system. These experiences—the degree of physical nourishment, psychological stimulation, social encouragement, and cultural enrichment—not only inhibit or advance the extension and the elaboration of the intellectual system but shape its course and direct its expression into specific channels. By early adulthood, therefore, the die is cast for life, and no amount of intervention from that point on can materially alter the basic structure and the function of the developed system.

4. The intellectual system is affected in important ways by other systems, both physical and psychological. Reading speed, for example, is a product not only of mental ability but of physical abilities such as eye movements and visual acuity. But it is affected most by motivation, which determines what a person will do with what he can do.

The Motivational System

Besides fostering the growth of intellectual abilities, early life experiences set their indelible imprint on the way a person chooses to satisfy his needs. What a person chooses to do depends, of course, on his physical and mental ability. Something else, however, intervenes.

A particular event may appear to one man as a challenge; to a second, as a threat. The man who sees it as threatening may fight, while another who sees it in the same way may run away. Of those who are inclined to fight, some will do it with spirit and energy; others, with timidity and fear. These differences in response stem from the unique motivational system each person possesses.

The motivational system, which is popularly referred to as the "personality," appears to be composed of many dimensions that have been given a wide variety of labels, such as extroversion, self-confidence, sociability, aggressiveness, masculinity, thoughtfulness, and hypermania. Basically, these traits can be reduced to three: attitudes, drive, and expression.

Attitudes. By the time he reaches maturity, each person has organized his intellectual and emotional processes with respect to certain aspects of his internal and external world that provide him with a readiness to respond to life situations. This organization contains *affective* elements (that is, a liking for or an aversion to particular activities) and an *evaluative* element (that is, a perception of some activities as desirable and others as undesirable).

Each of us, for example, has a set of hypotheses about people: They are to be trusted or distrusted; they are friendly or hostile; they are honest or dishonest. These hypotheses determine our behavior.

Attitudes are not the same as opinions or beliefs. The latter, which lie close to the surface of the personality, are readily expressed, are more lightly held, and are easier to change. As one gets closer to the core of the personality, however, these hypotheses become more generalized, more rigid, and more inaccessible to conscious control or articulation. For example, when asked for his views on honesty, a person will assert his *belief* that honesty is the best policy and declare that he always tries to behave honestly. His real *attitude* toward honesty can only be inferred from a careful observation of his behavior in situations that call for it, as when he completes his income tax return or applies for employment or sells his car. Often, when confronted with evidence, a person will be astonished at his attitudes.

From early life, attitudes are formed in such a way that they tend to dominate the whole personality. At the deepest level, a person develops either a positive or a negative attitude toward himself. This *ego* or *self-concept* is the most pervasive aspect of the personality. A weak self-concept is debilitating. At its worst, it incapacitates the individual for almost any adaptive activity and drives him to the extremes of self-defense where he must concentrate most of his attention and energy on himself. In milder forms, it leads to the adoption of defense mechanisms that are aimed at warding off threats to self-esteem or to reducing the pain already generated by a wounded ego.

The self-concept interacts with the other basic attitudes toward life, toward people, toward God, toward authority, toward country. Together they form a system that is either positive or negative.

Positively oriented people, referred to as optimists or extroverts, are usually cheerful, constructive, and supportive; they tend to view life as something to be acted upon and controlled. Negatively oriented people, referred to as pessimists and introverts, are cautious, apprehensive, and defensive; they are likely to view life as something to react to or be controlled by.

The magnitude, the intensity, and the salience of attitudes determine the situations in which people prefer to exercise their physical and their intellectual abilities and the degree of acceptance they will be accorded by the society in which they live. An innate ability will remain undeveloped unless the possessor has a positive attitude toward exercising it—unless, that is, he sees it as pleasing to him and clearly desirable. The development of such abilities as concert singing and marathon running requires long periods of hard work and self-denial. Consequently, the innate abilities of people will be brought to their full realization only by extremely positive attitudes toward them.

The attitudinal system gives direction and character to the total satisfaction of human needs. It influences a person's perception of his environment, his interpretation of it, and his response to it. In this process, certain aspects of the need system become salient and define the major behavioral orientation of the person in question and the environmental situation he will prefer. At present, psychologists have identified three major need orientations.[6]

1. Achievement-oriented people. People with positive attitudes toward life seek situations affording an opportunity for them to act on their environment, to grow in it, and to be recognized by it. The salient need here is called *achievement*. People motivated by this need generally are characterized by strong, positive feelings of self-regard and a belief that the environment can be mastered. They prefer situations in which they can take personal responsibility for finding solutions to problems, and they generally set modest goals, take calculated risks, and look for concrete feedback on how well they have done.

2. Power-oriented people. Other people are more ambivalent toward life, being both positively and negatively oriented toward themselves and others. They are active responsibility seekers, desiring to supervise and to direct the actions of others. Most salient here is the need for power, and people with this orientation derive satisfaction from controlling the means of influencing others. When the need for power is accompanied by a strong need for achievement, the combination results in constructive, responsible managerial behavior. But power orientation can be exhibited in a defensive, negative way. This manifestation is represented by a need to subjugate others, to control them, and to dominate them in an autocratic style.

3. Affiliation-oriented people. People whose attitudinal systems are negative are apprehensive about life and seek security from it. The salient need

[6] For more details on these orientations see Saul W. Gellerman, *Motivation and Productivity* (New York: American Management Association, 1963).

of such people is for affiliation. Such people fall into two categories: Those in the first group look for warm, friendly, compassionate relationships with others; and, as with teachers, welfare workers, and missionaries, they satisfy their needs by entering into helping relationships with others. Members of the second group look for highly structured situations with well-defined protective arrangements that include promotion by seniority, tenure of office, pensions, and fringe benefits.

Drive. A person has to expend energy to satisfy his needs in ways specified by his attitudinal system. The energy so expended can be both physical and psychical; the first refers to the absolute amount of energy available, and the second to the relative amount available for a specific activity. The absence of physical energy is known as *fatigue,* which represents the inability to act because of previous activity. The absence of psychic energy is referred to as *ennui,* which is the inability to act because the activity fails to stimulate action. Each of us has his own store of energy resources and a threshold for its activation. A worker may feel too exhausted to work overtime, but later he can spend his evening bowling with enthusiasm. The combination of physical and psychic energy that a person can mobilize for a specific task is called *drive,* and it can be general or specific.

Those with high general drive levels are usually vigorous, industrious, and action-oriented people. If, in addition, the drive can be mobilized into specific channels, the person can direct his energy constructively and purposefully at concentrated targets. The high-drive person who can harness his energy will not waste it on idle behavior that promises little return for his own need satisfaction.

Those who have high levels of free-floating energy but lack the ability to harness it are less effective. Often they appear as the whirling dervishes of the executive suite who send up clouds of dust out of which seems to come little in the way of constructive action.

People with strong inner anxieties must usually devote their energy to keeping their anxiety level under control. Consequently, they have less energy available for outward, constructive behavior. An insecure person, placed in a situation like a managerial post that requires high drive, will almost certainly be unequal to it.

The drive system, therefore, has two basic dimensions—the amount of energy available for positive, ego-enhancing activity and the degree to which it can be harnessed for maximum application to a specific objective.

Persons characterized by free-floating energy or a high level of inner anxiety are more effective in social and recreational areas of life where the roles are much more ambiguous and less demanding. In the complex and responsible positions at the upper echelons of the managerial world, incumbents not only must possess a high degree of drive but must be able to mobilize it for effective application. There are, unfortunately, not many individuals who have these characteristics—which is another dimension of the managerial crisis.

The outward expression of one's attitudes and drives constitutes the third stage of the motivational system where the man is joined to an occupational role and a career.

Expression. The chief means of acting out one's self-concept is an occupation. For centuries, the idea that man worked simply to satisfy his animal needs impregnated the fabric of the philosophical, religious, and economic thought of the Western world. But behavioral scientists have evolved a broader view of the motivation to work that is based upon a deeper understanding of human needs. The new view incorporates the following basic tenets:

1. The choice of an occupation is an expressive act that reflects a person's abilities, attitudes, and drives. An occupation, consequently, represents a way of life rather than a set of isolated work functions. It implies a certain status for the individual, prescribes a particular style of living, and denotes the individual's place in the community.
2. The choice of an occupation represents an active implementation of the self-concept. In holding or adjusting to a job, a person tests his concept of himself against reality to find out whether he can actually live up to his picture of himself.
3. The interaction of the person with the requirements of his work role creates for him a limited number of methods for dealing with environmental and interpersonal problems. Occupations that attract a person reveal his basic attitude and his preferred adjustment style; those that repel him reveal situations that he perceives to be distasteful.
4. The members of a specific occupational class have similar personalities and similar histories of personal development. Their grouping together in the same occupational and organizational environment creates an interpersonal climate that is typical of that profession or organization.

These principles have led occupational psychologists to project theories of personality based upon vocational choice. Essentially, these theories rest on the idea that people are happy and effective only in certain specific occupational and organizational roles; that, within the limits of the labor market, they will seek their favorite roles as persistently as water seeks its own level. Much of the exploratory job behavior of young adults represents an effort to find the ideal situation in which to express their own unique personality traits.

There are two dimensions to the expressive system: the horizontal (that is, the specific field or job family, such as accounting, medicine, or teaching, that the person chooses) and the vertical (that is, the level of responsibility at which he hopes to function). Some theorists add a third dimension, enterprise, that refers to the particular sector of the economy—public, private, or educational—in which the person finds it most satisfying to express himself.

Vocational choice, therefore, is a cumulative process of decision making begun in childhood and largely irreversible. Young people today, in the highly developed countries, have a latitude of choice never before experienced by any similar group in the history of mankind, and some authorities attribute the youthful unrest in these countries to a flight from the responsibility implied in this decision-making activity.

Whatever the decision, the fact remains that by the time he reaches adulthood, each person is able to function effectively in only a few of the wide assortment of occupational cells in the three-way matrix provided by society. As we shall point out later, the managerial role is only one of many available in the organization. Men with the ability, the attitude, and the drive to perform these roles effectively are difficult to find. When they are discovered, they often are labeled as misfits because they are self-confident, aggressive, outspoken, impatient, and highly intelligent. They are the kinds of persons that force a company to compete, to build, and to grow. Many companies avoid them because management is a little frightened of them and does not know how to handle them. But, as we said at the beginning of this chapter, adjusting to them is the name of the game. For organizations by themselves are helpless. It is only the human being who counts; only he can plan, dream, create, and decide.

The first lesson to be learned in the selection of managers, therefore, is that they are human. They have needs, attitudes, drives, and expressions that determine success or failure. But their humanness does much more than that; it goes far in deciding the climate of the organization: how it will achieve its goals and even what goals it will seek. The successful organization will then adjust to these men; that is, to those who have the intellectual and the motivational systems they need to become effective managers.

3

The Effective Manager

A FEW years ago a Montgomery Ward store in a small midwestern city was in deep trouble. A large army post nearby had been deactivated, a new throughway had been constructed two miles west of the store's location, and a major competitor had placed a new store in a modern shopping center on the new throughway. The regional planners in Kansas City had no alternative but to close the store down. Since the lease still had a year to run, they dispatched a young manager to the store to operate it, partly as a development experience for him and partly as a replacement for the experienced manager, who was needed elsewhere.

Somehow they forgot to tell the young manager that the store was to be closed down—or, if they did, he did not listen very carefully. He took over the store as though it were the latest merchandising complex in a modern shopping plaza. Sales volume soon began to pick up; the attitude of the store personnel shifted from apathy to excitement; in six months the earnings moved from the red to the black and stayed there. Plans to close the store were quietly dropped. Asked what brought about the abrupt shift from a loser to a profit maker, Montgomery Ward's regional vice-president shrugged his shoulders and said of the manager, "He just went down there and managed the hell out of that store."

It is often easy to enumerate reasons why an enterprise succeeds or fails. With so many variables that appear to have a make-or-break impact upon the outcome, there is a natural tendency to overlook the importance of the man, particularly the man in charge. Society subscribes to the idea that management is important, but society doesn't really believe it. Even top managers are dubious about the significance of their own roles in the success or failure of an enterprise. When things go wrong, they tend to blame the system; when things go right, they modestly give credit to "the team."

The only way to manage an organization effectively is to give managers authority to run it and then hold them strictly accountable for the results. This idea is hardly new to anyone, however rarely it is carried out in practice. But the idea breaks down because we know so little about picking men who have the capacity to manage. And, if we ask a blind man to drive our car, we can hardly blame him if he runs it into a tree.

The tendency to delude ourselves into believing that organizations largely run themselves is why there are so many counterfeits in the management ranks. An advertisement in the business section of a large metropolitan daily placed by an executive search firm very aptly describes this character. He will be glib, intelligent, and persuasive. He will be personable, even charming. He may have excellent references. But once on the executive staff he will produce little and destroy more.

Sometimes a counterfeit manager can get by for years in a company by the simple device of not remaining in the same job for more than two years. Rensis Likert points out that decisions have short- and long-range effects.[1] The short-range effects usually deal with the kinds of costs that show up quickly in the accounting system. Long-range effects usually are felt first in the intervening variables such as employee loyalties, attitudes, and motivations. These variables affect the end-result variables such as productivity and earnings much more slowly, so that the outcome is difficult to trace back to a particular decision or to a specific manager. Likert puts the time interval between a decision affecting the human resources of a company and its effect on investment return at about two years.

Managerial effectiveness becomes, thereby, an elusive quality, greatly to be desired but difficult to pinpoint. Advances in the behavioral sciences are making inroads. We now know that only certain types of personalities have the talent to achieve excellence in management positions. We also know that excellence is a quality admired in all societies but that societies differ in what they consider to be excellent. In postindustrial societies, excellence is construed as "talent and its triumphant fulfillment."

Most of us have a healthy respect and admiration for talented people

[1] Rensis Likert, *The Human Organization* (New York: McGraw-Hill, 1967).

because they are not only the leaders of society but its chief contributors. They are in the minority everywhere, but most of the world's accomplishments in the arts, sciences, government, philosophy, and religion can be attributed to this 5 to 10 percent of the population. The remaining individuals are nothing more than the consumers of the talent of the richly endowed few. It is no different with managerial talent. As Howard Johnson, the young chairman of the company bearing his name, said recently, "After all, how many really good men are there in a company . . . the really great ones? Five, ten, twenty? There are never enough, and you can never afford to lose a single one."

In our discussion of managerial talent we have already defined it to some extent by looking at the human side of the manager. Originally a word denoting a money unit, the word "talent" refers to a special skill. Opera singers, poets, and professional football players are people of talent, and so are managers. The crucial question is how to identify and to develop talent. Here the answer is more complex. Talent is a product of three interacting elements in a dynamic system: ability, attitude, and opportunity. The first two are possessed by the individual, but the third must be furnished by the social environment.

Regardless of ability or attitude, talent can never be achieved unless the possessor is given the opportunity to develop it and to exercise it. All the "mute, inglorious Miltons" who lie in country churchyards around the world are victims of a lack of opportunity. To use another analogy, a young man with a great arm, a fine eye, a good pair of legs, and a strong desire to succeed as a major-league baseball player will wind up driving a truck or selling soap unless he is discovered by a scout, has the benefit of top-flight coaching, and gets a chance to play his way up to and in the major leagues.

Success as a manager depends upon the organization in which one functions. The managerial role exists only in an organization. To bring managerial talent to the surface, we must understand organizational as well as human behavior.

Organizational Behavior

The Managerial Society is a society of organizations. Developing a theory of organizations, therefore, is as important as a theory of personality. The two are not as exclusive as would appear on the surface.

An organization is a cooperative system of people, acting together to achieve a common purpose that in some way contributes to the purposes of the society of which it is a part. While organizations vary widely in their purposes and their activities, they all have the common dimension of management, a common set of administrative ideas, and the common role of manager.

There are three basic elements in the organization system: purpose, people, and action. Let us look at each of these to get a clearer perspective of the manager's role and the management process.

Organizational Purpose

By far the most important element in the organizational system is its purpose, because—being its reason for existence—this purpose gives direction and meaning to all its activities. The articulation of the corporate purpose is a demanding, elusive task. But it will also be rewarding, for it raises fundamental questions about goals, member roles, and the value of many of the organization's activities.

Until recently, when the management-by-objectives approach was adopted by many corporations, the definition of organizational purpose was completely neglected. It was simply assumed that profits and a return on investment were the organizational purposes. The more astute managers have come to realize, however, that these are only indications of how well the corporation is achieving its purpose, whatever that may be.

Defining corporate purpose, therefore, is a vital exercise. Marketing authority Theodore Levitt of the Harvard Business School has noted that buggy-whip manufacturers went out of business because they thought their purpose was to make the highest-quality buggy whips at the lowest possible cost. Had they thought of themselves as being in the transportation business, they might still be in business today, because society has a continuous need of transportation and only a temporary need for buggy whips.

The delineation of purpose is only an exercise in philosophy unless the purpose is translated into tangible goals and programs for achieving them. It is generally agreed today that goals must be established throughout the organization in a two-way process of communication.

To implement goals and objectives, organizations have to develop standards, procedures, and practices. These have a tendency to be substituted for the goals and the objectives. When an organization is managed by objectives, it becomes performance-oriented; it grows and it develops and it becomes socially useful.

Organization Members

There are three classes of people that make up any organization, each identified by its reason for joining the organization, each making its unique contribution to the organization's purpose, and each essential to its continued existence. The first and perhaps the most important class is the *consumer* group—those who use the products or the services provided by the organization. Whoever they are—customers, clients, patients, students, or citizens—they are essential to the organization's purpose. The organization exists for them, and it cannot survive without them.

The second class of members is the *policy-maker* group—those who articulate the precise goals of the organization and furnish the financial resources with which to achieve them. In industry, stockholders comprise this class of membership, delegating their responsibilities to a board of directors. In government, it is the taxpayers, and they exercise their responsibilities through the legislature. In enunciating policies and defining goals, the needs of the other members must be taken into account or difficulties will ensue.

The third class of members is made up of the *employees,* who contribute their personal services to the organization in return for wages and salaries. Employees can be subdivided into *managers* (who direct the administrative process) and *operators* (who actually produce the organization's goods and services).

While the function of the managers is to make organizational decisions, they do not exercise it unilaterally or independently. Decisions have to be made within a policy framework, and they have to be carried out by operators. Managers must influence policy on the one hand and persuade operators to implement policy decisions on the other. Conflict often arises between policy makers and managers—as, for example, between the president and the Congress and between operators and managers (say, in a labor dispute).

One of the realities of organization life is the ever present tendency for the other two member classes to usurp the decision-making function. If the management group is weak, they often do, and then the whole organization suffers. From the previous chapter we can see why. People join organizations because they see in joining a way of achieving a personal goal. The immediate and personal goals of the three member classes vary. Policy makers desire a maximum return on their investments, employees want optimum rewards for their labors, and consumers look for the highest quality of goods and services at the lowest possible price. These logical but divergent goals represent a legitimate, unending conflict with which the organization must cope, principally by designating a strong and an effective managerial group to be the final decision-making body.

As an organization decision maker, the manager is thereby continually confronted with the task of *suboptimization;* that is, with the necessity of maximizing the satisfaction of organizational needs by less than optimal satisfaction of any member's needs. Furthermore, since a manager has at best only an imperfect ability to foresee the future, a decision that appears optimal for the present may turn out to be a serious error over the long run. Decisions that are long-run failures result in higher opportunity costs for the organization which represent penalties suffered for not having done the best possible thing.

The manager, consequently, plays a central role in the organization as the linking pin among policy makers, employees, and customers. He must view the organization as a whole, understand its purpose, influence its policy formulation, establish its goals, make its decisions, see that they are carried out, and evaluate the results. In a real sense, therefore, he constitutes the intellectual and the motivating force of the organization. This is why we can say with such assurance that an effective manager's worth is incalculable.

The Administrative Process

Managing an enterprise effectively is a great challenge representing the highest level of human talent, the end product not only of the individual's ability, personality, and experience but of civilized man's accumulated wisdom. To emphasize this principle, we must examine the third element of the organization—the action that joins the people to the purpose, the administrative process.

The administrative process is common to all organized effort, public or private, profit or nonprofit, civil or military. Although it varies in form, there is an underlying similarity to its substance wherever it is carried out. Building the pyramids, running the affairs of the Roman Empire, organizing great nations out of feudal rivalries and creating large land armies out of undisciplined hordes of armored knights were administrative feats that rank with the successful execution of the lunar landing mission. In fact, no political, technological, or social movement—not even the spreading of the Gospel—could flourish and maintain itself without adequate administration. The historical landscape is covered with the tombstones of magnificent ideas that died, not from irrelevancy nor because their time had not come, but simply because of weak administration.

The administrative process is often referred to as a "black box" because it simulates an intricate and complicated wiring system of decision and action that transforms inputs into outputs. If the administrative process is functional and productive, the basic inputs of ideas, men, money, and material are transformed into the intended outputs: job satisfaction for employees, return on invested capital for stockholders, and high-quality goods and services for customers. When it is dysfunctional or counterproductive, other outputs will be emitted that take the form of waste. Effective administration consists in maintaining a high ratio between functional and dysfunctional outputs.

In Exhibit 1 we remove the cover from the black box to show the details of the administrative process. It has three basic dimensions: *organizing, communicating,* and *managing.* The administrative process is therefore three-dimensional, with each dimension subdivided into more precise administrative tasks. Organizing refers to the structure of personal interrelaoperation of the members. When so viewed, the administrative process betionships in the administrative process; communicating, to the network of information links among them; managing, to the action taken to achieve cocomes a dynamic way of disposing the organization's resources to the maximum extent to achieve specific goals. Under the direction of competent managers, all the employees of the organization whose contributions (though equally vital) are not those of the manager are linked together in a unified effort.

Organizing. Organizing has two dimensions: *coordinating* (which extends horizontally across the organization) and *subordinating* (which projects vertically up through it). Coordinating includes the task of allocating responsibilities to each member and informing the others of his planned actions. Subordinating refers to the process of committing the organization's resources to a course of action. It naturally involves the use of authority; that is, the right to unify actions through rules binding on all.

Communicating. Communicating is the act of processing information and of facilitating organizational problem solving. As the power supply of the organization, these processes are so essential to the organization that it can function only as effectively as they permit.

EXHIBIT 1
The Administrative Process

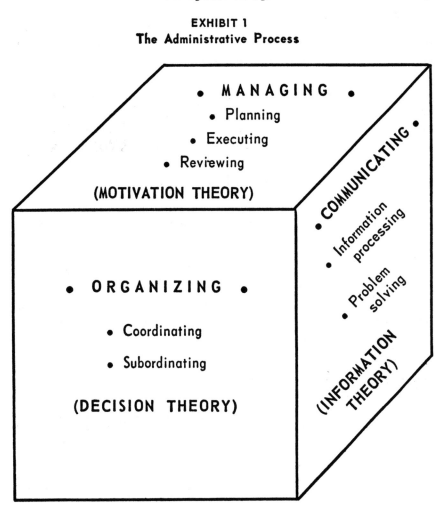

Managing. Managing, the task of directing the organization's activities, is a cyclical function that involves three phases: *planning,* establishing objectives and deciding how to achieve them; *executing,* implementing the plans; and *reviewing,* determining how well objectives have been attained.

Since the manager presides over and directs the administrative process, his role covers information handling, problem solving, coordinating, subordinating, planning, operating, and reviewing. But decision making lies at the heart of these processes. Organizing is the process of allocating the decision-making functions to the various members; communicating is the process of providing decision makers with appropriate information on which to base their decisions; and managing is the process of making, executing, and reviewing decisions. Consequently, it becomes clear from this brief review of the administrative process that the function of the manager is to make decisions and that all his other activities are subordinate to it.

The fact is that many organizations are not structured this way at all. Employees with the title of manager make few decisions or are involved in activities unrelated to the administrative process such as merchandising, banking, engineering, or accounting. When so engaged, they have no time for managing. This situation is the root of many of management's problems. To understand why, we must look further.

The Concept of Role

So far, we have examined an organization as a cooperative system. It can also be studied as a network of *roles*. Role analysis is useful because it helps to appreciate the importance of role definition, introduces us to such significant ideas as role enactment, conflict, and confusion, and suggests another cause of the managerial crisis.

The Importance of Role Definition

There are differences in the ideas of position, job, and role. A *position* (or a post or a station) is a precise location on an organization chart. The chart may be drawn formally on paper, or it may merely exist in the common understanding of the organization members. But the position will be a reality as a reference point showing its relationship to the positions of other employees.

Groups of positions with roughly the same tasks are called classes or *jobs*. Generally these tasks are given the same job title, such as "sales representative," and are put into writing in the form of job descriptions which provide the basis for compensation and promotion plans. Since job descriptions customarily contain information concerning what is to be done and with what degree of discretion, they are limited in scope to the more formal, external aspects of a role.

A role, however, covers all the behavior expected of an incumbent, formal and informal, personal, social, and cultural. It includes not only what is expected of the incumbent but his perception of this expectation.

Some forms of behavior critical to success in a position are never mentioned in a job description. For example, it may be imperative for a manager to refrain from profanity in certain social settings, to be temperate at cocktail parties, and to join certain community organizations. These duties are hardly ever written into a job description and are rarely considered in the compensation plan, but a man could get fired for failing to live up to them.

After the formulation of purposes and goals, the next logical step in the management of an organization is the definition of tasks and the clarification of roles. These flow from the organization's purpose; they are independent of the personalities who enact them. This very important point is usually expressed by the phrase "The position seeks the man." A person can change his role only by modifying or ignoring organization purposes and goals, which is a common practice. But, unless tasks are clearly defined and roles clarified, there is no way of establishing the criteria of effective job performance. You cannot evaluate a man's performance unless you know what he was asked to do. And, if you cannot evaluate performance, you have no way of determining the personality traits necessary for it.

This "for the want of a nail, the shoe was lost" argument explains the confusion and the difficulties encountered in the selection, development, and motivation of managers. In the absence of a clear idea of the dimensions of the managerial role, it is impossible to evaluate managerial performance or to identify the personal traits of the effective manager.

The logic of this argument has in no way hindered the flood of literature describing the qualities of a good manager. Some of the role specifications have been temporarily valid in certain eras, leading men to deduce incorrectly that they were absolute and universal. The accumulation of these erroneous deductions becomes embodied in a tradition that is widely accepted as true for all times and all situations. The conflicts, power struggles, and institutional upheavals that follow are attributed solely to the persons involved rather than in good measure to the erroneous assumptions about managerial role requirements.

Role-Theory Principles

The task of managerial selection begins with a careful definition of the manager's role. This task is more than an exercise in job evaluation. It involves an understanding of the principles of role theory.

Role theory is a highly elaborate system with many concepts and propositions that are useful for the study of human behavior in social structures. We are concerned with only a few ideas here: role enactment, identification, ambiguity, confusion, and conflict.

Role enactment. Enacting a role requires at least two people, the one who acts and the other for whom he acts. For role behavior is distinguished from personal behavior by the fact that in a role a person behaves according to his understanding of what others expect of him, as when he pays his taxes, provides food for his children, or performs his job. In personal behavior, on the other hand, he acts strictly to satisfy his own needs, as when he eats, watches television, or plays golf.

Roles are assigned by groups (for example, the father of a family), by organizations (a vice-president), and by society (a citizen). No one can escape from some form of role behavior if he wishes to live and work with other people. The more he wishes to belong and to be approved by a specific group, the more he has to adapt his behavior to its expectations. Conversely, if a group wishes to maintain harmony and coordination within its membership, it must agree on its role assignments and requirements and communicate them to each member.

Role identification. Sometimes personal behavior so blends into the role that the two become indistinguishable. This is known as role identification, a common example of which is a man's identification with his role as a father. His son finds it difficult to see the man as anything but his father, and thus his father's personal qualities become synonymous with the role of father everywhere. If his father is strict, all fathers are strict. Role identification often misleads observers into confusing personality traits with role requirements. Lists of the qualities of effective managers contain numerous personal traits that are specific to individual managers and not to all managers.

Role status. In particular social settings, roles acquire attributes that make them more or less desirable to the group members. This aspect of role is referred to as *status.* High status stems from the capacity of the role to influence the actions of the other group members. The ability to influence others, to bind their wills, to get them to do what they otherwise might not do is called *power,* and the possession of it is referred to as *leadership.* The social status of power seems to be universal, and it is eagerly sought after by men of all cultures. But its presence in the managerial role is an important reason why people seek it, and it plays havoc with the way they are selected for it.

Role ambiguity. Since the expectations of people in any social system are often unarticulated and are constantly changing, many if not most role requirements are ambiguous, confused, and even contradictory. The role of a first-line supervisor, for example, has evolved over the past 50 years from its high-status perch approaching that of an absolute monarch to that of a mere figurehead today. A supervisor's role in many companies is now so ambiguous that the incumbents are uncertain of what is expected of them; and, even when they are certain, they find that the expectations of their superiors conflict with those of their subordinates.

Role ambiguity and confusion breed irrational and even superstitious behavior. In the absence of a clear understanding of what is expected of them, group members will behave in ways that are dysfunctional in terms of group goals. Take, for example, the manager's role in performance evaluation, which is essential to effective management. Because so few managers or their subordinates really understand what is expected of them in this regard, they go through the formalities of performance evaluation, sometimes with apprehension and embarrassment, sometimes in a ritualistic manner, but always without achieving its objectives.

Role conflict. There are several types of role conflict. The most elementary form is that which occurs *within* the role; that is, when it includes two incompatible tasks. A common example of intrarole conflict occurs in many managerial positions where the incumbent is required to *judge* his subordinates and at the same time *counsel* them. Careful role definition is one way to eliminate this type of conflict.

Another type of role conflict occurs when the requirements of the role are incompatible with the *personality* of the incumbent. A newly promoted sales manager finds that the very traits that contributed to his effectiveness as a salesman seriously limit his effectiveness as a manager. Role-personality conflict is probably the most frequent cause of managerial ineffectiveness. It can be prevented only by careful selection and placement.

A third type of role conflict occurs when two interdependent roles are incompatible. Interrole conflict is inescapable in functionally aligned organizations. The role of the comptroller, for example, clashes with that of the personnel director. The management-by-objectives trend is designed to minimize this form of interrole conflict. However, a more subtle but more insidious form of interrole conflict occurs between a manager and his assistant of the same unit who in a one-over-one design supervise the same subordinates. This form of conflict can be minimized only by sound organizational planning.

Role-Theory Implications

Organizational conflict and managerial-selection inadequacies can often be traced to role ambiguity, confusion, or conflict. They show up in many forms, some of which are as follows:

1. The failure to relate the functions of each managerial position to organization purposes and goals. This failure is usually due to a prior and more serious error, the failure to establish clear and meaningful goals and objectives. Consequently, role specifications tend to stress procedures and techniques and attract incumbents who are procedure-oriented and technique-bound.

2. The position description, which is the formal expression of role behavior, is written primarily to establish the basis for a socially acceptable and a financially practical compensation plan. It thereby reflects the market value of the skills involved rather than the worth of the contribution the role makes to the organization's goals. The job description of an engineering manager, for example, will emphasize technical knowledge and skill even though they influence overall managerial effectiveness only indirectly because the availability of technical skills in the labor market determines compensation levels.

3. The social status and power of a position often obscure its true role dimensions. Because the power and high social status of such top executives as a corporation president, an army general, or a university president are so desirable, the specifications of their positions are defined in the broadest and most ambiguous terms. This ambiguity then may blind people to the incumbent's actual ineffectiveness in enacting the role until long after he has vacated it.

4. The impact of the environment and the incumbent's personality on a role is often so strong that it is quite difficult to isolate its exact demands. This influence is particularly strong in high-level positions where greater role identification is possible. It is relatively simple to think in the abstract about a drill-press operator's role, but we can think of the American presidency only by recalling a specific person such as Lincoln, Roosevelt, or Eisenhower.

The fact remains, however, that each organization role contains certain irreducible limits and unchangeable elements to which the incumbent must adhere if he is to be effective in it and if the organization is to fulfill its purpose. These irreducible limits, which flow from the nature of the organization, prescribe the types of personalities that can successfully perform the managerial role. In the next chapter we shall examine these dimensions, but before doing so we must put together the two models of organization and individual behavior that we have constructed to arrive at a third model.

Managerial Role Effectiveness

Peter Drucker has pointed out that management theory has given little attention to the idea of managerial effectiveness.[2] He says that we have stressed the manager's ability, training, and knowledge but not his specific attribute, his effectiveness. But the trouble goes deeper than this. Broadly speaking, insufficient attention has been paid to the general notion of role effectiveness. Role effectiveness is based upon role-personality compatibility, and it leads to the satisfaction of the needs of both the individual and the organization.

Role-Personality Compatibility

The idea of role-personality compatibility is beginning to attract the attention of management as the evidence piles up demonstrating that satisfaction of animal needs does not motivate workers to perform in other than a mediocre fashion.[3] It is becoming apparent that to obtain and to sustain high-quality job performance a person's psychological system must be engaged. So far, though, no one seems to know exactly how to put this idea into effect.

The trouble has been that both vocational counselors and personnel managers have misunderstood what role effectiveness really implies and how it is achieved. Vocational counselors stress the fact that role effectiveness lies in the satisfaction of the incumbent's human needs. They urge their clients to look for jobs that will enable them to "do their own thing." The clients have thus turned away from many important social roles because they appear to be unattractive, require long hours and hard work, and may tend to dehumanize them. This is one of the reasons for the disenchantment of American youth with the idea of entering on a business career.

[2] Peter F. Drucker, *The Age of Discontinuity* (New York: Harper & Row, 1968), p. 200.
[3] See, for example, Frederick Herzberg, *Work and the Nature of Man* (New York: World Publishing Company, 1966).

Personnel managers, seeing only the other side of the coin, have stressed the contribution that the worker makes to the achievement of the organization's goals. They look for potential employees who have the minimum amount of ability and skill to do the job. Their criterion is whether the man is right for the job; they ignore the equally important corollary of whether the job is right for the man.

Underpinning both approaches is the unquestioned assumption that there is a direct and positive relationship between role performance and role satisfaction, that one accompanies the other in a one-to-one relationship. It has been demonstrated repeatedly that this is not necessarily so. It holds in one direction, in the sense that it is impossible for a human being to sustain high-quality performance in a role that is incompatible with his expressive needs, but it is quite possible for a person to perform a job poorly while he is getting a fair degree of satisfaction from it. When a person finds himself in a role that is incompatible with his needs, he can respond in one of three ways:

1. He can first try to shape the role to his personality. Thus a highly achievement-oriented person who finds his greatest satisfaction in an engineering role will, if promoted to a managerial role, restructure it to de-emphasize or eliminate its entrepreneurial and social responsibilities. This maneuver may so disturb his relationships with his superiors and his subordinates that he finds himself in considerable disfavor. A frequent solution to this conflict is to hire an assistant to handle the social aspects of the job and leave the manager to his first love, engineering. But then he is no longer a manager.

2. If the demands of the role are so inflexible that the incumbent cannot shape them to his own personality, he will leave it or he will be asked to leave it. Although this outcome is the most common cause of resignations and dismissals, it is seldom recognized as such.

3. If the incumbent cannot mold the job to his satisfaction or leave it, he will respond with low-caliber performance and with covert or even overt resistance to the organization's demands. He then becomes a problem to himself and to his employers. Managers often get locked into jobs by pensions, stock options, high salaries, high mortgages, and braces on the children's teeth. The resulting bind creates an inner tension that can be reduced only by such negative behavior as malingering, arguing, and excessive drinking or by the development of ulcers, hemorrhoids, and coronaries.

The Orthogonal Approach to Role Effectiveness

The way to view role effectiveness is to treat performance and satisfaction as two separate and independent outcomes of effective role enactment. Treated orthogonally, each outcome can be represented by a vector running from low to high which, when placed on a chart, forms two of the coordinates of the life-space on which any organization member can be located. As shown in Exhibit 2, the two vectors cross at 90° angles, because they are independent, to form four separate quadrants. It is important to note that each vector is not necessarily unidimensional. Role satisfaction may be a combination of attitudes toward the role context and the role content. The

EXHIBIT 2
A Model of Role Effectiveness

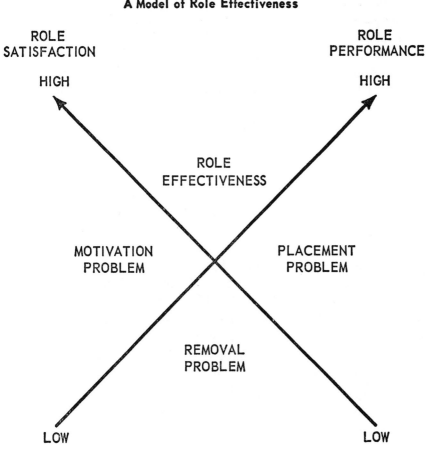

ROLE
SATISFACTION

ROLE
PERFORMANCE

HIGH

HIGH

ROLE
EFFECTIVENESS

MOTIVATION
PROBLEM

PLACEMENT
PROBLEM

REMOVAL
PROBLEM

LOW

LOW

role-performance vector is also a combination of factors, such as performance standards, perception of rewards associated with effort, and the effort extended. It is also true that these vectors represent mean levels of the variable obtained over periods of time. Each individual's role satisfaction and performance fluctuate daily, but they usually fluctuate within a fairly restricted range.

The role-effectiveness quadrant. The upper quadrant, whose occupants enjoy high levels of role satisfaction and performance, constitutes the role-effectiveness area. This is where all employees ought to be, but the evidence suggests that, of those who are there, most are managers who have a greater opportunity to merge their personal goals with organization goals. If an employee is not situated in this quadrant, then he can be termed a problem employee. There are three kinds of problems that may be involved here, each defined by the particular quadrant in which it occurs.

The placement-problem employee quadrant. In the right-hand quadrant are employees who perform at reasonably high levels without experiencing true personal need satisfaction. We name this sector the placement-problem employee quadrant because the problem stems from the fact that the employee has been placed in a role that is incompatible with his personality. Putting managers in this quadrant can really hurt a company. Sooner or later they will let it down, and when they do the crash usually reverberates throughout the organization.

People who find themselves in this quadrant are advised to remove themselves, for, if they cannot (because of the labor market, their high salaries, or other considerations), they will develop the symptoms of maladjustment: ulcers, alcoholism, neuroses, or invalidism that will seriously inhibit their effectiveness and cause them eventually to slide into the lower quadrant.

The motivation-problem employee quadrant. In the quadrant at the left are those employees who, while achieving moderate satisfaction from the job, perform at a mediocre or substandard level. In this quadrant dwell the majority of American workers. We call this quadrant the motivation-problem employee quadrant because people in this category are insufficiently motivated. Their lack of motivation stems from two sources—the rewards are directed at their animal needs, and the role demands are subhuman. Their satisfaction is not genuine because it is based on a varied assortment of fringe benefits that can be enjoyed only off the job.

Many psychologists have argued that role satisfaction and role performance are related to a third variable, rewards. A person's tendency to undertake a particular activity will depend on his expectation that performing that activity will produce certain consequences (rewards) and the attractiveness of those consequences (values) for him. Each person's motivational system determines not only the activities that will satisfy him but his perception of the value of the consequences.

The major rewards offered employees are benefits that are enjoyed by not working; therefore, they are not associated closely enough with job performance. The jobs themselves often have been so simplified that they require intellectual abilities well below those possessed by the average person. Thus they are monotonous and unchallenging and offer no opportunity for enhancement of the self-concept. To motivate employees, then, management must enrich and enlarge the role to engage more of the psychological need system.

One of the problems is a lack of attention paid to employee attitudes. This variable should be monitored as continuously as output data are. Professor Rensis Likert has shown that a drop in employee attitudes usually precedes a drop in performance levels.[4]

The removal-problem employee quadrant. The bottom quadrant, which we have termed the removal-problem employee quadrant, is where all problem employees ultimately land. When a person performs ineffectively or is seriously dissatisfied with his work, his behavior will eventually become a burden for the other members of the organization. Usually, the other members will find a more or less humane way to remove him from the job—or at least from their presence. The principal method is early retirement on or off the job.

We have placed the role-effectiveness quadrant at the top to demonstrate that staying there requires considerable effort by both the organization and the person involved to overcome the gravitational pull of the forces implicit in human nature and organization systems. Some conflict between individual needs and the demands of the organization is inevitable. As we pointed out in the previous chapter, there has to be adjustment on both sides. So far, it has been the individual who has had to do most of the adjusting. As we shall indicate later, there is a powerful tendency in organizations to stifle individualism and to enforce conformity, particularly in the managerial ranks.

Yet the truly effective manager has to be his own man. He must take control of his own career; and, when he finds he cannot satisfy his needs in one organization, he should leave it. And he always does. Thus many

---

[4] Rensis Likert, op. cit., p. 85.

companies by their present practices are actually retaining inferior managers and forcing the better ones out.

Role effectiveness begins with adequate role definition. Lyman Porter and Edward Lawler have constructed a theoretical model, based on the motivation-value-expectancy concept, in which performance is associated with the manager's perception of two types of rewards: *extrinsic* (for example, pay and promotion) and *intrinsic* (something that satisfies self-actualization needs). But performance, they declare, depends upon what effort is expended and on whether it is correctly applied. They found in their studies of seven organizations that, even when a manager exerts a high degree of effort, the resulting job performance may be relatively mediocre because his role perceptions are inaccurate.[5]

To find the answer to the question "Can he become an effective manager?" we therefore have to know what it takes to be one; and, to know what it takes to be one, we must first know what a manager is expected to do.

[5] Lyman W. Porter and Edward E. Lawler III, *Managerial Attitudes and Performance* (Homewood, Ill.: Richard D. Irwin, 1968).

4

The Managerial Role

THE managerial role has probably been misinterpreted more than any other in history. Because its dimensions depend, not only on what is to be done, but on the personality of the doer and the cultural milieu in which he does it, they have been difficult to pin down. It is not surprising, therefore, to find that the definition of the job in the management literature reads like something out of the Boy Scout manual. One trade journal, for example, recently listed these as the attributes of an effective manager: inspirational leadership, broad background, motivational enthusiasm, pride and patience, a sense of timing, and good judgment!

To select, train, motivate, and reward managers equitably, we have to have more than platitudes to go on. No one can be termed an effective or an ineffective manager unless we know what is expected of him. Yet even a superficial inspection of the prevailing practices in public and private management reveals a consistent indifference to the implications of this common-sense notion. And the indifference seems to increase with the importance of the role. In fact, it appears that as a role increases in complexity, significance, and status its dimensions become more ambiguous and vague. There are few corporations that have taken the trouble to analyze the functions of the manager and answer these critical questions: Who is a manager and who is not? What is a manager supposed to do? What are the characteristics of his role that make it uniquely different from others in the corporation?

61

The few studies that have been made, however, afford a clearer insight into the true nature of the managerial role. These studies allow us to begin constructing a more rigorous model of the manager's job on which to base a program of effective utilization of managerial resources. The new model will be quite different from the traditional ones, and it will suggest a reason why there has been so much error in managerial selection.

What Does a Manager Do?

Before discussing the new model of the manager's role, and to illustrate its practical implications, let us examine the management structure of a professional baseball club. The purpose, the people, and the administrative processes of athletic organizations are so clear-cut that they provide an excellent and unusually lucid view of the management process.

A major-league baseball club is organized for the purpose of entertaining a certain sector of the community. There are other social purposes, such as enhancing civic pride, keeping younger people off the streets in the summertime, providing them with adequate male models, and bringing business to the community; but these are byproducts. The primary purpose of a baseball club is entertainment.

The club achieves this purpose by winning the world championship, a goal that is its ultimate test of success. No other goal can be substituted. The attainment of this goal satisfies, first, the team's clients—otherwise known as the "fans." Satisfied clients fill the stadium for every game, and a repeatedly filled stadium insures a substantial return on the club owner's investment. The players themselves reap many benefits in the form of fame and the financial rewards that accompany athletic success in our society. In this way, the three member groups of the organization are tied together by a common purpose that fits in nicely with the personal goals of each.

Championships are won, not necessarily by the most talented teams of players, but by the most effectively run organizations. The amazing success of the New York Yankees during the period from 1920 to 1960 is proof of this assertion. The most effectively run organization is characterized by three clear-cut levels of management, each with different role requirements.

On the first level is the field manager whose task is to make decisions about who will play and how the game will be played. He decides the batting order for the game, selects the pitcher, and during the game makes on-the-spot decisions as to who will pinch-hit and whether to sacrifice or to hit and run. For maximum team effort, everyone above and below him must defer to him in this responsibility.

It is to be noted that the field manager is not necessarily the team leader nor does he have to be particularly charismatic. Indeed, the better field managers generally are a fairly colorless lot, who usually were not highly talented as baseball players themselves. On and off the field, the team leader usually is the star player, the idol of the fans, or at least the player who commands the most respect of the other players. Quite often such a leader fails to become a successful field manager. The reason is simple: The effective field manager must be a master tactician, a person who can make the soundest decisions with the resources available according to the situation. And this skill has nothing to do with popularity, playing talent, or leadership.

Above the field manager we find another managerial role, that of the general manager, a role for which the field manager may or may not be qualified. The general manager's task is to provide the field manager with a steady supply of player talent. His decisions, therefore, are much broader in scope, covering the negotiation of player salaries, the operation of farm teams, the scouting of new recruits, and player transactions with other baseball clubs. He also chooses the field manager and evaluates his performance.

The general manager is, therefore, a strategist rather than a tactician, and his decisions require a much longer time sequence between their making and their consequences. The field manager who decides to pitch to a hitter rather than put him on base learns quickly how good his decision is. The general manager who gives a large bonus to a bright young prospect must wait five or six years to find out whether he made a good decision. This is probably why general managers last longer than field managers.

The general manager reports to the president of the team, who is rarely involved with the team's operations. Should he inject himself into the general or field manager's decision spheres, he will hamper their effectiveness, a lesson that many club presidents have not yet learned. The president's concern is with the sport of baseball itself and its relationships to other activities and organizations in the community. His decisions involve franchise shifts from city to city; the operation of league affairs; relationships with political and business leaders in the community, with the board of directors, and with investors; and the public image of the game. Consequently, while the field manager and the general manager are required to be experts in the intricacies of baseball, the president has to know little more than the average fan. He is an organizational statesman whose primary talent lies in his organizing ability and his skill in selecting good managers.

When all the parties—the president, the general manager, the field manager, and the players—understand the dimensions of each managerial role and govern themselves accordingly, the organization prospers according to the player's talents. But, when the star player attempts to tell the manager where he should play, or the field manager comments on the operation of the franchise, or the general manager tells the field manager when to relieve a pitcher, disorganization follows. Everyone soon finds out in the number of games lost and the dismal standing of the team in the league how poorly the club is managed.

Managerial Role Definition

Unfortunately, such relationships are not as obvious in other areas of business and government, where the goals and the results are not nearly so explicit. Few organizations, consequently, have paid adequate attention to the task of managerial role definition.

A recent survey of many large corporations revealed that less than a quarter of them possessed well-developed managerial position description programs and these were all among the larger concerns. Among the reasons for this anomaly, according to Matthew J. Murphy,[1] are these: (1) The duties of higher-level jobs range so broadly that managers cannot see how any evaluation plan can cope with them. (2) There is a widespread feeling that at higher levels "the man makes the job." (3) Higher-level jobs are politically "sensitive."

Despite these objections, defining the role of the manager formally is important, not principally to justify the executive compensation program or to establish territorial preserves within the corporation, but to determine the requirements of the incumbent and to evaluate his performance. A job description should define the scope and the functions of the job, the responsibility and the authority of the man in the position, his prescribed relationships with others in the company. It should be a guide, not a law, and it should be designed primarily for manpower planning. Essentially, a job description of a management position consists of two broad functions: those that are unique to the department, organization, or industry and those that

---

[1] Matthew J. Murphy, "A Flexible Approach to Management Job Evaluation," *Personnel*, Vol. 37, No. 3 (May/June 1960), pp. 36–43.

are common to *all* managerial positions at that level and which justify the use of the title *manager.*

Without an adequate job description we are left with nothing but tradition to define a role. And there is a tradition that goes back hundreds of years, even though the literature on management is of fairly recent origin. Aristotle, Plato, Augustine, Aquinas, and Machiavelli all discoursed on the art of governing and the requirements of leadership, and their ideas have fashioned the traditional concept of the managerial role that is still woven tightly into the fabric of current organizational theory and practice.

Current Views of the Managerial Role

Basically, there are three views of the manager's role today: the father figure that holds sway in highly traditional organizations; the group leader, advocated by many liberal social scientists; and the coordinator–project leader, who is particularly prevalent in the aerospace industry.

The manager as a father figure. For centuries, the managerial role was so simple that it was understood by everyone with the slightest social experience. The manager was a father figure, the *pater familias,* the sometimes benevolent, sometimes ruthless, but nearly always absolute master of his domain. He possessed unquestioned power and social status and confronted few problems of organization, communication, or supervision. The archetypes of this role were the lords of the great estates, the dukes and generals of the armies, the archbishops and princes of the church, and the owner-managers of the nineteenth-century factories.

Admittedly, the simplicity of this role has an irresistible attraction for men. What problems a father-figure manager confronts are of a philosophical or moral nature: how to use most equitably the power he possesses, how to reward and to punish fairly, and how to keep subordinates usefully employed.

Today, no educated person seriously holds to this perception of the manager's role. On the contrary, it is roundly repudiated. But the fact that it held sway over the minds of men for over 3,000 years and dominated their social institutions forces one to acknowledge its strong, pervasive, and subconscious influence on present-day management attitudes and practices. Despite social upheavals, technological revolutions, and political transformations, this autocratic model of the manager continues as the most widely accepted in every sphere of public and private administration. In somewhat softer tones it is the basic model in the military, in the church, in government, and in private industry. It underlies most of the traditional principles of organization and administrative theory, including the ideas of the unity of command, span of control, and line-staff relationships.

Its obvious shortcomings, particularly in a knowledge society, have led to the development of alternate models, each of which has so far attained only the most tentative acceptance by a small number of organizations.

The manager as a group leader. Beginning in the late nineteenth century, the increasingly liberal trend in economic and political affairs encouraged the rise of employee organizations, government intervention in the employer-employee relationship, and the birth of the behavioral sciences. These three developments led to the decline of overt authoritarian management.

Management increasingly became a science, heavily influenced by the methods of mechanical engineering and physics. In this view, man is a machine—a unique machine but a machine nonetheless. The function of the manager is simply to create the kinds of conditions that maximize his output. The pursuit of this idea led to the discovery that the machine works better when it operates in an environment that is socially conducive. Thus the manager's job is to create a climate in which the maximum amount of work can be performed.

The manager, therefore, is a teacher-trainer-consultant, concerned with maximizing his subordinates' opportunities for social gratification on the job. His function is to develop a cohesive work group by giving his subordinates a feeling of recognition and appreciation for a job well done, by permitting them to participate in the decisions affecting their work, by rewarding them properly, and by helping them realize their life's goals on the job.

This democratic view of the manager's role is currently being tried in a variety of situations with varying degrees of success. Its popularity stems from the fact that it coincides with the best traditions of Western ethics. But it is also extremely difficult to apply because it raises many knotty problems (to be described later). While it offers the attractive idea that a manager is a combination teacher and therapist, it has proved to be generally ineffective in achieving complex organization goals.

The manager as a project leader. The difficulties with the group-leader concept have led to a counterreaction by those who see the organization technologically as a complex network of groups with an intricate pattern of interrelationships. These authorities consider the essential feature of the manager's job to be that of meshing his unit's activities with those of the others that impinge on it, rather than that of maintaining internal harmony within his own work group. The manager, they say, is neither an autocrat nor a democrat; he is a technocrat, a coordinator-expeditor, an ambassador at large to those groups that, although they are in the same organization, do not have the same objectives and the same payoffs. Since the hierarchical order among these groups is quite ambiguous, effective interaction among them requires a good deal of persuasion and personal interaction on the part of the manager.

Adherents of this view of the manager's role claim that being skilled in human relations or in supervision is superfluous. The manager must first of all be highly trained technically and possess the ability to maintain lateral relationships, to be able to negotiate under stress, and to be effective in ambiguity. The manager spends his time in eliminating sources of disequilibrium, in maintaining organizational continuity and regularity.

The manager is neither a father figure nor a group leader. He does not have the time—he is too busy setting standards for his group and formulating and reviewing objectives. The organization is not really a pyramid but a matrix composed of project teams created to solve the problems of coordination and work scheduling. Once a problem is solved, the team is disbanded or given a new assignment. Thus it is possible for a worker to report in the course of the year to many managers. However, despite the success that the project-leader concept has achieved in some industries, it too is very difficult to put into general practice.

There is, of course, a degree of validity to each view of the manager's role. But, like the three blind men who feel different parts of the elephant in an effort to describe the beast accurately, they miss his totality and his essence. The essence of a manager lies in his role in an organization. As Chester Barnard has demonstrated so masterfully, the function of the manager is to make decisions.[2] The answer to our question "What does a manager do?" is quite clear: He makes decisions.

Manager or Leader?

For all the simplicity of this statement, it is fair to ask why the role dimensions of the manager are misunderstood so widely. The reason is that all

---

[2] Chester I. Barnard, *The Functions of the Executive* (Cambridge, Mass.: Harvard University Press, 1938).

three views see the manager as a leader; and, as we pointed out in our analysis of the management of a baseball club, a manager does not *have* to be a leader.

Although it was not until the twentieth century that scientific studies of leadership were initiated by serious thinkers, man has for centuries attempted to analyze the exercise of power which is implicit in the managerial role. Bertrand Russell said that, of all of the desires of man, his chief desires are for power and glory. And the easiest way to obtain glory is to obtain power.

This view of power represents the philosophical foundation on which most concepts of the phenomenon of leadership and authority are based. By and large, however, these theories have not kept up with the rapid advances in the physical sciences that have transformed the power base from land to knowledge of the secrets of nature. Not so long ago, when Russell wrote his treatise, power consisted of being able to decide, by the use of armed force if necessary, who should be allowed to stand on a given piece of land. Later, as the Industrial Revolution changed the source of wealth, power consisted of the ownership of the capital required to finance large enterprises up to and including the financing of a worldwide armed force.

Today, however, the fact that power is now vested in the possession of knowledge is shaking traditional establishments to their foundations. When power was based on possession of land or capital, it was relatively easy to retain; it could be overthrown only by revolutions of the most violent form, a course from which all but the most frustrated tend to shrink. But the power that emanates from technological superiority is so tenuous that it can be lost overnight by the introduction of a superior technology. The development of a new weapons system, for example, can alter the worldwide balance of power, and the marketing of a better product by a competitor can stagger even the most profitable corporation.

Given the appeal of power, its changing base, and its unquestioned possession by those in authority, it is easy to understand the unprecedented discussion and analysis of leadership and authority that have been carried on in recent years. Out of this introspection have emerged several theories as to the leadership behavior that will be most effective in organizations.

The behavioral sciences, in particular, have developed the notion of leadership *style*—a term that refers to the way the formal leader exercises power over his followers. In the next chapter, we shall examine some typical styles. To put it briefly, however, most theories of leadership focus on the group and the situation rather than on the leader himself. Most are oriented toward a group- or project-leader notion of the managerial role. They emphasize the importance of subordinate involvement and participation in decision making. The effective leader is one who acts as a catalyst, a consultant, and a resource for the group. The successful manager is the one "who is keenly aware of those forces which are most relevant to his behavior at any given time" and "who is able to behave appropriately in the light of these perceptions." [3]

Inherent in these theories is the notion that leadership is the same as management. Although it is probably true that the more well-adjusted personalities prefer a democratic-participative style of management, they do not want it on every occasion. While a game is in progress, the baseball manager cannot call the team together to find out whether he should take the pitcher out. And, although the democratic-participative style of leadership is most effective in small-group situations, its value diminishes with the size of the organization. As few as 25 may even be too many people. These two observations make the selection and development of managers hard to square with current leadership theory and research. The problem can be resolved, however, by treating leadership and management as two distinct phenomena. A manager is not necessarily a leader, and a leader does not necessarily have to be a manager.

What is a leader? An indication of the complexity of the problem of leadership can be found in the attempts to define it and the changes in the definition that have been made over the years. Sometimes it is viewed as a personal trait or a combination of traits, sometimes as a process, sometimes as a relationship, and sometimes as a role. A leader is defined variously as the one in a given office, the one who is preferred most by the other members of the group, the one who exercises the most influence over the group, the one who voluntarily receives authority from others, or, most often, the one who engages in leadership behavior. Implicit in these divergent perceptions of leadership are two central ideas: (1) The leader develops a positive bond with his followers; and (2) the influence the leader has over his followers is conferred on him by them willingly and freely.

Leadership, therefore, is a personality characteristic based to a large extent on the charisma the leader possesses for his followers. Thus his appeal must be to the emotional and the personal life of the group. Joan of Arc, Ghengis Khan, Napoleon, Winston Churchill, and Martin Luther King were leaders in the charismatic sense because their power lay in their ability

[3] Robert Tannenbaum and Warren H. Schmidt, "How to Choose a Leadership Pattern," *Harvard Business Review*, Vol. 36, No. 2 (March–April 1958), p. 101.

to unify and to inspire their followers. True leaders are often poets, philosophers, or actors by nature. They crystallize and personify the values of the
group or of a whole society. They shape its purpose and direct its attention.
Leadership, then, is associated primarily with ideas and ideologies, and every
social innovation requires it.

Leadership can also be shared by many members of a social unit, and it
can frequently pass from one member to another. A few years ago, the
bankers and the investment fraternity were the leaders of American society.
Today, the leadership baton has been passed to the intellectual-scientific community. Tomorrow, it will undoubtedly go to someone else.

What is a manager? A manager, on the other hand, has been entrusted
with the responsibility of decision making, which has nothing whatsoever to
do with leadership. It is not a personal trait; it is a role that is purely administrative and based upon the process of choosing a course of action and committing the group's resources to it. The manager's function is to define
goals and objectives, to select a course of action to achieve them, and to
evaluate realistically the results of that action.

There is little charisma in such a role. On the contrary, there is a certain
facelessness to it that is underscored by a recent survey showing that few
businessmen could identify the presidents of America's top 25 corporations.

Revolutions are started by leaders; but, unless their initial impetus is
sustained by managers, they will fail. Leaders depend for their success on
personality, a characteristic that has nothing to do with management. It has
been noted recently, for example, that few of the present heads of the larger
states are leaders in the charismatic sense. James Reston has noted that the
day of such spectacular leaders as Churchill, Roosevelt, Stalin, Adenauer,
Nehru, and Kennedy is gone and in their places are political and economic
technicians. The reason for this, he said, is supposed to be that the problems
of the modern world are too complicated to be resolved by personality leadership and must be left to a new managerial class which he described pejor-
atively as "political and economic mechanics." [4]

Consequently, leadership and management are most appropriately treated
as separate phenomena that are effectively handled simultaneously but not
necessarily by the same person. Leadership, implying as it does the notion
of inspiration and influence, is more a characteristic of a person or a group
of persons. Management, implying the notion of decision making, is a role
embedded in an organizational context.

The problem today is not one of leadership. As John Gardner pointed

[4] *The New York Times,* March 26, 1969.

out in his introduction to the 1965 annual report of the Carnegie Corporation of New York, many managers in business and government are falling victim to the "modern art of 'how to reach a decision without really deciding.'" "The sad truth," he declared, "is that many of our organizations are badly managed or badly led by either men of destiny who think they know all the answers or nervous nellies who lack confidence in their ability to decide."

The attempt to define styles of management is really irrelevant. The only test of a decision is how well it turns out, which has nothing to do with how others in the organization are attracted to or repelled by the personal magnetism of the decision maker. If a decision contributes to the common purpose, then all the members will benefit from it, regardless of whether they participated in it or whether they liked the decision maker. Every baseball player and every combat soldier knows this principle well.

Decision making naturally presupposes adequate information. One way of giving and getting reliable information is to engage in face-to-face discussion with those who are affected by a decision or have to implement it. To this extent, a participative-democratic style of communication can contribute to more effective decision making. We shall return to this idea in the next chapter.

In modern organizations, leadership is better left to the policy-making group, that is, to the board of directors or to the legislature. Here, it would seem, democratic-participative leadership may best be applied; and perhaps it is here that representation by other member groups, clients and employees, may reasonably be considered. Students, for example, may be placed on a board of trustees to give voice to their interest in policy formulation. But it would be impractical to appoint a student dean of admissions or of faculty. The development of managerial competence is a matter of time that precludes student participation in the decision-making process.

This idea is being put into practice in Europe, where experiments are going on with putting workers and union members on the board of directors. The nationalized British Steel Corporation has appointed a full-time scrapyard foreman to its board of directors. German companies have pioneered this idea since the early 1950s; and France, Israel, and Norway are carefully watching the experiment. Within the framework of our model of an organization as a cooperative system, it makes good sense to have representatives of all the member groups on the policy-making board to shape its values and to define its purposes. But decision making is best left to professional managers.

The Manager as a Decision Maker

Not so long ago, an engineer was promoted to the top spot in a large municipal agency. The day he was appointed, he unwittingly declared his own incompetence for the job when he told the press that he would rather design a rocketship to Mars than make a decision to go there in the first place. "I'm a problem-solver," he said. "Of course, I prefer a job with problems that can be solved with the slide rule. But I'm realistic enough to know that can't always be the case."

A manager is no more a problem solver than he is a leader. He can do both, but they are not essential to his role. Decision making is, and it is different from both although it frequently is confused with both. Let us look at the notion of the manager as a decision maker in more detail, therefore, particularly as it affects selection and promotion.

Decision Theory

Since selection always implies a choice, it necessarily involves a decision. Hence the most appropriate model of selection must be based on decision theory. (In Part Two we shall make proposals which will represent a substantial departure from the prevailing models that are based on measurement theory.)

While there is general agreement on the importance of the decision-making process, there is considerable disparity in the approaches utilized to explain it. Recently a discipline termed *decision theory* has emerged that is largely mathematical and rational in nature, is based on the laws of probability, and utilizes concepts drawn from information theory, operations research, and other related disciplines.

Most organization theorists, however, contend that the resulting models inadequately represent the way in which managers really make decisions. They assert that, far from being the coldly calculating weigher of events, the manager is more or less an opportunist who tends to muddle through decisions. Though he muddles with a purpose, he is forced to do so by the decision situations he faces. Decision theory is of little help to him, they say, because the decision-making models deal essentially with isolated decisions in static situations such as betting on a horse race or on the turn of a card.

Dynamic models including sequential decision situations in a constantly changing environment become so unmanageably complex that they are diffi-cult to conceptualize and almost impossible to verify experimentally. Thus, while integrated decision theories have in fact made distinct contributions to the development of improved organization decision making, they have been necessarily limited.

A dynamic model, on the other hand, is far more typical of the everyday decision situation confronted by the average manager. What is necessary is a broader model of decision making that is perhaps less elegant mathe-matically but that takes into account the psycho-social variables that play a crucial role in the making and implementation of decisions.

What Is a Decision?

Herbert Simon suggested that, in any study of the administrative process, the proper unit of analysis is the decision.[5] Noting that traditional admin-istrative theory emphasized *action,* the process of getting things done and the so-called principles that are laid down to help in achieving such action, he very properly pointed out that a decision always precedes an action. An adequate analysis of organizational behavior, therefore, must focus upon the decision-making process, and we would add that adequate analysis of managerial behavior must do likewise.

The unfortunate confusion over decision-making processes has led to the treatment of problem-solving and decision-making behavior as identical processes. Consequently, decision making is usually described as an analyt-ical activity amenable to mathematical or computerized manipulation. De-cision making is, however, not a purely intellectual process. A decision rep-resents a judgment; a final resolution of a conflict of needs, means, or goals; and a commitment to action made in the face of uncertainty, com-plexity, and even irrationality. It always implies a degree of freedom on the part of the decision maker and contains conscious and unconscious aspects.

The choices of a rat in a maze or of alternative solutions to a problem by a computer are often referred to as "decisions." But they are really only crude paradigms of the human decision-making process. They are pro-grammed (one by instinct and the other by logic), contain no degree of freedom other than that provided by the laws of chance, and imply no ego-involving considerations. Decision making is uniquely human and, therefore, cannot be computerized.

[5] Herbert K. Simon, *Administrative Behavior,* 2d ed. (New York: The Free Press, 1957).

Problem-solving activities may precede or emanate from a decision, but the optimal solution may not necessarily be chosen by the decision maker, nor is the soundest decision always based on an optimal solution. In fact, problem solving may not involve a decision at all.

The Decision Situation

The pivotal element in the decision process is the commitment made; consequences are secondary. An organization decision commits a portion of its present resources to an action with a partially unknowable and uncertain future. Thus each decision involves both a "cost" and a "risk." This commitment to uncertainty defines the properties of the decision situation: *complexity* and *magnitude*.

Decision complexity. Decision complexity refers to the possible number of courses of action available to the decision maker. Since a decision involves a choice, there must always be at least two options, but there can be many more. The more there are, the more complex the evaluation task required of the decision maker. A decision with two options, *A* and *B*, requires only one comparison between *A* and *B*. The addition of another option, *C,* triples the number of comparisons, *A* with *B*, *A* with *C*, and *B* with *C*. A ten-option decision requires 45 separate comparisons; a 100-option decision, 4,950! This is why the selection process becomes so complex when there are many candidates for a position.

If the option number exceeds the ability of the decision maker to compare them or even to perceive them all, the decision situation becomes too complex for him. He will then use either random techniques (pick one out of a hat) or, more probably, a ritual that appears to make his decision rational (promote on the basis of seniority). To reduce the confusion and uncertainty, the more effective decision maker, consciously or unconsciously, will resort to sequential decision making. He narrows his range of options down by a series of two-option decisions in a decision-tree network. He then traces a critical path through the series of two-option choices to the soundest decision. But decision trees are complex, requiring dependable information and time to work out.

Decision magnitude. The magnitude of a decision refers to its size with respect to the commitment of organization resources and the certainty of the outcome. An organization decision sets in motion a train of events that encompasses its economic resources and the energies and the attitudes of the human beings affected by it. A decision to raise prices, for example, affects not only a firm's production, sales, and profits but its customers', employees', and stockholders' attitudes and behaviors. These decision consequences are difficult to determine because they are usually affected by other decisions and influences not within the control of the decision maker.

Current decision-theory models treat decision making primarily in terms of the expected outcome. They also attempt to maximize a mathematical expectation of profit. But, in a survey of 217 vice-presidents of 109 large firms, Professor Ross Stagner found that many goals other than profit maximization are important in decisions. These goals include promoting the company image and adhering to its traditions.[6]

The decision maker, moreover, has only a general idea of the exact consequences of his decision. He is concerned more with how much of the company's resources are committed to the action regardless of the certainty of the outcome. What he is committing plays a much more significant role in the decision-making process. Reflecting the utility of the outcome to the decision maker, the size of the commitment depends upon the organization's financial position, public image, and value system. A $100,000 decision made by a $100 million firm involves a smaller commitment than one made by a $1 million firm.

The magnitude of a decision is the product of (a) the economic and (b) the human factors modified by (c) the degree of uncertainty and (d) the time available to make it. We can develop a crude index of a decision's magnitude by assuming that each of the four factors has equal weight, scaled into a gradient of ten equal intervals. We are not asserting that this assumption of equal weight is actually so, but it serves our purpose in demonstrating how these factors interact to escalate or to reduce decision magnitudes. A decision of minimum economic and human commitment—say, the purchase of paper clips—would have a commitment magnitude of one times one, or one; a decision of maximum economic and human commitment—for example, granting a general salary increase to a firm's employees—would constitute a commitment magnitude of ten times ten, or 100. Thus, in terms of the commitment, a decision magnitude can range between one and 100.

But the uncertainty as to the commitment or the consequences sharply accelerates decision magnitude. Uncertainty is a function of the information and the time available.

Information reduces the uncertainty of a decision. The less information

[6] Ross Stagner, "Corporate Decision-Making: An Empirical Study," *Journal of Applied Psychology*, Vol. 53, No. 1 (Feb. 1969), pp. 1–13.

the decision maker possesses, the larger the decision uncertainty. If we place values on the amounts of information available to the decision maker in the same way as we did with human and economic commitments—that is, from one to ten, with the value of one denoting all the possible information that the decision maker would require and the value of ten denoting no information at all—decision magnitudes can now range between one and 1,000.

A decision involving a high commitment of capital and human resources with an index of 80 sharply increases to 800 if the decision maker has little accurate information on which to base his decision. On the other hand, a major-commitment decision of 80 can be held to a figure of 160 if information is available to give this factor a value of 2. It can be seen, also, how a low-commitment decision of 25 could escalate rapidly to a magnitude of 250 if there is no information available and could outweigh a decision involving greater commitments but with much more information. In short, decision, information, and probability theories can make distinct contributions to the decision-making process by increasing the information the decision maker needs and thereby making decisions more manageable.

But the application of these theories through decision-tree analysis and operations research involves time—time to accumulate the necessary data, time to analyze them, time to interpret them, and time to feed them back to the decision maker. Thus a fourth major factor contributes to the magnitude of a decision: the pressure of time.

Lack of time can raise the magnitude index to its maximum value, 10,000. If we assign a value of one to ten to the time factor, with one denoting an almost unlimited amount of time to make a decision and ten indicating that an immediate decision must be made, it is quite obvious that ordinary decisions on which adequate information is available can escalate sharply for lack of time. Planning, which is in reality advanced decision making, plays a key role in minimizing time pressure and making decisions more manageable.

Management by Crisis

The crisis-ridden company is simply one where the uncertainty factors are completely out of control. Decisions are made under severe time pressures and with inadequate information. In the collective bargaining process, for example, decisions often reach extremely high magnitudes because the negotiators for each side are required to make decisions involving high financial and human commitments with little information and almost no time to reflect on them. Unsound decisions are thereby generated that require additional hasty decisions to remedy matters. Without realizing it, an organization can become locked into a cycle of randomized or even superstitious decision-making behavior.

Curtis Jones makes the point that the minimization of demands on a manager's time is a useful criterion for evaluating alternative courses of action. He also makes the often overlooked point that many decisions can be more meaningfully related to the return on a manager's time rather than to a return on investment.[7]

It would appear that a good strategy for organizations would be to structure their decision making so that decision makers have access to sufficient information and time in proportion to the commitments involved. In some corporations, sufficient time is given to the higher levels of management, but down below what appear to be ordinary decisions are escalated to a crisis stage by lack of information and the necessity of making on-the-spot decisions continually.

Without adequate structure and control over the time and information variables, decisions tend to escalate in magnitude to the point where they become unmanageable and beyond the comprehension of any single human being. In some cases, a decision's complexity, commitments, and uncertainties require that it be made by a *group* of decision makers. An excellent example of how sufficient time to deliberate can make a decision of extremely high magnitude manageable is described by the late Senator Robert Kennedy in his account of the 1962 Cuban missile crisis.[8]

The spectacular magnitudes of modern decisions account for the trend in many top corporations toward assigning long-range decisions of far-reaching implications to committees. General Motors, Westinghouse, and Armco are among the many major corporations that have, in recent years, moved to broaden their top decision making and place it in the hands of committees. These committees can be very effective provided proper attention is paid to the personal qualifications of those involved in the decision-making process and the organization is structured to facilitate information flow and the proper use of managerial time. One effect of the managerial crisis has been to place severe demands on a manager's time and to distort the organ-

[7] Curtis H. Jones, "The Money Value of Time," *Harvard Business Review,* Vol. 46, No. 4 (July–Aug. 1968), pp. 94–101.

[8] Robert F. Kennedy, *Thirteen Days* (New York: W. W. Norton, 1969).

ization's structure and climate. As Curtis Jones shows, the concept of maximizing time can be applied to the total organization to provide a framework not only for its analysis and design but to formulate managerial recruitment and development plans.

The function of the executive, then, is to make decisions. It is the skill that most clearly differentiates managers from all other organization members, and it is the skill that also differentiates top-ranking from lower-ranking managers. Decision making is, however, much broader than merely making a commitment after weighing alternatives. It involves the entire process of establishing goals, defining tasks, searching for alternatives, and developing plans. It includes all the activities of coordinating, information processing, problem solving, and evaluating that precede the decision. It is a science and an art, involving both the intuitive and the deductive powers. Part of it can be learned, but part depends upon the personal attributes of the decision maker.

To understand and hence to improve an organization's decision-making capacity, it is necessary to examine the variables involved: the nature of the decision-making situation, the climate in which decisions are made and implemented, and finally the personalities of the decision makers themselves. We have already examined the first and third variables; now we must examine the second, the organizational milieu in which decisions are made and implemented.

5

The Managerial Milieu

It was a company that prided itself on the high caliber of its management group, which was carefully selected, well paid, and highly trained. Every opening in the management ranks was filled either by promotion from within or by direct college recruitment.

The annual college recruitment program was a textbook model of excellence. It was well planned, meticulously executed, and carefully researched. The results justified the effort. Over 80 percent of those to whom employment offers were made accepted them and the most frequently given reason for acceptance was "I was impressed by the selection process."

Every spring, the company president gave the keynote address in the three-day training program for those managers selected to participate that year in the campus interviewing activity. "Find me the uncommon man," he would say. "Bring me the maverick, the individualist, the innovator with new and fresh ideas!" It was an inspiring address that deserved to be reprinted in the *Journal of College Placement* and in every campus newspaper.

But the company psychologist, who heard this speech year after year, knew better. His carefully analyzed data told a story that belied the president's high ideals. In that company an uncommon man had no more chance of survival than a mackerel in a school of sharks. The organizational milieu was irresistible and unrelenting in its rejection of mavericks and innovators.

In the first place, most of those who applied were generally of the same type as those who already populated the organization. Secondly, those who

were different tended to be disqualified—for the most part, unconsciously—
by the campus interviewer. Third, if somehow an uncommon man was invited to the home office for further assessment, he tended to lose out there.
And finally, if he managed to make it all the way, he consistently received
the lowest performance ratings from his supervisors. The system operated
like a silent but powerful cookie cutter, stamping out organization men and
driving out uncommon men.

The organizational milieu is a product of the personalities that inhabit it
and the tasks that have to be performed in it, creating a value system, a
structure, and a climate that is conducive to both. There is no uncommon
man except in reference to a particular milieu. As many an industrial
manager has learned to his dismay, the management practices that are most
effective in business are positively disastrous in government. The milieu of
an advertising agency will be unlike that of a research laboratory, and both
will differ from that of a manufacturing company. And it is difficult for a
human being to find satisfaction in an atmosphere that is alien to his own
interests and ideals.

The manager's milieu, therefore, is the third variable that we must account for in our model of selection, not because each organization requires
its own brand of manager, but rather because the organizational milieu has
its own prescription for effective management. We use the term *milieu* rather
than environment to include all the environments—physical, psychological,
and social as well as internal and external—in the concept. The milieu consists of two separate aspects, the way the organization is structured for
decision making and the value-and-reward climate surrounding its activities.

Organizational Structure

The definition of the role of the manager as a decision maker and its
corollary that decision making lies at the heart of the administrative process
have profound implications for the social structure of the organization. If
the manager is a decision center, his location in the organization has to be
strategically placed according to the magnitude and the complexity of the
decisions he must make. The decisions involve proper information and later
implementation. So there is current concern, not only with the decision-
making structure, but with decision implementation.

Behavioral scientists have devoted considerable attention to the information-processing and implementation phases of the decision-making process. The results of their work have fostered a theory of participative decision making that has implications, not only for organizational structure, but for managerial selection and development.

Participative Management

The underlying assumption of participative management is that the more a subordinate participates in a decision, the more he will be committed to it and the harder he will work to insure a successful outcome. During the 1960s, organizational development became the "in" thing and participative management the hottest phrase in the management lexicon. Almost every manager who calls himself progressive will agree that the more participative he can get, the better manager he will be.

The interest in participative management parallels the social and economic trends in the overall society. It arises out of the obvious conflict between the traditional American political and religious values that stress democracy, individual freedom, and human dignity and the authoritarian climate, organization structure, and values of nearly all its institutions. Since World War II, behavioral scientists have conducted a concerted drive to "democratize" human relations in industry.

The Western Electric studies of the 1920s and 1930s paved the way by discovering the impact of social factors on production. The supervision and productivity studies of the University of Michigan's Survey Research Center in the early 1950s attested to the superiority of the employee-centered supervisor over his production-oriented counterpart. Then, in the late 1950s, techniques originating in Bethel, Maine, fed the flames of participative management and fired managers with a new humanitarianism.

Sensitivity training. Sensitivity training is the currently popular name for the new techniques—a kind of experience-based learning originally known as T-group training (the *T* stands for "training"). There are presently many variations of sensitivity training with names like encounter groups, personal-growth groups, and marathons. The programs vary in length from two days to two weeks; the object is to teach the participant human relations, communications, and leadership skills.

The exciting but sometimes questionable events that occurred in training laboratories all over the country stimulated a flood of books, pamphlets, and conferences. Each carries the same message: Involvement of the group members in a decision results in both maximum support and higher-quality decisions through an increase in resources.

American management quickly became interested. Sensitivity-training programs were conducted in many parts of the country with varying formats. Some groups were made up almost entirely of members of the same firm. Sometimes they were "family" groups consisting of members of the same unit; sometimes they were "vertical" groups composed of many layers of management from the same unit; sometimes they were "oblique" groups composed of several layers of management from different units in the same group. For the most part, such programs were and are popular, but all share the same problem: the difficulty of applying the new skills to the everyday situation. The trouble is, as was asserted, that you cannot apply democratic techniques in what is essentially an autocratic organization structure.

New theories of management structure. The structure of an organization, it was argued, depends almost solely on its decision-making apparatus. MIT's Douglas McGregor was one of the first behavioral scientists to draw a sharp line of demarcation between two contrasting philosophies of management which he termed, respectively, *Theory X* and *Theory Y*. The Theory X philosophy of management (the traditional autocratic approach), he said, is based on the idea that people have an inherent dislike of work, are by nature lazy and ignorant, and therefore have to be coerced, controlled, directed, and even threatened to get them to put forth the effort necessary to achieve organizational goals. Theory Y, on the other hand, a democratic-participative approach, is based on the assumption that people are *not* by nature resistant to organization needs. They have become so, McGregor asserted, as a result of experiences in organizations. The motivation, the potential for development, the capacity for assuming responsibility, the readiness to direct behavior toward goals are all present in people. The real task of the manager is to arrange organizational conditions and methods of operation so that people can satisfy their own needs best by directing their efforts toward organizational objectives.[1]

McGregor's view was endorsed repeatedly over the following 15 years by many other behavioral scientists. Yale's Chris Argyris, for instance, asserted that the organization strategies of most American companies are best suited to the capacities and characteristics of a child, rather than to those of

[1] Douglas McGregor, *The Human Side of Enterprise* (New York: McGraw-Hill, 1960).

an adult, because employees are asked to become passive, submissive, and subordinate to their leaders.[2]

California's Raymond E. Miles expounded a human-resources theory of management.[3] He declared that a manager's job cannot be viewed as merely one of giving direction and obtaining cooperation; rather, it is one of creating an environment in which the total resources of his department can be utilized. In this environment, the manager shares information and discusses departmental decisions with his employees and encourages their self-direction, not to improve their role satisfaction, but to improve the decision making and the total performance efficiency of the organization. Many decisions are made more efficiently by those directly involved in and affected by them. In fact, Miles added, the more important the decision, the greater the manager's *obligation* to encourage subordinate self-direction.

The development of participative management as an alternative to the traditional approach does much more than simply establish a potentially more effective approach to decision making. It establishes a totally new organization milieu. Each organization follows a particular philosophy of management selected from a spectrum ranging from authoritarian to participative. If it adopts an approach in which the manager makes all the decisions and passes them on to subordinates for execution, it follows an authoritarian philosophy that determines its organization structure and climate. Its structure will follow closely the classic organizational principles of unity of command, many levels of management, tight spans of control, and formal channels of communication. The direction of information flow will be downward, supervisors will have little trust in subordinates, and a high degree of emphasis will be placed on management controls.

If management adopts an approach where subordinates are fully involved in decisions related to their work and where decision making is widely disbursed throughout the organization, it will follow a democratic-participative philosophy. The organization structure will be open and problem-centered, supervisors will have confidence in their subordinates, the direction of informational flow will be up and down and across organizational lines, and control data will be used only for guidance and problem-solving.

The University of Michigan's Rensis Likert has subdivided this decision-making spectrum into four management systems.[4] System I, which he

---

[2] Chris Argyris, *Personality and Organization* (New York: Harper, 1957).

[3] Raymond E. Miles, "Human Relations or Human Resources," *Harvard Business Review*, Vol. 43, No. 4 (July–Aug. 1965), pp. 148–163.

[4] Rensis Likert, *The Human Organization* (New York: McGraw-Hill, 1967).

originally entitled *exploitive-authoritative,* corresponds to McGregor's Theory X, and his System 4, which he termed the *participative* style, corresponds to McGregor's Theory Y. In between, Likert places System 2, *benevolent-authoritarian,* and System 3, *consultative.* Likert's data indicate that high-producing departments are seen by managers as using systems that tend toward System 4, whereas low-producing units use systems tending toward System 1. His research also shows that most managers manage according to System 2 but would prefer to manage and be managed by System 3 or System 4.

Models of managerial style. Paralleling the growth of sensitivity training and of these new theories of management was the development of models that attempted to classify managerial behavior in easily understood terms. Robert R. Blake and Jane S. Mouton developed what they called the *managerial grid.* It includes two dimensions, vertical and horizontal, each of which is subdivided into nine units.[5] The vertical dimension represents concern for people; the horizontal, concern for production. The managerial style of any manager can be characterized in terms of where he falls on each dimension, reading the horizontal dimension first. The "9:1" manager is a "slave driver," an exponent of Theory X and System 1. On the other hand, the "1:9" manager is a "paternalist," a follower of the purest form of Theory Y and of System 4. To Blake and Mouton, the "9:9" manager is perfect.

Blake and Mouton expanded their model into a six-phase-grid organization-development program. The objective is to gain corporate excellence, defined as the situation in which high concern for production is fused with high concern for people based on the use of empirical data for problem solving and open, objective communication for understanding the emotional components of conflict.

But the Canadian professor, William J. Reddin, contends that there is no such thing as an ideal style of management, because different situations require different styles.[6] He has developed a *tridimensional grid* by adding a third dimension, effectiveness, to Blake's production-people axis. Effectiveness appears to be related to the ability of the manager to make sound decisions. The effective 9:1 autocrat becomes a benevolent autocrat, the effective 1:9 missionary becomes a developer, and the effective 9:9 manager is simply an executive, while the ineffective 9:9 manager (an impossibility, according to Blake) is a compromiser.

[5] Robert R. Blake and Jane S. Mouton, *The Managerial Grid* (Houston, Tex.: Gulf, 1964).
[6] William J. Reddin, "The Tridimensional Grid," *Training Directors' Journal* (July 1964), pp. 9–18.

Blake and Mouton also have expanded their managerial grid to include a third dimension, thickness, which they define as resistance to change from a particular management style.[7] And Chris Common has proposed a three-dimensional model, the *managerial surface,* composed of the following dimensions: concern for people, concern for output, and concern for commitment. His total model is visualized as a constantly changing surface in an ever changing force-field.[8]

The neat simplicity of these models and their reduction to numbers and catchy labels have made them exceedingly popular in management circles in the English-speaking countries. Managers who are exposed to seminars devoted to grid or laboratory approaches quickly acquire a new vocabulary which they use in their "back home" situations freely. There is, however, a long distance between the acquisition of a new vocabulary and a change of managerial behavior. Managers who describe themselves as 9:9ers are often referred to by their subordinates as "massive 9:1ers."

This perceptual dissonance is widespread. Miles reports that while the typical modern manager broadly endorses participation and rejects traditional autocratic concepts of management, he seems to have adopted two different models of participation, one for himself and one for his subordinates. He is for participation by subordinates only as a way of raising their morale and making them more docile and content. The full implications of participative management are reserved, in his view, for his superiors in dealing with *him.*[9]

Problems with participative management. Despite its ideological attractiveness, there are problems with the assumptions underlying participative decision making. These problems are attested to by the fact that, so far, not a single business corporation in the United States has been able to apply it on a large scale and very few have attempted to do so. The Century Life Insurance Company, of Chicago, is one of those attempting to give the whole staff a voice in running the company. Corning Glass, General Electric, Olin Corporation, and B.F. Goodrich are among the major companies that are trying forms of participative management at specific plants, but not in the whole company. And Texas Instruments, among others, is applying some of the democratic techniques to the whole company.

Probably the most notable effort at an all-out application of participative management is occurring in the TRW Systems Corporation, in California,

[7] Robert R. Blake and Jane S. Mouton, "The Managerial Grid in Three Dimensions," *Training and Development Journal,* Vol. 21, No. 1 (Jan. 1967), pp. 2–5.

[8] Chris A. Common, "The Managerial Surface," *Training and Development Journal,* Vol. 23, No. 10 (Oct. 1969), pp. 12–19.

[9] Raymond E. Miles, op. cit., p. 148.

where a nine-year organization-development effort has been in progress under the direction of Sheldon A. Davis.[10] This company's employee population is about one-third professional engineers, half of whom have advanced degrees. Because of the nature of the company's work, which is essentially project-oriented, it has adopted a matrix structure with project offices and functional areas of technical capabilities. The resulting complicated matrix of interdependencies among the various functional units creates problems of relationships and communication that make participative management and what the company terms the method of *confrontation* most effective. But it is apparent that the very nature of this company's products, its task structure, and the level of education of its employees make engaging in this type of experimentation more appropriate than would be the case with a manufacturing company, a retail corporation, or a public agency.

One drawback of the participative-management approach is the lack of solid research to document its contentions. What has been collected is either inconclusive or negative. Laboratory experiments have repeatedly demonstrated that groups that are organized to emphasize interpersonal comfort, openness, familiarity, and cohesiveness perform poorly. And at least one study, in a large insurance company, of different styles of management revealed that while greater acceptance of leadership and higher morale were present in the division led by the permissive, employee-centered manager, this division's performance results were no better than those achieved by the authoritarian production-centered leader. And, after a review of experiments using participation in decision making by subordinates, Jay R. Galbraith concluded that high-quality decisions can be reached under participative conditions if there is a low need for expertise, a low need for coordination, small conflict of interest, and a problem that lends itself to creating new ideas.[11]

It is important to note that, in discussing the TRW Systems experience, Dr. Davis warns of the risk of overgeneralizing the McGregor hypothesis, of confusing it with a soft, mushy, "sweetness and light" approach to management. It must also be emphasized that the proponents of participative management for the most part have not advocated explicitly that decision making be delegated to subordinates. Likert. for example, states quite plainly that the manager is accountable for all decisions, for their execution, and for the results. And UCLA's Tannenbaum points out that the amount of

---

[10] Sheldon A. Davis, "An Organic Problem-solving Method of Organizational Change," *Journal of Applied Behavioral Science*, Vol. 3, No. 1 (1967), pp. 3–21.

[11] Jay R. Galbraith, "The Use of Subordinate Participation in Decision Making," *Journal of Industrial Engineering*, Vol. XVIII, No. 9 (Sept. 1967), pp. 521–525.

freedom the boss gives to his subordinates for decision making cannot be greater than the freedom which he himself has been given by his own supervisor.[12]

THE DECISION-MAKING STRUCTURE

By and large, participative-management theorists have tended to overlook the main features of the decision-making structure: the task and the personalities involved.

Despite the interest in participative management and the talk about organizational innovation, few departures—let alone radical changes in overall corporate structure—have been reported. The innovations that are occurring are in process or technology and few of these show up in radical structural modifications. Some writers attribute the lack of changes in organizational structure to the deeply embedded belief in the necessity of maintaining highly structured organizational arrangements. The truth is, however, that the intrinsic natures of the decision-making process and of the human personality determine ultimately how an enterprise will be organized.

An organization is, in many ways, a system of decision centers placed at strategic points in the information-feedback network to provide an orderly flow of information essential to decision making. As decisions increase in magnitude and complexity, they must be processed at higher and higher levels in the organization where wider access to information is possible. Higher decision centers make only those decisions that require information not available to the lower decision centers.

One implication of this requirement has escaped many organization theorists. Higher-level decisions involving greater information processing are broader in scope, require more time, and will necessarily be more abstract and generalized. The time span between the making of a higher-level decision and the feedback on its effectiveness will be much longer. Therefore, the decisions emanating from higher-level decision centers cannot always be clear to those who must implement them.

The dimensions of higher-level positions are different in kind, rather than in degree, from lower-level positions. Top-level decision making includes tasks related to long-range planning, the preservation of corporate assets, and the exercise of broad power and authority. Lower-level decision making includes the administration of day-to-day affairs, the direct super-

[12] Robert Tannenbaum and Warren H. Schmidt, "How to Choose a Leadership Pattern," *Harvard Business Review*, Vol. 36, No. 2 (March–April 1958), p. 101.

vision of operations, technical markets, products, and people. These are quite different concerns that call for quite different managerial practices; they cannot be incorporated in a homogeneous organizational philosophy.

Decision making also connotes power, because a decision necessarily commits all the members of the organization to a particular course of action. The organization confers authority in the role, and those who are subordinate to it transfer it to the role incumbent. The authority emanating from the role is called *objective* authority; that which is implicit in the person is *subjective* authority.

Being essentially authoritarian in nature, decisions made on the basis of objective authority must be implemented by appeals to obedience, by respect for law and order, or by fear. They are exercised mainly through written policies, rules, and regulations, and they require a power structure to secure cooperation through the security and dependency needs of its members. Objective authority, therefore, is most effective with people whose security needs are salient.

Decisions made on the basis of subjective authority are essentially democratic and can be implemented on the basis of respect for the competence of the decision maker. The appeal here is to the intelligence and to the free choice of the implementer, obtained through two-way communication, an essentially democratic social structure, and satisfaction of his achievement needs.

An organization, therefore, in ordering its decision-making centers and in peopling them, has a choice of emphasizing either objective or subjective authority. The choice is usually determined by the task of the organization and the differing intellectual and motivational systems of the organization members. Since these vary widely, not every member is able or willing to participate equally in the decision process. In some instances, in fact, the inability to comprehend either the magnitude or the complexity of a decision can be quite threatening and lead to resentment at being involved in it at all.

The success of any decision-making structure depends on the tasks involved, the personality systems of the organization members, and the organizational climate.

The Organizational Climate

In the enthusiasm for organizational development and participative decision making, the real dimensions of the organizational climate have often been overlooked. Studies have indicated a strong tendency of subordinates to gravitate toward managers whose attitudes and philosophies of management they share. They have also revealed an equally strong tendency of managers to recruit personality types who they feel share their views. Thus John B. Miner, of the University of Maryland, concluded that a man who succeeds in one company may very well not succeed in another because the value-reward structures may be at odds and the factors that make for success frequently differ from one organization to the next. While a company may value initiative, independence, and concern for people, it often tends to reward other characteristics that are typical of authoritarian or bureaucratic management.[13]

Motivational Climate

According to George Litwin and Robert Stringer, organizational climate is the pattern of the expectations and incentives that impinge on and are created by a group of people who work together.[14] It molds and shapes the motivation and the behavior of each member of a workgroup through its effect on his perception of what is expected of him and what he will "get" for doing a job a particular way.

Organizational climate, they say, makes salient one of the three attitude orientations referred to earlier: achievement, power, or affiliation. Their research has tended to confirm this hypothesis; it shows that distinctly different organizational climates can be created by varying management patterns: (1) high performance–high satisfaction (the achieving business); (2) low performance–high satisfaction (the democratic-friendly business); (3) low performance–low satisfaction (authoritarian-structured business). A particular climate remains relatively stable over time, has a dramatic effect upon worker performance and satisfaction, and arouses a different kind of concern or motivation. The first climate will act to increase concern for achievement; the second climate will act to increase concern for affiliation; and the third climate will act to increase concern for power.

[13] John B. Miner, "Bridging the Gulf in Organization Performance," *Harvard Business Review*, Vol. 46, No. 4 (July–Aug. 1968), pp. 102–111.

[14] See George Litwin and Robert Stringer, *Motivation and Organization Climate* (Boston: Div. of Research, Harvard Business School, 1968).

Organizational Choice

The climate not only arouses a particular need, it also attracts people with those needs and repels people with different needs. This process is the force underlying occupational choice, which is in many respects the same as organizational choice. We have already established that success in an occupation depends, not only upon a person's ability, but upon his attitude, his drive, and the means by which he prefers to express them. The best way of determining the dimensions of an individual's personality is by exploring the occupational roles he prefers and those he rejects.

The most well-developed and most empirically based theory of vocational choice has been advanced by John L. Holland.[15] His theory states that there are in the Western culture at least six basic personality types, to which he has given the labels *realistic, intellectual, social, conventional, enterprising,* and *artistic.* There may be more than six, but there certainly are not fewer. Each is the product of the physical, psychological, social, and cultural forces that influence a person to adopt habitual ways of coping with the tasks presented to him by his total environment. A type is, therefore, a complex cluster of personality attributes.

Holland's classification is in general agreement with that of other noted occupational theorists, but he has continued to develop his theory by research to the point where it has become of significant interest to those concerned with the counseling, guidance, selection, and placement of people in occupations. His scheme is, therefore, worth examining in more detail because it has produced efficient predictions of vocational choice and job satisfaction, it contains a set of concepts (each with some unique variance), and it provides explicit interpretations of an individual's expressive directions.

Since people search for environments that will permit them to exercise their abilities and to express their attitudes and values, and since, to the same degree, environments search for people with similar propensities, there are six kinds of climate dominated by a given type of personality. Briefly, these six types can be summarized as follows:

1. Realistic. The realistic person copes with his physical and social environment by selecting goals, values, and tasks that entail the objective, concrete evaluation and manipulation of things, tools, animals, and machines and by avoiding goals, values, and tasks that require subjec-

15 John L. Holland, *The Psychology of Vocational Choice* (Waltham, Mass.: Blaisdell, 1966).

tivity, intellectualism, artistic expression, and social sensitivity and skill. People who fall into this class are generally masculine, unsociable, emotionally stable, materialistic, genuine, and oriented to the present time.

2. Intellectual. The intellectual person copes with the social and physical environment through the use of intelligence. He is the seeker of truth. He solves problems primarily through the manipulation of ideas, words, and symbols rather than through his physical and social skills. People in this class are generally analytical, rational, independent, radical, abstract, critical, curious, and perceptive.

3. Social. The social person copes with his environment by selecting goals, values, and tasks in which he can use his skills and interest in other persons so as to train them or change their behavior. The social person is typified by his social skills and his need for social interaction. His characteristics include sociability, social presence, capacity for status, and dominance. He is concerned with helping people, and in problem solving he relies upon his emotions and feelings rather than upon his intellectual resources.

4. Conventional. The conventional person copes with his physical and social environment by selecting goals, tasks, and values that are sanctioned by custom and society. Accordingly, his approach to problems is stereotyped, practical, correct. It lacks spontaneity and originality. His major values are economic, and his personal traits are consistent with this orientation. He is somewhat conservative, inflexible, and persevering.

5. Enterprising. The enterprising person copes with his world by selecting goals, values, and tasks through which he can express his adventurous, dominant, enthusiastic, energetic, and impulsive qualities. He is oriented toward people, but he is persuasive, verbal, extroverted, self-accepting, and self-confident and likes to be the center of attention.

6. Artistic. The artistic person copes with his physical and social environment by using his feelings, emotions, intuitions, and imagination to create art forms or products. For the artistic person, problem solving involves expressing his imagination and taste through the conception and execution of his art. He is a seeker of beauty. The artistic person is characterized by complexity of outlook, independence of judgment, introversion, and originality.

Holland offers a more detailed description of his scheme that shows the similarities and the differences in each model type. Of course, no person is a pure "type," falling completely and exclusively into one category of this expressive system. Rather, he has tendencies in each of the six categories, usually peaking on the one that represents the primary direction of his vocational expression. The second-highest peak determines his choice of a role within the major area and becomes his secondary vocational expression, representing a narrowing or focusing of his choice.

It is possible to develop a classification scheme based on the first four peaks with which to match people to jobs. For example, most successful salesmen will peak first on "enterprising" and then on "conventional"; accountants, on "conventional" and then on "enterprising"; biologists on "intellectual" and then on "social"; journalists on "artistic" and then on "social"; and secretaries on "social" and then on "conventional." Our major concern is with managers, who, for the most part, peak on "enterprising" and then on "conventional." There are, however, exceptions to this.

The expressive system that emerges as the outward manifestation of needs, attitudes, and drives will determine the direction into which a person will channel his energy and seek opportunities to implement and to enhance his self-concept. This is an important idea, vital to the development of an adequate selection and placement program. But this is not all there is to the story.

People with similar expressive systems tend to congregate together, like birds of a feather, because they are attracted by similar tasks. Clusters of tasks become roles, and a network of roles forms a structure inhabited by personalities. The resulting interactions create the third dimension, the organizational milieu. If a person fails to find a milieu that is compatible with his intellectual and motivational systems, he will experience, at best, a sense of ennui—that is, a considerable reduction in the amount of energy he can mobilize for his task—or, at worst, a deep frustration that will incapacitate him. In either case, he cannot respond to the demands of his environment in a constructive, adaptive way.

The organizational purpose, with its related value system, so attracts people with similar needs, personalities, and values that it gradually acquires a pervasive personality orientation that reinforces and sustains its milieu. Completely changing the decision-making structure and climate of an organization would require the removal of most of its people and the redesign of its tasks—large undertakings that cannot be accomplished overnight. They cannot be done by training or by organizational development. They have to be done first by changing the task and by selecting different types of people.

Decision Making and the Computer

The effort to change the decision-making structure will be largely unsuccessful unless it is begun at the top with the decision makers. This is what seems to be happening, though in a purely accidental fashion by the introduction of the computer into the decision-making process.

It is interesting to note that, so far, the impact of the computer on top-level decision making has been fairly limited. A major consulting organization reports studies indicating that computers are very much underutilized in today's corporations. One reason for this situation is that older managers, bred in rigid structures with clear lines of authority and chains of command, do not have the skills or the appetite to master the management-science tools necessary to make decisions with the information the computer spills out. As management positions adapt to the computer during the 1970s, the top management decision-making structure will change. The computer will turn out more alternatives and more strategies. Model building and risk analysis will become standard procedures. And these new tools will require men with the intellectual abilities to grasp the complexity and the magnitude of the decisions and with the motivational systems that will permit them to be comfortable in the presence of risk and uncertainty.

According to the Systems Development Corporation, the new computer technology will turn the whole management structure upside down.[16] This corporation has designed what it calls a *meta* system ("meta" meaning of a higher order or more comprehensive), which enables the computer to be utilized as an extremely knowledgeable and fast-thinking executive assistant.

"What will happen to decision making in a company when its data-processing resources include a meta-system capability?" asks SDC. The impact may be felt, not only in the way information is utilized, but also in the speed with which new requests for computer services can be filled. The company says that what will be required, though, is a new organizational approach to information processing and decision making. In the traditional view, the aim of a management information system is to look at the organization from the bottom up, relegating the manager to a practically passive role. Probably the traditional view is conditioned by the way information always has had to be processed—from the bottom up, with details condensed at each successive organizational level. Information goes up; orders come

[16] "Getting the Man on Top to the Bottom of Things," *SDC Magazine,* Vol. 11, No. 6 (June 1968), pp. 1–13.

down. This is how information got to the top executive before computers, and when manual systems were automated there was no obvious reason to consider a different way.

But, with the advent of the meta system, the whole approach has to be turned upside down, so that the executive looks at the information from the top of the organizational pyramid. This top-down view puts the executive in control of the machinery; the computer does not so much punch information to him as, in effect, it becomes a crystal ball, giving him the power of penetration through organizational layers. Thus, as the information flows down from the top to bottom, decision making can be moved as close as possible to the scene of actual operations.

The additional power of penetration will naturally carry additional responsibility to use that power properly. Decisions will require the evaluation of more facts, but then they can be more accurate. What new pressures the wide use of meta systems will bring to bear upon management only time can tell. "The future is no place for the timid," concludes the Systems Development Corporation. "For the bold, the prospect of working with a computer assistant should be an exciting one." And, we might add, it will revolutionize the managerial milieu.

It is doing so already, according to *Business Week*.[17] The new management is taking over, shattering the old organization chart and developing a new management style. Quoting management consultant Harold Wolff, *Business Week* says that, while the old management mainly concerns itself with the efficiency of the production process and the workforce, the new management seeks the optimal use of all corporate resources, including its executive talent. One of the major corporations involved in the new management is Pillsbury. Extensive use of the computer has changed the corporate climate in this company. "The essence of the change is in the style and thought and pattern of relationship among executives," the president is quoted as saying.

The Self-Renewing Organization

The new management is creating not only an innovative organization but a self-renewing organization.

Gordon Lippitt and Warren Schmidt have introduced the fascinating idea that, as businesses go through the stages of birth, youth, and maturity,

---

[17] "The 'New Management' Finally Takes Over," *Business Week* (Aug. 23, 1969), pp. 58–62.

they face a predictable series of organizational crises. Each crisis, they assert, requires new management capabilities. And probably another dimension of the managerial crisis is represented by the need of managements in the 1970s for new management capabilities.[18] This need will be met by changes in three variables: milieu, task, and personality.

The organizational milieu. Through its policy makers and its executive group, an organization establishes a set of values within which its decisions are made. These values reflect in part the values of the overall society, in part the purpose of the organization, and in part its internal climate. They prescribe the norms of acceptable behavior, the degrees of freedom permitted each member, the extent to which members participate in decision making, the risks encouraged, the rewards or punishments for effective or ineffective decision making, and the degree of error tolerated. The new approach is based on the assumption that effective organization decision making is not obtained by developing and disseminating a set of detailed procedures to be adhered to undeviatingly down the line. This strategy is too restrictive for all but the dullest and most disinterested employees. It is also impractical because it never covers all the contingencies and it usually results in excessive delays and the referral of routine decisions to higher authority.

A sounder strategy consists of establishing and communicating values in the form of policies and goals within which lower-level managers are free to make their own decisions. This approach leads not only to sounder decision making but more personally rewarding managerial roles. If each manager's role is designed to conform to his personal capacities, and if the climate is sufficiently supportive to provide incentives and to minimize fear of error, the net effect is a greatly enhanced facility for organizational decision making.

Role design. Centers for decision making must be designed and ordered according to the magnitude and the complexity of decisions. These decision centers must be placed at strategic points in the information processing–feedback network to provide the orderly flow of information required to make decisions. As decisions increase in magnitude and complexity, they must be moved higher in the organization to provide for greater access to information and more time. This is not to say that top managers will have a less complicated life or that they will know everything that is going on in the company, but it does say that they will have more time to devote to long-range planning and broader decisions. This realignment of decision-making

[18] Gordon L. Lippitt and Warren H. Schmidt, "Crises in a Developing Organization," *Harvard Business Review*, Vol. 45, No. 6 (Nov.–Dec. 1967), pp. 102–112.

roles can only be achieved by careful attention to the personalities of the role incumbents.

Personal capacity. The intellectual and the motivational systems of the decision maker are of critical concern to the decision-making process even though they are sometimes unnoticed. Each manager brings to his role a background of personal experiences in decision making that is independent of either his role or the organizational milieu. Individuals with low self-esteem or with rigid personalities characterized by a high need for security will tend to be cautious, conservative, and slow to decide. Other managers, because of immaturity, may be inclined to impulsiveness or to overdecisiveness. Still others, lacking the intellectual ability to comprehend decisions of more than average magnitude and complexity, will tend to focus on minor decisions and delay or evade responsibility for important decisions.

All of these, then, when put together give us a picture of the total life-space of the manager, which we will explore in the final chapter of this section.

6

The Managerial Life-Space

ONE of the world's largest corporations, a multinational firm with a sales volume in excess of $5 billion, was faced with a problem: the selection and development of top managers. Not that it lacked candidates; on the contrary, they were too numerous. From among the many nominated by the group vice-presidents, the president sought a way of identifying those few on whom the corporation could most profitably concentrate its development efforts. The only information this giant concern had to go on in facing this decision was that supplied by its supervisors. And each nominee, according to his supervisor, was doing a first-rate job and had all the qualities necessary for a top management position.

The difficulty was that each nominator had his own idea as to the qualifications of a top manager—and they conflicted. The marketing vice-president's list of requirements clashed with those of the systems vice-president, and his in turn were entirely different from those of the manufacturing vice-president. The president was unable to reach a consensus among his top managing group as to who should be designated for promotion.

Probably in no other area of management was this company so ill-equipped to make a high-level decision. It was quite research-minded and spent millions of dollars each year on its research and development efforts. It even maintained a competently staffed personnel research unit. But the company psychologists were assigned to salesmen selection research and to the validation of clerical tests. The idea of doing research on top management simply never occurred to the president and his vice-presidents—or, if it did, it was quickly dismissed as either impractical or a usurpation of top management's prerogatives.

This situation is one of the strangest anomalies of the Managerial Society. There are few corporate presidents in the United States who would argue with the statement that good managers are worth a lot to them. There are even fewer who would say they have all the good managers they need now. And there are *none* who would assert that they know all there is to know about selecting and developing managers.

In the light of these assertions, one would expect to find American management engrossed in a massive research effort aimed at the identification of managerial effectiveness and the best ways of predicting it. This simply is not the case. Comparatively little meaningful research has been or is being conducted, and what is being done is the work of a relatively few corporations.

We are left, then, with little factual support for the theories described in this book. There are, of course, a number of excellent reasons for this situation, not the least of which is the inherent difficulty of conducting appropriate research among managers. But the really surprising fact is that there is so little effort being made to identify the characteristics of the effective manager at a time when so much money is being spent on his development. All we have is the survey findings reported in the business journals; and these, while interesting, lack the rigor on which to build a promotion and progression program.

Nevertheless, by piecing together the data scattered through the research literature, by extracting what we can from business magazines, and by discounting much of it on the basis of the inherent limitations in studies of managerial effectiveness, we can arrive at a tentative idea of what can be considered to be the *managerial life-space*.

Life-space is a concept developed by social psychologist Kurt Lewin to measure the person and the psychological environment as it exists for him. It includes such factors as his needs, goals, motivations, mood, anxiety, and ideals. The environment includes both consciously and unconsciously perceived forces that have an effect on the individual. Our model of the managerial life-space would consist of three concentric circles: The characteristics of the personality would be in the center, surrounded by a middle ring consisting of the requirements of his role and an outer ring constituting the milieu in which he operates. Managerial effectiveness has to be determined by reference to this total life-space.

Defining and measuring the life-space is a formidable task fraught with many problems. Nevertheless, there have been breakthroughs. We shall examine the problems first and then review the research to underline the significance of these breakthroughs.

Research Problems

In recent years there have been several surveys of the research conducted on managerial qualities and effectiveness. All have reached the same conclusion: It is unimpressive and unenlightening. The vast majority of industrial and governmental organizations have made no effort at all to determine whether their management selection and development programs are useful. What little research evidence has been compiled on the effectiveness of managers is less than satisfactory.

This situation is due to the problems encountered in conducting studies of this kind. One basic problem is the fact that there simply are not enough individuals in managerial positions to meet the requirements of statistical inference. But an even more serious problem than that of numbers, which can be overcome, is that of identifying an effective manager. Defining managerial effectiveness is compounded by the basic criterion problem and the effects of role and organization milieu on managerial performance.

The Criterion Problem

Not long ago a researcher was asked to embark on a study of the managers of a major corporation. In presenting his design to top management, he mentioned that of course he would require an objective method of identifying the company's most effective managers. The corporate executives whom he consulted assured him that there was no problem; they had ample records of each manager's performance extending over the previous five years. But, as they began discussing each measure—sales performance, salary history, supervisor's ratings—they fell to arguing among themselves over its reliability. Not a single one of their measures could stand on its own feet. What they were left with finally was the personal judgments of the group vice-presidents as the sole indicator of a successful manager.

The investigator then interviewed each vice-president to ascertain the traits he looked for to determine who was an effective manager. Each vice-president came up with a set of characteristics that was at odds with the one proposed by his peers. This is what psychologists refer to as the *criterion problem,* and defining and developing adequate criterion measures is one of the most elusive problems of managerial research. Most predictor validation studies are suspect because the criteria used—such as supervisory ratings, position level, and salary—are inadequate. The failure to obtain correlations between selection instruments and criteria may be due more to the inadequacy of the latter than to the shortcomings of the former.

The basic problem with the classic model of criterion-centered research is that the index used to represent successful job performance is usually quite limited—first, by its subjectivity; second, by its partial representation of an individual's total performance; and, third, by its reference to performance at a single point in time

Obviously, management must assess the effectiveness and the relevance of the techniques it uses in selecting managers to determine whether they are useful tools or just window dressing supported more by custom than by their effectiveness. But what are needed even more are relevant criteria of managerial performance. Relevant criteria are *reliable;* that is, consistent. They are *multidimensional;* that is, they cover all aspects of a manager's performance. Finally, they are *longitudinal* in that they include measures taken at different points in time. But we also need to know whether the instruments predict success at the junior management, the middle management, the senior management level, or all three.

Criteria of managerial effectiveness, therefore, are complex in their structure and in their relationships. A real effort has to be made to understand and to explain these interactions and their relationships to other behavioral measurements. Recent emphasis has, in fact, led to a different concept of the criteria of managerial effectiveness than has so far appeared in the management literature:

1. The trend is no longer to accept what management views as the most desirable job performance but, rather, to establish as desirable what is most effective in terms of individual and organizational growth.
2. More attention is being paid to what a person is required to do and how he does it than to what he accomplishes.

These new criteria emphasize what a manager does with what is in his control. The emphasis is not so much on the achievement of objectives as on the soundness of the decision he makes with the information and the time that he has available to him.

Defining Managerial Effectiveness

The first problem that has to be overcome is the identification of managers. A good many studies of managerial effectiveness are misnamed. High-talented people are not necessarily managers. Studies have indicated that many managerial roles are overloaded with tasks that have nothing to do with managing. Engineers with managerial titles, for example, spend most of their time on engineering problems rather than on decision making. The same situation holds true in banking, in retailing, in manufacturing, and in a whole host of other industries and occupational functions.

The error in confusing the function of a manager with the function of a specialized discipline confounds the results that have emerged even from the most well-controlled studies of managers. The picture that emerges is not so much that of a manager as that of a composite engineer, accountant, salesman, or lawyer who has been given, through the selection process, managerial responsibilities. Therefore, we are told little about the characteristics of the effective manager.

Studies of managers have also been hampered by treating the managerial role as identical with the leadership role. There is nothing at all amiss in studying the nature of leadership or of the effectiveness of leadership styles. The error lies in applying the results to the managerial role.

Another question that has to be answered deals with the effectiveness of the managers included in the research studies. How do we know that a man who reaches the top is really an effective manager or a master politician? The answer is, of course, that we do not. But it *is* possible to get a feel for the answer to this question. Experience in administering a decision-making exercise to over 8,000 managers from all over the world and from every sector of society leads inescapably to the conclusion that most managers are really poor decision makers: They are poorly organized; they tend to make decisions without adequate information; they avoid important decisions and concentrate on the smaller, less important ones; and they put off making decisions wherever possible. Moreover, Ross Stagner's study of 217 executives in 109 firms indicates that profit maximization in the decision-making process is often offset by many other considerations, not the least of which are social role and personal bias.[1]

What comes through in both these studies is the suspicion that many "successful" managers are noteworthy more for political maneuvering than

[1] Ross Stagner, "Corporate Decision-Making: An Empirical Study," *Journal of Applied Psychology*, Vol. 53, No. 1 (Feb. 1969), pp. 1–13.

for their competence as decision makers. This would explain why these men falter so badly in front of the computer. As responsibility seekers, with strong needs for security and an aversion to rocking the boat, they have reached their positions by interpersonal rather than decision-making skills.

In his study of organization values and rewards, John B. Miner points out that many companies do a poor job of attracting, retaining, and developing managers who possess the characteristics conducive to success.[2] Their managers are men who have played to organizational reward systems rather than to organizational values implicit in effective performance.

H. Edward Wrapp reflects this attitude in his list of the attributes of a good manager: keeping well informed, focusing time and energy, playing the power game, and practicing the art of imprecision. The last two attributes are of real significance. In playing the power game, Wrapp says, the manager must be able to plot the position of various individuals and units in his organization with regard to any proposal. And, as for developing the art of imprecision, the successful manager must know how to satisfy the organization's need for a sense of direction without ever actually getting himself committed publicly to a specific set of objectives.[3]

Many managers develop an elaborate set of defenses against the proper performance of their jobs. To them, management by goals is a threatening exercise with which they cope by artful hedging. Long-range planning is a concept to which they pay lip service and which they avert by a flight into busyness, into the "don't have enough time" syndrome. The very weight of the duties that a manager loads on his shoulders is his first line of defense against the anxieties that stem from his lack of confidence in his capacity.

Other favorite ploys of the pseudo-manager are the business of selecting impossible standards or goals (no one can fault you for trying so gallantly) and the search for the perfect solution to a problem (rather than an acceptable and a workable solution). In such ways, many if not most managers control their inner anxieties and survive in the organizational milieu which is known popularly as "the rat race."

Sooner or later, of course, events in the outside world overtake such managers, and the organizations they serve pay a handsome ransom to extricate them from their own incompetence. But their prevalence in managerial roles in industry and government casts a pall over nearly every

[2] John B. Miner, "Bridging the Gulf in Organizational Performance," *Harvard Business Review*, Vol. 46, No. 4 (July–Aug. 1968), pp. 102–110.

[3] H. Edward Wrapp, "Good Managers Don't Make Policy Decisions," *Harvard Business Review*, Vol. 45, No. 5 (Sept.–Oct. 1967), pp. 91–99.

study of managerial effectiveness and of the identification of management potential.

The Effects of Role and Milieu

So far, there have been few studies that have taken the organizational milieu into account. Yet there is evidence from several experiments to show that the milieu has an important effect upon a manager's behavior. And, as we have already pointed out, effectiveness depends upon the structure and the climate of the organization.

The result of these two omissions is to make all simple one-to-one studies of managerial behavior suspect. They deal with noninteractive relationships or main effects, with the linkage of specific measures of individual difference to indices of managerial effectiveness. There are almost no studies concerning the measurement and the exploration of variables that meaningfully describe the dimensions of the role and the organizational milieu.

BUSINESS-JOURNAL STUDIES

These problems with research have left a serious informational vacuum as to the personal qualities of a successful manager. By and large, the vacuum has been filled by the business press.

Naturally, businessmen and government officials are keenly interested in the qualities of an effective manager. Every corporation is plagued by the problem of picking the wrong man or of promoting what looks like a top-flight prospect and watching him turn sour in a job obviously over his head. Hardly an issue of a well-established journal goes by without some article on managerial selection, motivation, or development. And, from time to time, "studies" are reported on the managerial profile. These generally consist of questionnaires sent to managers asking them to describe the qualifications of a top executive. Of course, these surveys are so seriously deficient in methodology that they really represent a social consensus of current fashions in the executive suite. But, by examining enough of them over a period of time, we can obtain a glimpse of what the managerial life-space looks like.

Most of the studies agree on one fact—that the manager is intelligent—although some feel he is not "brilliant." One study of 33 top executives of companies doing at least $25 million annually found that the single most significant identifying factor was intellectual ability. The group ranked higher than 96 percent of the general population of business and industrial workers. Another study of 1,700 top executives reported that, though managers did well above average in college, only one in twenty made the dean's list.

With respect to motivational traits, there seems to be a general consensus that such qualities as initiative, job knowledge and skill, dependability, ability to get along with people, stability under pressure, personal wholesomeness, and good work habits distinguished the managerial elite from the inferior managers. One prominent magazine asked 75 high-ranking executives to define the personality traits indispensable to the good executive. Their replies cited judgment, initiative, integrity, foresight, energy, drive, human relations skill, decisiveness, dependability, emotional stability, fairness, ambition, dedication, objectivity, and cooperation.

These studies, overall, seem to be in agreement that the characteristics of an effective manager are as follows:

1. Intellectual ability. Managers at all levels have the ability to think, to reason, to solve problems, to make sound decisions, and to spell out ideas with precision.
2. Organizing ability. Managers have the ability to bring things, ideas, and people together to accomplish some goal.
3. Initiative. Managers show more imagination, self-starting behavior, and confidence than the people they direct.
4. Drive. Managers have more energy, especially of the type that is directed toward clearly identified goals.
5. Leadership. Managers have the ability to win the interest and the respect of other people.

These characteristics, more or less intuitively arrived at, are similar in many respects to the more empirically derived traits to be described later. There is, however, a possible change in emphasis taking place. As we have already noted, the computer is having its impact on managerial characteristics. The new manager may be more closely akin to the older, more entrepreneurial types of the early twentieth century than to the professional manager of the past 25 years. It is possible that we may be returning to the risk takers of yesterday, although the new managers of course have a broader view of their social responsibilities in today's knowledge society.

While interesting and even helpful, the judgments arrived at through a survey of managerial opinion are hardly specific enough to develop a selection and development program. They do not tell us how to measure the qualities of an effective manager, nor do they describe how they can be spotted early. What is needed is a more rigorously designed and controlled experiment conducted by competent behavioral scientists to afford a deeper insight into the personality dynamics of the effective manager.

Behavioral-Science Research

With all the caveats that have been already mentioned, it is not possible by any means to lay down a rigorously defined description of the managerial life-space. Nevertheless, we now have indications of what it may be like, enough indications to suggest the broad outline of the managerial selection and progression strategy that we shall develop in Part Two. There has been sufficient work in the areas of the managerial role, organization climate, and the managerial personality to suggest at least some tentative descriptions of what it takes to maintain an effective managerial staff.

The Dimensions of a Managerial Role

While the manager is essentially a decision maker, the illustration of the baseball-team structure presented in Chapter 3 indicates that he performs a number of other functions to support his essential responsibility. The illustration also suggests that, at different levels, the nature of the decision-making process changes drastically. These two observations lead to the question whether there are enough common functions in the managerial position to postulate a set of universal dimensions for all managerial positions. This question addresses itself to the crux of the matter of managerial selection and development and suggests why many selection and progression programs fail.

If we hold, as many do, that managerial roles differ from company to company, from function to function, and from level to level, we are left with the uncomfortable conclusion that no systematic approach to selection and development is possible. Each role, then, has to be filled by intuition, a process that leaves too much room for error. It also opens the door to many types of irrelevant employment practices.

If, on the other hand, we assume that the managerial role is essentially the same regardless of the situation and changes only with level of responsibility, then we can identify those similarities by studies across many managerial roles in many organizations. There have been a few studies that have attempted to do this, to identify objectively the common dimensions of managerial positions. This has been difficult because managerial roles can only be studied in a specific organizational setting as they are enacted by role incumbents. Once again, we confront the confounding problem. The role demands so blend with personality and organizational variables that it is difficult to separate them.

Several studies have been conducted that tend to confirm the view that there is a great deal of similarity in managerial roles. One study of 452 managers employed in 13 companies ranging in size from 100 to over 4,000 employees was based on the idea that the managerial role can be divided into two basic areas—function and competence. The *functional* categories encompass related responsibilities requiring similar or basic skills such as planning, investigating, coordinating, and supervising.[4] The *competence* area refers to the specific and technical information required, as on finance, purchasing, and marketing.

Each manager's performance was measured in terms of the proportion of time he spent in each area and the relative importance of each to job success. The investigators found that there was a minimal core of a manager's job, comprising about 55 percent of his working time, that was devoted to the functional areas. The remainder of his activity involved some specific competency such as employee relations, manufacturing, or engineering. The higher the level of the position in the organization, the greater the emphasis on planning more general activities.

Another study of 355 officers in a large metropolitan bank utilized the same approach but sought to obtain an estimate of how managers thought they *ought* to spend their time.[5] Owing to imperfections in the organization's structure and the design of managerial positions, the study found, most managers were plagued with the problem of doing things that subordinates should have been doing and not spending enough time on what the managers should be doing. In general, the earlier results were confirmed; there was an almost unanimous desire on the part of bankers to spend more time planning and less time processing information. In other words, they wanted more time to manage and less to be bankers.

[4] Thomas A. Mahoney, Thomas H. Jerdee, and Stephen J. Carroll, "The Job(s) of Management," *Industrial Relations*, Vol. 4, No. 2 (Feb. 1965), pp. 97–110.

[5] John A. Haas, et al., "Actual vs. Ideal Time Allocations Reported by Managers: A Study of Managerial Behavior," *Personnel Psychology*, Vol. 22, No. 1 (Spring 1969), pp. 61–75.

Both studies tended to confirm the major dimensions of the managerial role. But they were based on asking the manager how much time he spent on various activities, an approach with several weaknesses. First, as already has been indicated, the imperfections in the notion of what a manager does cause him to spend time on things he ought not to be doing. Second, managers are not very accurate in reporting how they spend their time; they tend to overestimate time spent on production and underestimate time spent on interpersonal relations. Third, managers waste a good deal of time even though they may not realize it. This is particularly true during business hours when interference from telephone calls, meetings, visitors, reading chores, and "crises" so often occurs. But a good deal of a manager's work is done in the evening hours and on weekends when things are quiet. One study showed that the typical American executive puts in a minimum of 60 hours a week, including one night working in the office and two at home.

For these reasons, John K. Hemphill used a different approach to the analysis of managerial positions.[6] He asked managers in several companies to complete a questionnaire dealing with four aspects of managerial work: (1) position activities, (2) position responsibilities, (3) position demands, and (4) miscellaneous position characteristics. It will be noted that this approach represented an attempt to get at the real dimensions of the managerial role by focusing on the demands of the position as well as the functions and the responsibilities. When the results were analyzed, a profile of managerial positions with ten dimensions was obtained:

1. Providing a staff service in nonoperational areas: gathering information, selecting employees, briefing superiors, checking statements, verifying facts, and making recommendations.
2. Supervision of work: planning, organization, and control of the work of others.
3. Business control: cost reduction, maintenance and inventories, preparation of budgets, justification of capital expenditures.
4. Technical aspects of products and markets: development of new business, marketing, anticipation of changes in demand for products.
5. Human, community, and social affairs: concern with the goodwill of the company, maintenance of the respect of important persons.
6. Long-range planning: plans for the future of the company, company goals, evaluation of new ideas.

[6] John K. Hemphill, *Dimensions of Executive Positions,* Research Monograph 98, Ohio Studies in Personnel (Columbus: Ohio State University, 1960).

7. Exercise of broad power or authority: recommendations on very important matters, interpretation of policy.
8. Business reputation: product design, quality and improvements, delivery schedule, complaints about products or services.
9. Personal demands: concern about the propriety of the manager's behavior.
10. Preservation of assets: capital expenditures, large expenditures (as for taxes and operations).

Hemphill's conclusion that some combination of these ten factors can be found in every management position has been confirmed in several studies. One or more of them is dominant in a particular managerial role according to its level in the organization, the function for which the incumbent is responsible, and the type of enterprise engaged in by his employer. Higher-level managerial positions, for example, emphasize such factors as long-range planning, the exercise of broad power or authority, and the preservation of assets, while lower managerial positions are more inclined to be involved with the supervision of work, the provision of staff services, and the technical aspects of products and markets.

It is also noteworthy that the studies referred to were conducted in organizations where the positions were titled "managerial" or "executive." Not all of them were, in fact, managerial positions within the meaning established earlier, but they tend to support the basic idea that managerial positions have much in common regardless of the organization and differ only according to level.

The data, then, begin to suggest the role requirements of the manager. The lowest-level manager is concerned with activities directly related to people, with providing staff services, and with the direct supervision of work. He has the greatest face-to-face contact with people, and his decisions generally involve the activities of subordinates. We would therefore suppose that the personal requirements needed at this level would be social skills and the ability to establish effective working relationships with others. Many of the characteristics associated with leadership are to be found at this level.

The second-level manager is concerned with business control, with the technical aspects of products and markets, and with human and community relations. He is more concerned with functions and processes, and his decisions are mainly of a technical or functional nature. It would be expected that the dominant characteristics of the middle manager would be problem-solving skills and technical competence.

The top-level manager is concerned with long-range planning, the exercise of broad power and authority, and the reputation of the firm. At this level, therefore, a manager deals for the most part with broad ideas and abstractions. Conceptual ability, a high degree of fluid intelligence, and good judgment would be essential for effective performance.

It can readily be seen, then, that the decision-making activities of the three levels are very different, calling for distinct talents not needed at the other levels. It is to these differences above all else that a managerial selection program must address itself.

The Effect of Organizational Milieu

To date, there have been few studies of organizational milieu. We have, however, referred to Rensis Likert's human-resources accounting system, which is an attempt to account for the effect of organizational structure and patterns of management behavior on productivity, costs, and earnings. The University of Michigan, along with the management of the R. G. Barry Corporation, is now engaged in the development of the first such system.[7] This system measures investments in the firm's 96 managers in terms of outlay and replacement costs. So far, the data indicate that the replacement cost of the firm's entire managerial staff is about $1 million.

This approach should yield some interesting financial information on the effect of the managerial team on the organization. But it will not tell us what kind of managers function best in which kinds of environments.

We do have some idea of the importance of this problem. By comparing organizations with different levels of performance in three different industrial environments, Professors Paul Lawrence and Jay Lorsch showed that the more successful businesses can be distinguished from the less successful in the way they adapt to their environments.[8] Two characteristics were studied: differentiation and integration. The more different the patterns of thought and behavior of the managers in two departments that had to work together, the more difficult it was for them to achieve integrated action. In the higher-performing organizations, the tensions between the states of differentiation and integration were resolved more effectively.

It is clear that people with similar motivational systems gravitate not

---

[7] R. Lee Brummet, William C. Pyle, and Eric G. Flamholtz, "Human Resource Accounting in Industry," *Personnel Administration* (July–Aug. 1969).

[8] Paul Lawrence and Jay Lorsch, *Organization and Environment* (Boston, Mass.: Div. of Research, Harvard Business School, 1967).

only toward certain occupations but toward certain organizations and toward certain departments in those organizations that offer the promise of catering to their particular need systems. We can obtain some information on this phenomenon from Holland's research. By reviewing the profiles of the six personality orientations referred to earlier, he found that he could predict with considerable accuracy not only a student's choice of college major but the likelihood of his transfer from one college to another with a student body more compatible with his personal characteristics and interests. Indeed, Alexander W. Astin published a book of college environmental profiles similar to Holland's personality dimensions to enable students to select the college with the environment that suits them best.[9]

There is some evidence that the same process determines a college senior's choice of occupational career and the organization in which to pursue that career. It appears that certain personality types are attracted to an organization, that the selection process weeds out those persons who do not fit into its organizational climate, and that the after-employment experience tends to mold the individual to the organizational personality orientation or to eliminate him.

It is likely, therefore, that managers in the accounting department will have needs, values, and a frame of reference that will differ in major ways from those of managers in the research and development or marketing divisions, thereby creating opposing organizational cultures that make cooperation and communication difficult. Without some way of resolving this conflict, the organization will suffer.

The interaction of the managerial personality with the organizational milieu was clearly shown by a study of a major European household-product industry. Psychologist Ken Rogers identified firms with a clear pattern of success and failure. Using as a basis the transcript of more than 600 interviews with executives of these firms, he sought the reasons for each firm's position.[10]

In both the successful and unsuccessful companies, he found remarkably consistent managerial personality patterns. Although all the companies were in the same business, operating similar organizational structures under similar marketing conditions, their results not only differed markedly but continued in the same direction through time. Furthermore, the personalities and attitudes of top-level managers reflected themselves throughout

---

[9] Alexander W. Astin, *Who Goes Where to College?* (Chicago: Science Research Associates, 1965).

[10] Ken Rogers, *Managers—Personality and Performance* (Chicago: Educational Methods, Inc., 1963).

the hierarchies of their organizations. Rogers noted that this process was reinforced by selection; management tended to hire in its own image, and employees gravitated toward certain companies because, consciously or intuitively, they felt "at home" there. Once they joined the organization, the prevailing managerial atmosphere demanded of these men a close adherence to company philosophy.

Rogers also reported that in the successful companies there was a basic harmony between the actual job performed and its symbolic value for the manager, while in the less successful companies strain and tension of a purely disharmonious kind were evident. The executives' conscious purposes in the unsuccessful companies were often at odds with their unconscious needs.

Studies of the Managerial Personality

It is fairly clear that organizational performance can be reduced ultimately to individual men and to their motivations, conscious and unconscious. For decisions, obviously, are made not by organizations—they have no reality outside of the minds of men. They are made by men, by individual personalities acting out the roles assigned to them in accordance with the dynamics of their own needs systems.

Research, then, must ultimately boil down to studies of the work-motivated adult manager. This of course creates great difficulty because of the many uncontrollable variables that the researcher encounters. Studying executives is not like observing the behavior of albino rats in a maze. Efforts to date have been conducted within such large companies as Humble Oil; Sears, Roebuck; IBM; General Electric; and the Bell System. Most of these studies have been undertaken by comparing the background data and test performance of managers with selected criteria over a period of time. The conclusions of these studies can be summarized in the following categories: biographical data, intellectual measures, motivational measures, and measures of the decision-making process.

Biographical information. Personal-history data have generally been associated with managerial effectiveness. They are fair predictors for first-line managers but somewhat less useful for higher-level managers. The most notable success has been achieved by the Humble Oil Company with a biographical information blank that will be described in more detail later. It has proved to be valid with European as well as American samples. On the other hand, Sears, Roebuck researchers have not had very much success with this instrument as a measure of managerial potential.

The various studies show that biographical data that reflect achievement motivation, drive, and perseverance are among the more valid indicators of managerial potential. Successful managers are better educated than less effective managers; they were exposed to a much less restrictive upbringing in their early lives; they showed greater conscientiousness in school and a more purposeful approach to college. Over all they manifest a total life pattern of successful endeavor.

But the question remains as to whether these data are effects or causes. They represent social facts that emanate from a basic psychological-need system that thrived in a supportive early developmental environment. To understand the psychological factors more clearly, it is necessary to examine the human traits of the successful manager.

The intellectual system. Naturally, the decision maker must have the intellectual and the technical competence to understand the variables involved in a decision. This requirement has been treated so extensively in the literature that it is almost superfluous to mention it here. We may note in passing that this aspect of human performance receives most of the attention in the selection of potential managers. But there are other more important considerations.

First, if the concept of decision complexity and magnitude is valid, it is probable that decision making is subject to the same psycho-physical principles by which physical stimuli are interpreted by the brain. This process occurs in the perception of the magnitude of the decision and the ability to differentiate a number of alternatives. While we have posited a decision-magnitude index ranging from one to 10,000, it is quite likely that this spectrum exceeds human capacity. Human beings undoubtedly have minimum and maximum levels of decision-magnitude comprehension just as they have in their ability to hear sound frequencies. While sound frequencies range from 10 to 100,000 cycles per second, human beings have a potential for hearing only in the 20-to-20,000-cycle range, and few persons have even this wide a range.

Although we can speculate that human beings can grasp the implications of a decision of no more than a given magnitude, we cannot establish the upper limits. But this human peculiarity explains why, in board rooms, executive chambers, and legislative assemblies, expenditures of millions of dollars are often approved in minutes while purchases involving only a few hundreds are haggled over for hours. And it also explains why many serious thinkers today are of the opinion that international events and a rapidly expanding technology confront heads of states and corporations with decisions that are beyond the ability of any single mortal.

Besides the ability to comprehend the magnitude of decisions—and there are many individuals whose ability to perceive the consequences and the commitments of a decision is quite low—the ability to deal with decision complexity also differs from person to person. Most human beings are comfortable only with a two-option decision, seeing reality in terms of black or white and hardly ever noticing the gray. Even when there is a choice of three or four pretty well-defined options, a human being will consciously or unconsciously reduce them to two. It takes a good deal of training and education plus a highly developed intellectual structure to handle multi-option decisions and, when faced with a two-option decision, to actively seek a third or fourth alternative. It is this characteristic that is of keen interest in the selection of managers.

There appears to be quite impressive evidence demonstrating the superior intelligence of managers. Historically, intelligence tests have been most useful for identifying managerial potential, and it is only recently that other measures such as the biographical information blank and situational tests have caught up with them. Many studies have shown that intelligence, typically measured by verbal ability tests, is a fair predictor of first-level managerial performance but not of higher-level managerial performance. But studies using more intensive measures of mental ability, particularly when they attempt to get at fluid rather than crystallized intelligence, have uniformly shown intelligence at a fairly high level to be important. The Sears, Roebuck studies, for example, concluded that the effective executive is characterized by an orderly, structured intellect of considerable power.

The motivational system. So far we have viewed decisions from the standpoint of the organization, even though we have already noted that a decision is made only by human beings. It is obvious, therefore, that every decision in some way and to some degree commits the decision maker himself. His personal fortunes and his self-esteem are inevitably bound up with the decision he makes. It is logical to assume that this consideration will be so salient in the decision-making process that, consciously or unconsciously, the decision maker will weigh carefully the personal risk involved in making an organizational decision. This subjective consideration constitutes the "What's in it for me?" factor that cannot be treated too lightly. It is often this aspect of the decision that gives it its air of irrationality.

An organization decision of whatever magnitude or complexity becomes completely transformed by the motivational system of the decision maker. His total attitude or response set will be a product not only of his internal personality dynamics but of the organizational value system in which he operates and of his perception of his role in that organization. Thus a routine organization decision may be viewed by an individual manager as quite risky, particularly if he expects that a poor outcome will incur punishment either from the organization or from within himself. If he sees a high risk in making a decision, he will try to reduce that risk by procrastinating, on the theory that many situations decide themselves, or by spreading the risk among his superiors, peers, or subordinates on the theory that the smaller the personal risk, the more objective and rational becomes the decision.

One would expect, therefore, that the effective manager would be characterized by a generally positive attitude toward life motivated by achievement, power, or autonomy needs; that he would be self-confident, dominant, and assertive, have strong drives mobilized for concentrated action, and be interested in power, political manipulation, and recognition. By and large, these characteristics do come through in the research that has been conducted. To cite a few studies: Lyman Porter found that forcefulness, imagination, and independence are more typical of large-company managers than small-company managers; that line managers feel they receive more autonomy, esteem, and self-realization than do staff managers. They are sure that forcefulness, self-confidence, and decisiveness are among the key needs satisfied in their jobs. The major finding of Porter's study was that the demand for conformity comes from the small company rather than the large, from lower management rather than from top management. The individualist is much more likely to be found in a top management position in a large company than anywhere else.[11]

Zygmunt A. Pietrowski, in a study of 110 vice-presidents and presidents, half of whom were successful and half failing, found that the former could be contrasted to the latter on the basis of their motivational characteristics.[12] The successful top executive strives more intensively for personal achievement, sets more difficult work goals for himself, is a better gauger of his

[11] Lyman W. Porter, *Organizational Patterns of Managerial Job Attitudes* (New York: American Foundation for Management Research, 1964).

[12] Zygmunt A. Pietrowski, "Consistently Successful and Failing Top Business Executives: An Inkblot Test Study," in George Fisk, ed., *The Frontiers of Management Psychology* (New York: Harper & Row, 1964), pp. 18–28.

work, can work longer hours under pressure, can adapt emotionally to a variety of people, is more original, and has less insecurity and self-doubt.

Edwin E. Ghiselli found in his study of 287 managers that the effective manager showed less need for job security and less desire for financial reward than did less effective managers.[13] The desire for power over others was about the same in both groups. But the effective managers showed the strongest desire for self-actualization, for the opportunity to utilize their talents in creative ways.

In summary, the studies indicate quite clearly that the successful manager has a total life pattern of successful endeavor. He was good in college; he had high socioeconomic aspirations; and in his early years, extending back through school to the home situation, he was forceful, dominant, assertive, and confident.

Decision making. Only recently have studies been aimed directly at relating the personality characteristics of managers to their decision-making behavior. In one study, the profiles of 726 management people, covering all levels from first-line supervisor to company president and including a variety of occupations and ages, were obtained.[14] The results show that differences in performance on the decision-making exercise were definitely related to level and type of education and to size of company but were less clearly related to age and level in the organization. The younger manager in a higher-level position with at least a bachelor's degree, preferably in the administrative or the social sciences, who was employed by a large company and who presently held a position involving managerial or administrative responsibilities, achieved a more desirable decision-making profile. He showed good verbal skills and an affinity for social ambiguity and enjoyed situations involving power, status, and leadership. Older managers from smaller companies, with less education, whose training had been primarily in engineering or in general business administration, tended to obtain less desirable decision-making profiles. From this study it was concluded that the self-assertive manager with a high self-regard was a better decision maker than the more conventional, cautious person. He produced more work, and he seemed to enjoy the stimulation of the exercise.

The managerial life-space. To obtain a final view of the managerial life-space, however, we must cite the work of Jon Bentz and his staff at Sears, Roebuck. There is no question that Bentz has conducted the most

[13] Edwin E. Ghiselli, "Some Motivational Factors in the Success of Managers," *Personnel Psychology,* Vol. 21, No. 4 (Winter 1968), pp. 431–440.

[14] Felix M. Lopez, *Evaluating Executive Decision Making,* AMA Research Study 75 (1966).

thorough, systematic, and objective work in this area.[15] Concern for the measurement of executive behavior has a relatively long history in Sears, going back to 1942.

The managerial role in this company has very little technical overlay; most managers are generalists, and development takes place largely through job rotation. However, Sears' executive population is no run-of-the-mill group, differing markedly from the average man in many respects. Sears managers are intellectually superior; they appear to be socially aggressive and goals-oriented, with unusually fine personal adjustment and confidence and ambition that enable them to carry responsibilities.

Through a battery of well-researched psychological tests over a dozen years or more, Sears developed an executive battery that predicted management success at Sears. The effective executive was shown to be an energetically active man with aggressive sociability. He is further characterized by an orderly, structured intellect of considerable power, strong administrative leadership skills, considerable emotional strength, and a highly competitive orientation. These factors are given support and direction by a strong competitive drive and a practical, business-centered turn of mind.

But the executive battery, as far as Sears is concerned, has only tapped one dimension of the managerial life-space. Since Sears, like many other companies, is undergoing a dynamic metamorphosis as it keeps pace with the radically changing structure of the Managerial Society, it is apparent to management that the demands made upon executive personnel have been altered subtly but significantly. To fill out all the dimensions of the life-space, the company believes that it needs to measure additional abilities and motivational characteristics in the following areas:

1. The use of mental ability. Sears will need managers who are several notches above the current quality. The company is looking, therefore, for measures of the use of intelligence without the binding influence of personality, the quality of thinking that is without intellectual rigidity. It wants a measure of flexibility in the use of intelligence.
2. Qualities of intelligence and personality that would measure openness to change and identify those individuals having the unique capacity to function as the initiators of change. Here Sears needs measures that will assess the ability of the personality to maintain an open mind to new

---

[15] For an account of this work see V. Jon Bentz, "The Sears Experience in the Investigation, Description and Prediction of Executive Behavior," in F. R. Wickert and D. E. McFarland, eds., *Measuring Executive Effectiveness* (New York: Appleton-Century-Crofts, 1967), Ch. 7.

things and the tendency toward initiation of change, creativity, and flexibility in thinking and acting.

3. Factors related to administrative skill and decision making. Here are needed measures of the ability to think through complex situations, both in isolation and in association with others. In popular terms, Sears feels it must assess such qualities as "breadth of vision" and "the ability to integrate parts of the business through the utilization of sound business-like judgment." This is akin to something that might be called "intellectual organization."

4. Assessment of emotional strength as a part of the competitive personality. It is Sears' belief that there is a continuing need to assess the personality variables of emotional strength and/or control, personal aggressiveness, and the desire to contribute.

To measure these additional characteristics, Bentz and his associates have developed a multiple-assessment program. Initial efforts have been extremely fruitful and so very promising that Sears is now studying the attitudes of managers and is considering a major organizational study.

In summary: To assess a managerial candidate adequately, four major clusters of instruments are required: (1) a battery of traditional instruments to measure the personal characteristics just cited, (2) an in-basket exercise to measure administrative and decision-making skills, (3) a group situational exercise to measure social skills and leadership in small-group situations, and (4) performance-evaluation procedures to measure a person's impact on his superiors. Each of these measurement instruments will be described in detail in Part Two. One thing is clear, however: The vast amount of data generated by the Sears research, as well as that of others cited earlier, suggests that the dimensions of the managerial life-space cannot be effectively assessed by the measurement methods and tools of the past. The new findings do not necessarily contradict earlier studies; they only suggest how complex the problem of assessing managerial potential really is and how naive early approaches have been.

The task ahead for all major organizations is to build a new program based on the realities of the managerial life-space. Only in this way can they keep up with technological expansion, and only in this way can they approach a solution to the managerial crisis. What this new managerial assessment model may look like will be described in Part Two.

In practical matters the end is not merely speculative knowledge of what is to be done, but rather the doing of it. It is not enough to know about virtue, then, but we must endeavor to possess it, and to use it, or to take any other steps that may make us good.
—ARISTOTLE, *Nichomachean Ethics*, BOOK X

PART TWO

Programs, Procedures, and Practices

7

The Managerial Manpower Plan

THE absence of a theoretical base to reflect the realities of human and organizational behavior forces American business and industry to follow selection and promotion practices that smack of either the courtesies of a gentlemen's club or the law of the jungle. A splendid example of the latter approach was offered by the widely publicized executive shuffle that occurred in late 1968 in the Motorola/Fairchild/Philco-Ford triangle. Motorola's executive vice-president started the ball rolling by resigning to become president and chief executive officer of the Fairchild Instrument Company. He brought to his new company not only a strong background in semiconductor-manufacturing technology but seven other managers of Motorola's semiconductor division. Noting these moves, the financial community shifted $60 million dollars along with the new president; Fairchild's stock went up 20 percent, and Motorola's dropped 10 percent.

Motorola promptly announced that it had sufficient depth in its management to cover the loss of these executives. But in a short time it hired the general manager of Philco-Ford's micro-electronic division to replace the executive vice-president it had lost. Later on, it filed complaints against Fairchild and its ex-managers to prevent Fairchild from obtaining and using the Motorola trade secrets known by these men.

This is, of course, only one of many cases that typify the confusion in numerous contemporary managerial selection programs caused by the long tradition of bad theory and even worse practices. In contrast to these practices, we shall present in Part Two a decision-making model of selection and promotion embedded in a new personnel system that is based on the following propositions:

1. Effective managers are essential for the achievement of organizational purposes.
2. Only a small proportion of the labor force possesses the intellectual and motivational qualifications to enact the role of manager effectively.
3. The possession of an adequate supply of effective managers depends on an organization's ability to attract them and to identify them correctly.
4. The attraction, selection, and retention of effective managers depend upon the opportunities for personal growth and fulfillment offered by the organization.
5. The identification of men with the potential or actual skills of an effective manager depends upon the assessment methods employed.
6. The creation of growth opportunities in an organization is a function of its personnel system.

In essence, these propositions call for the development of a brand-new approach to the utilization of the corporate manpower resources. This, we realize, will not be easy. For, in developing a new approach, a company is faced with the realization that it has a history, a tradition, and a cultural setting in which it must operate and out of which has evolved a set of personnel practices and procedures that greatly restrict its ability to utilize its human resources maximally.

Analysis of the personnel practices and procedures used by modern corporations and public agencies, however, reveals one central characteristic: diversity. It is possible to make sense out of this diversity only by viewing it from the perspective of systems theory, looking for patterns that cut across organizational boundaries. We must thereby identify personnel *systems,* rather than *programs,* and apply them to every organization. Because, while an organization may have neither a personnel structure nor a formal personnel program, it does have a personnel system. This may be haphazard and informal, but it is still a system.

The actual personnel system, which is nothing more than the way in which an organization utilizes its human resources, is as vital to it as the central nervous system is to the human body. For over the long pull it determines the kinds and qualities of people who are brought into the organization. It also provides the avenues for advancement, it conditions the attitudes and the values of the employees, and it modifies the public's view of that organization.

The extent to which various personnel systems have developed and are now in control of the organizations of which they are a part has created blocks to the development of comprehensive manpower plans even when they are deemed to be in the public interest. The operation of poverty programs, for example, has been seriously hampered by union regulations and other characteristics of the country's collective bargaining system. Thus it will be difficult to change the existing personnel systems in many organizations. Management nevertheless has a golden opportunity to innovate and to institute change in one group. It has always been free to manage its own members. There are few compelling reasons to inhibit it in hiring, promoting, and firing within its own ranks.

The development of a managerial personnel system, therefore, can be a logical and an essential first step toward the development of a comprehensive personnel system. After it has been tested and implemented, it can be extended to other high-talent employees, to the technical and professional people, and ultimately to the entire labor force. As a matter of fact, it would be impossible to change a personnel system by starting anywhere else but at the top.

In other words, the institution of the managerial personnel system proposed in Part Two can be considered a pilot program for the whole corporation. Once the managerial group is covered by a more enlightened system, it will be only a short step to the point where the other members of the organization can be invited to join in.

Contemporary Managerial Personnel Systems [1]

Before examining this new system, however, we must look briefly at the major features of contemporary managerial personnel systems.

The various personnel policies, practices, and procedures in the United States can be grouped into five major systems. Of these five there are actually only three that apply to managers: the political, the career, and the competitive systems. While none is found exclusively in a single organization, it exists in part in nearly every company or public agency.

---

[1] Some basic ideas in this section are drawn from Frederick C. Mosher, "Careers and Career Services in the Public Service," *Public Personnel Review*, Vol. 24 (Jan. 1963), pp. 46–51.

The Political System

By far the oldest, the political system is based fundamentally on a manager's loyalty to his superior. This system, which is in effect very loose and informal, can be traced to man's earliest experiments in social organization. The political system permeated the tribal structure of nomadic days, gave power to the lord of the manor of preindustrial society, and reinforced the position of the royal house in the political monarchy. The principal characteristics of this system are two: Qualification for a particular office is secondary to loyalty to the chief, and performance is judged by the way the chief's interests are advanced.

Modified to some extent by modern technological and democratic requirements, the political system still retains at its core the idea that appointment to and retention in a position stems from membership in a specific social group, such as a family, tribe, political party, or ethnic class. In the early days of the American republic, and in many public and private enterprises throughout the world today, political appointments and the political system are an accepted way of life.

It is argued that in certain situations the political system is essential. If the chief executive, who is ultimately responsible for the fulfillment of the organization's purposes, is to implement his decisions effectively, he needs lieutenants who are responsible to his orders. Thus cabinet officials and other high government and business officials are subject to the machinery of the political personnel system.

In its cruder forms, as in the early years of the federal administration and in many of the late-nineteenth-century business enterprises, the political system meant that positions were filled on the basis of patronage or nepotism. But increasingly, and especially at the higher levels of government and business, political appointments are no longer partisan; they are not necessarily "plums," and the incumbents are usually well qualified for the positions they occupy. However, the political system still goes against the grain of the American ideal of egalitarianism. According to one study not long ago, large numbers of managers consider nepotism undemocratic, and some of those who feel this way are themselves "nepots" or patrons of "nepots." In actual fact, a great many business executives consider nepotism outmoded and claim that it causes many subtle and distasteful problems. Yet the survey showed that most managers accept it.[2]

[2] David W. Ewing, "Is Nepotism So Bad?" *Harvard Business Review,* Vol. 43, No. 1 (Jan.–Feb. 1965), pp. 22–48.

It was discovered a long while back that the political system was useful only at the apex of an organization, and there only if it was supported by a cast of career members who furnished the continuity in administration and technical expertise. For, no matter how excellently endowed they may be, they are looked upon both by themselves and by others as expendable unless, like bishops and Supreme Court justices, they are assured of life tenure. By its very nature, therefore, this system creates a sense of expediency that colors every decision. Short-term objectives will be favored over long-range goals in decisions that may spell the difference between the success and the failure of the organization. In addition, political appointees often are so out of tune with the traditions and the values of the organization that they find it difficult to establish effective working relationships with their subordinates.

The Motorola/Fairchild case cited earlier is an example of the operation of the political system. And there are other cases, such as the Texaco/Occidental Petroleum Corporation dispute over the geologist who mapped out Peruvian oil concessions for Texaco and then went to Occidental and the Du Pont/American Potash affair where the Du Pont manager went to American Potash shortly after developing a new titanium-dioxide-manufacturing process. These affairs, plus the ouster of Semon Knudsen from the presidency of the Ford Motor Company in 1969, point up the high costs that can be encountered in the political personnel system.

Increasingly, in the more progressive corporations and government agencies, it is acknowledged that the political system has represented more trouble than it is worth. The trend seems to be away from it. We have referred to the decline of the charismatic business leader, which is attested to by the fact that few knowledgeable persons can identify the heads of top corporations, and to the tendency in large companies to appoint top decision-making committees. The emergence of a top executive committee composed of career managers who possess a long-range view of the corporation both fore and aft results in a somewhat anonymous chief executive who functions more as a prime minister subject to the directions of his cabinet or presidium. And the members of this group are, more often than not, products of the organization's career system.

The Career System

The career system is both an extension of and a reaction to the political system. Long ago, monarchs and other hereditary leaders recognized the more vexing disadvantages of the political system, realizing that to acquire stability in their regimes it was necessary to build a manpower structure that gave certain assurances of tenure and reward to its lower but essential officers. The principal reward held out was the guarantee that higher-level positions would be filled exclusively from their ranks.

Thus, in the career system, loyalty is transferred from a chief to a service. Personnel are recruited early, during or immediately following secondary education, given a thorough indoctrination in the demands, customs, virtues, and rewards of the service, and then launched on their lifetime careers. The principal qualification for admission to the service is potential for advancement to higher levels. Once admitted to the fraternity, the selectee can anticipate reasonable progression upward through a variety of assignments to a top level—unless, along the way, his conduct flagrantly advertises his unfitness for service. Rank in the organization is determined by the manager's career status rather than by the duties of the position he holds.

In moving up, the career man is constantly engaged in keen competition with his fellow careerists. But, on the other hand, he is comforted by the prospect of not having to compete with those outside the service. Classic career systems are found in the officer group of the military and the foreign services, but they also are strongly ensconced in the managerial ranks of private industry and in nearly all the professions. They differ primarily in the object of their loyalty; the professional's loyalty is to his science or profession, the manager's to his company, and an officer's to his service.

The career system maintains its characteristic exclusiveness, not only by eliminating outside competition for higher positions, but by enjoying a monopoly on the services it renders. A pattern of loyalty and a respect for tradition are thereby perpetuated that make a virtue out of conformity and a hero out of the organization man. The system is rarely found in an undiluted form; but wherever it prevails, and however it is modified, its most serious drawback remains. That is, it tends to discourage the innovative and enterprising management that is the backbone of an organization.

The impact of social and technological changes has therefore brought deep disturbances to most career systems. Since most careerists are by definition "generalists," qualified to fill any billet, the necessities of specialization in the new technostructure make them obsolete. Consequently, the classic model of the career system has passed from the scene, but in some form and despite efforts to break it up it still persists in both industry and government.

Our modern foreign service, which dates only from the Rogers Act of

1924, is a good example of how the career system persists in adversity. In the past 40 years there have been many proposals to improve and to strengthen the service. These proposals, submitted at the rate of one every two years, have all agreed on the issues that are important to the development of a more relevant and effective career system:

1. In staffing the service, recruitment should be conducted at all levels instead of at the bottom. The concept of "lateral entry" should be encouraged.
2. The staff should be consolidated under a flexible personnel system.
3. The career system should give greater scope and meaning to specialization on the one hand and to a growing need for managerial talent on the other.

In spite of these recommendations, the effort at improvement has succeeded only marginally. By 1965 a special task force set up by the secretary of state reported that the changes implemented were very modest in their scope and that the older problems were reemerging.

The difficulties of effecting change in the foreign officers' personnel system is just an example of the difficulties encountered in trying to break through the traditions, the status symbols, and the structure of a service that is continually reinforced by "in"-group loyalty. Modern secretaries of defense have encountered the same obstacles in their efforts to overhaul the promotion machinery of the officers corps of the armed services. And many corporation presidents have found it to be a formidable task to break up the patterns characterized by the company's career system. As one top personnel vice-president put it: "No matter what innovations we introduce into the management progression plan, the system grinds them down to the point where they become ineffective, and back we go to the status quo."

The Competitive System

In contrast to the political and career personnel systems, the competitive system is relatively new. In the public service it is known as the civil service system and traces its origins to the middle of the eighteenth century in Europe. In private industry it is known as the skills inventory or management replacement program, and its origins go back only to a date somewhere between the two World Wars.

In essence, the competitive system provides for appointment and promo-

tion to a particular position on the basis of fairly rigorous standards measured by a series of tests or other objective devices. The system developed as a
reaction to the more flagrant abuses of the political system and traditional
mistrust of the career system, which, with its rank and privileges, is imbued
with aristocracy and nepotism.

In the competitive system a premium is placed on the ability of the
individual to perform the duties of a specific job. Rank in the organization
stems from the responsibilities of the position rather than from the qualifications of the incumbent. Once appointed to the position, the incumbent usually acquires a proprietary right to it that makes him virtually impossible
to remove without a formal hearing. The basis of the competitive system is
the classification of positions into various grades based, usually, on job evaluation. In the public sector, appointment is usually by competitive examination; in private industry, the competitive system depends upon one of the
three following methods.

The personnel-records approach. A strategically situated personnel manager maintains effective internal contact and communication with various
company units. He also maintains a system of personnel records. When a
vacancy occurs, the unit manager contacts him for advice and information
on likely candidates, which he furnishes from his records or out of his head.
He becomes a center of information on applicants and job vacancies to
assist managers in filling positions.

The management-replacement approach. Information about the qualifications of current managers and their promotability is collected and stored
on various forms, and a manpower-inventory chart is constructed to identify
candidates for prospective openings. Each manager is expected to maintain
his own management-replacement chart. This shows the structure with the
names, not only of the incumbents in all positions, but of two or three
others who are listed as backups, each name being coded in a color to
signify the owner's readiness for upgrading.

The records information referred to can be maintained in a computer
storage mechanism. Openings are fed into the computer, and the names
and personal profiles of those meeting the requirements of the positions
are printed out. These names are then referred to the supervisors who will
make the eventual selections.

Although the intention of the competitive system—to eliminate the
favoritism that led to its establishment—was certainly laudable, the results
have not been satisfactory. The chief difficulties with the competitive system
stem from the basis on which selection and promotion decisions are made and
on the way they are related to other corporate programs. The system does

not place enough emphasis on present job performance, on the career aspirations of individuals, or on potential for performing at a higher level.

In the public service the way to advance is to pass an examination that usually measures only a small part of the skills needed in the higher-level job. In private industry the only way to advance is to influence the supervisor with the vacancy to accept you. In either case, the employee has little incentive to perform his present duties in any but an ordinary way, or to develop his skills for greater responsibilities that may or may not come.

In addition, a very subtle but very real seniority effect is present in this system. Because of the experience requirements built into most minimum qualifications for promotion, the effect on upward mobility is almost as strong as the seniority clause in a union contract. Over all, the competitive system lays down a series of restrictions on upward mobility that dampens ambition, solidifies lines of promotion, and encourages mediocre performance.

The Human-Resources Personnel System

The weaknesses in all these systems have led to a flow of innovations and improvisations tending toward the convergence of the three models into a more extended and complex system that is supported principally by the theories and the research findings of the administrative and behavioral sciences to which we have already referred. The new system is also receiving strong impetus from the rapidly changing social, economic, and cultural conditions in the external environment.

We have named this new system the *human-resources personnel system* because its emphasis is upon the full utilization of manpower resources rather than upon the implementation of a strategy of containment, which is implicit in the other systems. It is based on the notion that the manager's job as a decision maker is to optimize the use of all corporate resources, both financial and human.

For, to accomplish its mission, an organization has only two resources, capital and men. Peter Drucker says that, of the two, the latter is infinitely the more important. Yet, until recently, both institutions and society have behaved as though the situation were reversed, as though capital were the central source of power and were vastly more valuable than men. But now knowledge makes people productive, and knowledgeable manpower is the organization's most critical asset.

Manpower Planning

Since human beings are so valuable, the utilization of human resources must be planned as carefully as that of financial resources. Manpower planning, therefore, has become the key to the human-resources personnel system.

In the past ten years, we have witnessed a genuine phenomenon in mankind's history—manpower planning on a national scale in a free society. This planning is still imperfect in many respects: It is crippled by political and regional interests and prejudices, and it is disrupted by the American distaste for anything that smacks of social manipulation on the part of the government. Yet the GI Bill of Rights, the Manpower and Development Training Act, the various poverty programs, and the operations of the U.S. Employment Service are instances of governmental efforts at manpower planning that have been to a large extent successful. It is up to each institution now to key into these national manpower-planning activities. Most top managers believe that manpower planning will become a critical function in the next five to ten years and that companies that carry it out successfully will be distinguished from those that do not on the basis of their profit picture.

Since we have already said that planning is advanced decision making, it follows that manpower planning is a form of advanced decision making about the human resources of the organization. It has been defined rather widely as the process by which a firm insures that it has the right kind of people at the right place at the right time, doing things for which they are most economically useful. This is a good definition as far as it goes, but in a certain sense it is rather like saying that a rose is a rose is a rose.

Manpower planning actually represents a corporate strategy, a master battle plan that the chief executive follows to insure the maximum utilization of his human resources. It is a complex but comprehensive integration of all the decisions related to the deployment of his people. It is a combination of plans, policies, programs, and reviews that keeps the organization on course toward its objectives and, at the same time, in continuous touch with the realities of its internal and external environments. It is more than simply deciding in advance; it is a way of forcing the game, of making things happen.

So far, because of its recency, manpower planning is only dimly understood and practiced completely almost nowhere. It applies, of course, across the board to all employees, but its point of departure lies with the managerial group. Where it has been tried, it has often failed for lack of understanding of its importance or because of procrastination, operational pressures, and an absence of clearly defined responsibilities. But, above all else, manpower planning has failed because it takes hard work—lots of it—and the development of a clear view of exactly what it implies.

Attending a seminar on manpower planning is instructive because it underscores the lack of clarity in current understanding of the process.[3] To some firms, manpower planning really means manpower development, and their approach is purely qualitative; that is, they aim to make men better managers by undergoing certain experiences. Making managers better managers today is their goal.

To other firms, the stress in manpower planning is exactly the reverse; that is, on its quantitative aspects. Here the problem is defined as determining how many managers will be needed at some period in the future. The goal is to insure that the company has the right number of managers at the right places at the right time.

To a third group of companies, the emphasis is not so much on *manpower* planning as on *organizational* planning. They stress the structure and the climate within which managers function most effectively. Creating the proper climate and adapting it to current social, economic, and market influences are their goals.

While each of these approaches is naturally an important part of the overall manpower plan, it is not *the* manpower plan. Rather, the human-resources personnel system is a process not unlike the "fractional distillation" process used to refine oil. We begin with raw materials, and by a series of optional interventions we reduce these to a refined product. In the manpower plan, the optional interventions consist of the whole battery of personnel techniques, including recruitment, selection, training, pay, and promotion. Traditionally, however, American management has utilized these techniques in an unintegrated way. Within the human-resources system, manpower planning refers to the management of a coordinated and an integrated plan designed to meet the needs both of the organization and of the people who work in it.

Essentially, there are two kinds of variables that affect a company's resources, the controllable and the uncontrollable. The controllable variables refer to those interventions that the company makes to assure itself of a high-quality labor force: selection, training, performance evaluation, organi-

[3] For a clear exposition of the techniques of manpower planning see Eric W. Vetter, *Manpower Planning for High-Talent Personnel* (Ann Arbor: Bur. of Industrial Relations, University of Michigan, 1967).

zational structure, and management style. The uncontrollable variables include both the physical, economic, social, and political events that occur in the larger society, such as depression, war, or civil rights movements, and the strategies of competitors.

Manpower planning requires the establishment of a strategy to deal with the controllable variables and to forecast the effect of the uncontrollable variables on them. An integrated manpower plan enables management to act upon its environment rather than to react to events; to create change rather than to be managed by crisis. Even though it will never be perfect, the development of a managerial manpower plan has a number of advantages:

1. It focuses attention on specific manpower problems.
2. It clarifies the kinds of changes in the system that management is trying to effect.
3. It forces management to accept the interdependence between the various programs in its overall personnel system.
4. It forces management to make an explicit statement of the movement of personnel through its structure.
5. It clarifies the differing time sequences of manpower decisions, distinguishing between short- and long-range objectives, between productivity and morale, and between the maintenance of present job effectiveness and the development of potential for advancement.

To develop an effective manpower plan, three steps are necessary. First, a realistic set of policies must be formulated at the top based upon what the human-resources personnel system actually implies and implemented as a top management responsibility. Second, an integrated manpower-information system must be devised to supply facts rather than opinions or conjectures. And, third, a series of interrelated and integrated personnel programs must be established and implemented vigorously.

Policy. The human-resources personnel system must be based on an underlying philosophy that can be translated into a series of clear-cut and widely disseminated policies. It must be geared to the organization's purposes and goals. This basic philosophy places major emphasis on the evaluation and the development of the whole man. It considers the personal and emotional needs and satisfactions of the entire management group and their relationship to long-range organizational goals.

The system must be dynamic and flexible, open and responsive to its environment, not only within the organization but outside it. As changes occur in the social system, the organization must automatically respond by adapting its structure and processes to the transformed reality. Inevitably, such a plan will be complex. Different programs will have to be designed and applied not just according to occupational groups but by level and geographic area. The resulting unity in variety will require a multilevel functional arrangement with many vertical and horizontal relationships that will place a premium on cooperation and communication.

Above all, the policy incorporating this philosophy must be articulated and published. All members who are covered by the plan must be aware of and understand its basic features. It is entirely insufficient, for example, to publish a statement in a handbook saying, "It is the policy of this company to promote from within." This policy must be supported by a program that *guarantees* that this will happen and that it will be understood and accepted by those to whom it applies.

Responsibility. The responsibility for the administration of this system clearly rests with the chief executive and his top operating managers, working within a policy framework established by the board of directors. They are assisted by appropriate staff members in the personnel, systems, and other staff departments who develop and maintain it. The central personnel staff acts as internal consultant and change agent, its role encompassing three functions:

1. It serves as a *technical resource,* advising operating units on the most effective recruitment, selection, and development techniques.
2. It serves as a *central clearinghouse* by maintaining the manpower-information system.
3. It acts as an *auditor* to insure that operating units are adhering to corporate policies and standards with respect to the manpower plan.

The system must be highly centralized. Manpower planning—like finance —is a management function that cannot be delegated or decentralized. What has often been overlooked in studies of decentralization is that no successful firm has ever decentralized the financial function. Since there has rarely ever been more than one treasurer in a firm, the centralized control of finances exercises an ultimate power over all members in a decentralized organization. And, just as the management of financial resources is regularly centralized, so the management of human and, in particular, managerial resources must be centralized and the primary responsibility accepted by the chief executive. In fact, he should consider the direction of the managerial manpower plan to be his top responsibility.

The Impact on Managers

When fully operational, the plan we shall present is unlike any that has been so far available to top management. Since the information and the services it provides have simply not been available, managers and employers have operated without them, substituting their intuitions for facts and their opinions for a solid projection of future trends. To some, the plan may even smack of an invasion of privacy or constitute a "big brother" approach.

If it is to be maximally effective, however, managers will have to learn how to use it and how to live with it. In particular, they will have to realize that the plan is not a substitute for managerial decision making; it is merely a means of helping them make sounder decisions with longer-range effects by increasing the information needed and by making more time available. It certainly will be no substitute for the personal rapport that must exist between managers and their subordinates. It will not, therefore, eliminate the need for high-level managers to devote considerable attention to the performance and the needs of their subordinate managers. As a matter of fact, it should encourage them to spend more time in what is their primary task of coaching and evaluating the work of their subordinates.

Individual managers in turn may raise the objections that the plan represents an invasion of their privacy, that it will depersonalize the entire management-progression process. In their minds, the proposed management inventories and assessment procedures, pulling together, as they do, the scattered statistics about them, may constitute an unforgiving and an unforgetful judge who will never give them a second chance. Since it will expose managerial inadequacies quite clearly, it will be somewhat threatening. Managers may be properly concerned that the plan will not always be used for benevolent purposes.

It is important, in short, to ease everyone's doubts by explaining carefully the system's ultimate purpose to utilize managerial talent most effectively and to give everyone a better opportunity to grow. In line with this thinking, it is necessary to give consideration to the question of who has access to the data accumulated under the system. A security program will have to be established to determine who is authorized to seek what information. Someone in the organization—a director of organizational and manpower utilization, for example—will have to be assigned the ultimate responsibility of monitoring the system to make certain that no unauthorized use is made of it.

An Integrated Manpower-Information System

Often the human commitments in a decision situation lead to greater and longer-lasting consequences than the financial. But, just as often, managers make decisions solely on the basis of financial factors simply because the firm's financial-information system is well developed and serves as the measuring rod of their success. Consequently, managers tend to underestimate the human commitment.

The accounting and budgetary system tends to overinfluence an organization's decisions. People pay attention to them. A manager can squander half the organization's human resources; but, if he stays within his budget or shows a modest profit, he will be left to his own devices and may even be rewarded. Unless, therefore, a manpower-information system is developed that has the same precision and the same accountability as the financial-information system, manpower planning will remain an occult rather than a hard science.

Objectives and Requirements

The objectives of the manpower-information system are as follows:

1. To provide management with sufficient information on which to base manpower decisions.
2. To provide management with an inventory of employee skills available for the accomplishment of its overall goals and objectives.
3. To facilitate a search for in-company personnel qualified for existing vacancies in special assignments.
4. To estimate the effectiveness and the capabilities of the present work-force.
5. To identify personnel-development needs.
6. To provide adequate positions and salary controls.
7. To project present and future manpower requirements.

The requirements of the information system are that it must—

1. Integrate with all other management-information systems.
2. Apply to all company units and occupational groups.
3. Permit future expansion and elaboration.
4. Avoid duplication with other processes and records.

5. Permit economy of installation and maintenance.
6. Adapt to data-processing equipment either now or in the future.

The Three Elements

An integrated manpower-information system combines knowledge of past events, the present situation, and future probabilities.

PAST EVENTS

A manpower-information system must provide accurate information about historical trends in the company's manpower resources. In terms of rates and ratios, it must afford an accurate reading of present manpower resources. It is impossible to evaluate the effectiveness of present methods and procedures without adequate information on what has happened, who was involved, and with what effect.

Analysis of past events includes the following:

1. The compilation of statistics concerning the number of managerial positions filled annually by job title and organization unit; the median time required to fill these positions; the number of people who apply for jobs by certain demographic characteristics; the number interviewed, tested, referred, hired, and rejected for various reasons; the average length of time between application and final employment decision; and the cost of the company for each interview, test, and hire.
2. An evaluation of all instruments used in the selection and promotion program, including recruitment literature, application blanks, interviews, tests, and verification procedures.
3. Studies of terminations by job classification, length of service, organization unit, and reason; lateral transfers; reassignments; and promotions.

These statistics should be consolidated in charts showing trends in management-personnel movements and in flow diagrams of the management-procurement and development process showing where new managers are coming from, where they are going, and with what effect upon company operations. This is what Professor Eugene Jennings, of the University of Michigan, refers to as the new discipline of "mobilography."[4] It helps chart

---

[4] Eugene E. Jennings, "Charting the Difficulties to the Top," *Management of Personnel Quarterly*, Vol. 6, No. 2 (Summer 1967), pp. 13–21.

the routes managers take to the various levels in the corporation, the distribution and number of mobile managers, the slow and fast movers, and the delays and difficulties en route.

Analysis of past events will also contain structural information about ratios of management to nonmanagement personnel, direct labor as compared to indirect labor, and similar statistics. But this information, which in some manpower plans is looked upon as crucial, can be quite misleading. For example, Frank Cassell cites a study of manpower usage and deployment in American and German steel mills. American steel mills used three times as many supervisors and ten times as many technicians as comparable German mills. Yet American mills need only half the workforce of the German mills to produce a ton of steel.

Frederick Harbinson, after studying the relationship of nonproductive to productive employees, also concludes that such ratios can be very misleading.[5] Companies showing the greatest increases in nonproductive workers as a proportion of their total employment, he reports, are invariably those which have made the most spectacular changes in products, processes, and organization. His evidence indicates that the companies which originate new processes, products, or administrative methods invariably use a greater proportion of high-talent manpower than those which merely adopt the innovations that others have developed.

Thus it is probable that social and technical changes are requiring more managers and fewer workers, altering the traditional ratios materially. Indeed, there are those who say that future trends indicate the day is coming when *all* members of the organization will be managers!

THE PRESENT SITUATION

Information about the present situation reflects the state of the career structure and the characteristics of the company's manpower resources. The former is referred to as the *career plan* and the latter as the *human-resources inventory.*

The career plan. Every position in the company can be placed in a two-way matrix consisting of job family and level. *Job family* refers to a group of positions related by qualifications required and skills utilized—for example, accounting, personnel, and mechanical engineering. *Level* refers to the degree of skill required and its availability in the labor market. For larger

---

[5] Frederick Harbinson, "Manpower and Innovation: Some Pointers for Management," *Personnel* (Nov./Dec. 1959), pp. 8–15.

organizations it is possible to add a third dimension: *location*—for example, organization unit, profit center, or subsidiary. But, where possible, this should be avoided.

The career plan should be developed without reference to the salary plan or to outside competitive considerations. The only reference point should be the tasks that must be done and the skills required to do them. There are several methods of analyzing tasks and assigning positions to specific cells in the career plan. One way is to compile a skills dictionary by identifying the processes, products, and functions that go into each position.

1. Process. This refers to a series of actions that leads to a final result or product. We speak of a marketing or production process. An example of a process-skill listing would be:
   ENGINEERING, SCIENTIFIC AND TECHNICAL:
   Custom engineering, designing, drafting, field engineering, programming, mathematics, technical writing.

2. Product. This refers to the object or service created by the process—for example, an electric motor, a spindle, or purified water.

3. Function. This refers to a specific action in the process that leads to the final product. Some of the functions describing actions performed in a process and on a product are:
   a. Developing, conducting research.
   b. Installing, erecting, constructing.
   c. Performing tests, inspecting, analyzing, process controlling.
   d. Decision making, approving, reviewing, general directing.

Depending on the skills required, each position is assigned to a job level and a job family. For the management-manpower plan, of course, only those positions that are genuinely managerial positions—that is, have a high component of the functions listed in *d* of paragraph 3 above—would be included. By coding and classifying positions in this way and assigning them to a cell in the matrix, it is easy to identify logical *career paths* and to expose the gaps that may lie hidden in the existing job structure. This matrix, then, becomes the structural steel that supports the total personnel system.

The human-resources inventory. The human-resources inventory enables top management to determine, individually or in summary, the skills and other attributes possessed by its management employees. These can then be matched with the career plan. A useful inventory contains five categories of information:

1. Personal data, including age, marital status, and educational qualifications.
2. Occupational skills listed in terms of the skills dictionary.
3. Job performance as contained in performance-evaluation reports.
4. Potential for development as determined by appropriate measures to be described.
5. Career aspirations, based upon the employee's expressed wishes.

The inputs to this inventory will come from three major sources:

1. Personal-data and occupational-skills information supplied by the employee, generally on a biographical questionnaire which is updated annually.
2. Assessment data concerning intellectual and motivational characteristics, usually provided by an independent psychological assessment.
3. Performance-evaluation data accumulated under the performance-evaluation program.

The human-resources inventory is maintained by a central unit in the corporate headquarters of the company. Suitable methods of consolidating the data, preferably by computer, should be designed to furnish the following information to top management:

1. Profiles of employees meeting the specific requirements of a particular position.
2. Summaries of the process and products skills of company management personnel in specific units by job family and level.
3. Reports of special skills, languages, or training.
4. A management-succession report that enables top management to survey the adequacy of replacements for key positions, to isolate highly qualified performers blocked by lack of opportunity to progress, and to detect managerial and professional obsolescence.

The inventory can also furnish top management with a complete profile of a particular manager's background, work history, education, performance evaluation, and career aspirations.

Only when management possesses a data base approximating the one we have just described will it be in a position to make sound personnel decisions. Knowledge of past trends and the present situation with respect to the company's manpower resources and its skill requirements affords top managers a clearer view of the road ahead of the organization: whether it is growing, is stagnant, or is decaying.

In some organizations, a silent conspiracy can prevail that masks the facts about the managerial situation. Older managers who feel threatened by their advancing age, their creeping obsolescence, or their rapidly changing environment may try to hide their heads in the sands of yesterday. To support themselves, they may try many maneuvers—hiding promising young men, promoting incompetence, or making a farce out of the performance-evaluation program. Out of this mass anxiety an "establishment" is born, a highly structured "in" group that enforces manpower rules designed to insure its own security. This is the system that old men cherish and young men rail against, that blights a company like a creeping cancer and slowly destroys it as, all the while, its presence remains unfelt until it is fatal.

The antidote to this tendency is a realistic, up-to-date, and accessible system for providing information on managerial manpower that is not an end in itself but, rather, a powerful tool.

Manpower Plotting

Yet information about past trends and the present situation is really only of historical interest, much like the information given an automobile driver by his rear-view mirror. It tells him only where he has been, not where he is going. Information concerning not only his destination but the terrain over which he must go is provided by the manpower-plotting system.

By the term "plotting" we do not imply a conspiracy; rather, we refer to the process of mapping a course from one's present position to a desired destination. Plotting has more significance than the usual "forecasting" because, to answer the question "Where am I going?" I need to know my destination as well as the route over which I must travel.

Where are we going? Much has been written about management by objectives; the reader need only consult the many excellent books dealing with this subject. But a few words ought to be set down here concerning management by objectives in relation to manpower resources. An organization's goals must be based on an accurate appraisal of its manpower resources; otherwise they will be like the objectives announced by a last-place baseball-team manager in the spring—no more than pious hopes set down for their inspirational value. Public officials are quite guilty in this respect, establishing targets for full employment, tax reduction, and urban renewal that are totally unrealistic and hardly within the capacities of those on the payroll. And many businesses follow the same practice, establishing market-penetration or sales goals that are quite beyond the competence and the energy of their employees.

Setting goals, therefore, must take into account the probable course of events that is likely to unfold inside and outside the organization. This prediction of future events is known as *forecasting*.

Inside forecasting. Regardless of its purpose or its history, an organization experiences continuous changes which, taken together, tend to follow a course that can be defined and projected as a trend. Thus, after a company has accumulated sufficient historical data, it is fairly simple to project certain manpower trends. For example, to estimate within a fairly close margin the number of managers who will retire, die, resign, or be discharged in the succeeding 12 months is not so difficult. What is much more difficult and should not even be tried is to predict the names of those who will die, retire, or resign. But simply knowing that, according to present trends, the company must replace 23 managers in the next 12 months is a distinct advantage. And knowing within certain confidence limits how many must be replaced within the next five years affords an even greater advantage because, as we have pointed out, replacing managers is not like replacing desks or even typists.

Outside forecasting. In the past, management has done a poor job of plotting managerial manpower, partly because it has not tried, partly because it refused to believe its own figures when it did plot them, and partly because it failed to take into account the forces of change in the outside environment. For obviously there is a need to develop a strategy for the future, to face the reality of change in the external environment.

This strategy begins by examining the forces of change, by trying to understand how they originate and where they seem to be taking the company. In plotting its manpower course, a company has to make assumptions about changes ahead in the next 5, 10, 15, or 20 years in the following areas:

1. Psychological changes. The most profound changes will occur in people themselves, particularly in young people. The fact is that today's young people are much better educated than their counterparts of 20 and 30 years ago, are much more likely to react negatively to blind authority and to have different ideas about the motivation to work. While the transformation may not show up as readily in young business managers, they must be taken into account because they most certainly will have a profound effect upon management style and management potential in the next 20 years.

2. Technological changes. Much has been written about the rapid changes in technology, most of it dealing with the application of the computer and automation. We have already alluded to the impact of the computer on the emergence of a new manager group. A company must account for this impact in its managerial-manpower planning and in its managerial-progression program.

3. Social changes. As a result of psychological and technological changes, the patterns of the social system—particularly with respect to work— also are undergoing a profound transformation. Among the noticeable changes are, for example, shorter work periods and even shorter careers due to late entry into the labor market and early departure. There are more and more members of minority and disadvantaged groups in the workforce, and increasingly employees look upon the employer as the source of their total life security.

4. Political and economic changes. Whether we like it or not, the world is rapidly becoming one world in the sense of communication and transportation and in the sense of economic dependence. The immense changes that are already under way will have a profound effect upon the total managerial-manpower needs of the organization.

The effect of all these changes must be pulled together to plot the company's manpower course over the long range. Most firms—even those working within a very limited area—do a very poor job here. A study of employers' forecasts of manpower requirements made a few years ago showed that these were generally prepared by persons who had little knowledge either of future operating schedules or of forecasting techniques. The result was an exaggerated confidence in the accuracy of their predictions—which was particularly marked among those companies that did not keep any records of them!

In fact, the task of developing the manpower plot is so highly specialized that it should be assigned only to specialists. There are two methods of plotting: by mathematical projection or by making basic assumptions. Mathematical projections can be straight extensions of the growth of the workforce based on past and current trends, or they can be elaborate computerized formulations based on a mathematical model composed of many equations. So far it has not been practical to build a highly sophisticated mathematical model, but some are being experimented with in the universities.

The second approach, estimating the number and types of personnel to be needed in the future by each unit on the basis of assumptions inherent in one- and ten-year forecasts, seems to be preferable for the present. Projections based on alternative assumptions can be made for a period of years and then altered from year to year as indicated by actual events.

Key Manpower Programs

With the manpower plot, top management is in a position to administer its overall manpower plan, which will include three major elements: a manpower-information system, the manpower chart or course, and the programs designed to implement that course.

The overall manpower plan represents an integrated strategy that locks all the elements into one multifaceted system based on solid fact rather than on someone's conjectures or prejudices. Stressing unity rather than uniformity, it will contain four key programs:

1. A managerial procurement program designed to bring managers of vision, character, and ability into the organization on the basis of the organization's needs and plans.
2. A managerial progression program designed to provide for an orderly upgrading of managers in accordance with their capacities, their demonstrated achievements, and the organization's needs.
3. A managerial development program designed to enable each manager in the company to maximize his potential.
4. A managerial rewards program designed to compensate managers in direct proportion to their contribution to the achievement of the organization's goals.

The purpose of Part Two is to consider only the first two programs, the managerial procurement and progression programs. Later, after presenting these programs, we shall examine the managerial development and rewards programs briefly in relation to the first two. But, to understand fully the managerial procurement and progression programs proposed in Part Two, it is necessary now to examine some basic principles of managerial assessment.

8

Managerial Assessment

THE marketing vice-president of a large pharmaceutical firm was astounded one morning by a letter in his mail. It was from the chief of procurement of a federal agency with which the company did millions of dollars in business annually, and the simple request had the shattering effect of ten sticks of dynamite. Would the vice-president, the chief asked, kindly send the agency evidence of the validity of the selection techniques used to hire and to promote salesmen and detailers, such techniques to include but not be restricted to paper-and-pencil or performance measures, unscored interviews and application forms, and records of educational and work history used to judge applicants' qualifications?

Of course, it was entirely possible, the letter continued, that the evidence called for was not available, that perhaps efforts to secure such information were now in progress. If so, would the vice-president please notify the agency of the date of the completion of such studies and upon their completion forward two copies of the final reports? If the studies were not in progress, would the vice-president please inform the agency of the date when they would begin?

The vice-president put in an urgent call to his personnel director, and they spent a frenzied week examining personnel records, conferring with consulting psychologists, and composing a reply. In effect, they stated that while the company's selection techniques were progressive, fair, and impartial, they did not have the evidence of validity requested but that, as a matter of fact, a long-contemplated research program would begin immediately.

This letter, occasioned by Executive Order 11246 concerning guarantees of equal employment opportunity, served to bring forceably to the attention of this employer the flimsy basis on which his selection and promotion program was based. And while the Office of Federal Contract Compliance (OFCC) regulations do not apply to professional, technical, and managerial occupations, companies in their own best interests ought to comply with them.

Every organization ought to have evidence of the effectiveness of the methods and techniques it uses to select and promote managers. But most of them do not. Any survey of prevailing managerial assessment practices will show that they are largely intuitive, prone to wide margins of error, and based largely on the idea that the principal factor to be assessed is past experience.

The reason for this situation is not hard to find. Human assessment is by no means simple. On the contrary, it is so difficult and complex that it is fraught with controversy and is debated heatedly by experts. To assess another person, one must first obtain an accurate description of him in relation to the task for which he is being considered. No sensible person argues with this assertion. But, to describe a person accurately, we must obtain relevant information about him—and this is the sensitive area. Precisely what information is relevant to the role he is asked to play? And, if it is relevant, have we the right to it? Are there not some personal areas that are unavailable for public inspection?

These quite difficult questions are made even more difficult by the unfortunate way they have been raised recently by government agencies. The mishandling of inquiries into the personal background of applicants for positions has been so widespread that it has been necessary to pass laws at all levels restricting the amount and the quality of information that an employer may seek to obtain from a job applicant. And the trend is toward greater restrictions.

Most of these restrictions, however well intentioned, are unfortunate because they serve neither the applicant's nor the employer's best interests. They are designed to prevent abuses, but, as the proponents of the Eighteenth Amendment discovered, it is not possible to eliminate an abuse by forbidding a practice altogether. To the extent, however, that these restrictions stimulate employers to do some hard thinking with respect to their selection programs they will serve a useful purpose.

Assessment Issues

To develop a sound managerial assessment program, we must first consider the traditional assessment model that has been utilized before proceeding to the development of a new model, a model based upon decision making as the heart of the assessment process.

The assessment problem involves many issues: a definition of the term itself, an understanding of its purposes, the way these are best implemented, and a determination of the proper techniques to employ. These issues, either individually or in combination, occupy most of the literature on selection and testing. Some are very technical, but all are very important because the assessment outcome depends upon the way they are handled.

What Is Assessment?

As noted elsewhere,[1] the terms "evaluation" and "assessment" appear to be the most frequently used to describe and place a value on human characteristics. *Evaluation* refers to the determination of the worth of an individual's past performance in reference to a specific performance standard. *Assessment* refers to the prediction of a person's performance in a specific role. Thus "assessment" is the word that is proper to our discussion.

Assessment is a fourfold process:

1. Description. The systematic use of a variety of special techniques to describe the relevant characteristics of a person's intellectual and motivational systems.
2. Evaluation. The comparison of the description with a set of preestablished role standards or requirements.
3. Prediction. The statement of a hypothesis about the probable future behavior of the person assessed in a specific set of circumstances.
4. Decision making. The choice of a person for a particular position.

In essence, therefore, assessment is fundamentally a decision-making process and is subject to all of the observations made in Part One about this process.

This is an important assertion because it not only will affect the strategies employed in assessment but will determine the methods of evaluating the strategies used. It suggests an assessment model that so far has received little

---

[1] Felix M. Lopez, *Evaluating Employee Performance* (Chicago: Public Personnel Association, 1968), p. 38.

attention in the literature, which is mostly caught up in the attempt to explain human behavior in purely mathematical terms.

In the traditional assessment model to be described later, which is representative of most of the selection textbooks, assessment boils down to the verification of measurement instruments in terms of their reliability and validity. Consequently, it is not surprising that this model has been incorporated in the testing guidelines published by both OFCC and EEOC.

Respected theorists [2] have pointed out that this assessment model by no means constitutes the only model and is, in fact, subject to serious limitations. They suggest that, since the purpose of any assessment procedure is to help in making a selection decision, its utility must be evaluated in these terms, taking into account the particular decision to be made, the cost of obtaining the information, and the level of accuracy necessary for the decision.

Decision theory has been applied by operations researchers to the fields of economics and production to aid in making financial, operating, and sales decisions. It can also provide a useful frame of reference for assessment if it is viewed as a complicated game involving a great number of variables requiring many decisions at appropriate points. Some decisions are anticipatory; that is, they are of a "maybe" nature because they lead to further decisions. Others are concluding decisions because they are of the "go, no go" variety that ends the game.

To improve assessment decisions, principles must be elaborated, objectives clearly defined, data collected and analyzed, appropriate tools employed, alternative strategies analyzed, and the consequences of each evaluated. For example, traditional validation studies may indicate that an interview is useless. But a complete decision analysis may show that it reduces the number of applicants who are disqualified medically or rejected for background investigations; that the overall caliber of the group selected, as judged by management, is superior to previous groups that have been selected.

The Method of Successive Hurdles

Another feature of traditional assessment strategies is the successive-hurdle technique. The idea that an applicant should undergo a screening process

[2] L. J. Cronbach and G. C. Gleser, *Psychological Tests and Personnel Decisions,* 2d ed. (Urbana, Ill.: University of Illinois Press, 1965).

to save both him and the employer time and money is accepted unquestion-
ingly. The successive-hurdle technique requires a program by which an applicant passes through successively difficult obstacles in the form of biographi-
cal-information blanks, tests, and interviews on the way to a job. He is
eliminated at any point where he fails to qualify, even though the hurdle
measures only a minor portion of his total job qualifications.

This screening process resembles a funnel. The wide end, where the simplest and the most economical tools are used, permits many applicants to
pass through. But the narrow end, where the number of prospective employees is manageably fewer, is reserved for the complicated and costly tools.
Recent research has shown that this strategy is inadequate because it is
based upon a tradition that has little to do with the purpose of assessment.
The chief culprit is the instrument employed as the first screening device,
because, while it eliminates the unqualified, it also eliminates many of the
qualified. It is not that these instruments are invalid but that they are used
in the wrong way—as knock-out measures rather than as sources of information to form part of the applicant's total assessment.

Job effectiveness is a product that can be achieved by varying mixtures
of personal attributes. One person may succeed in a task because of his intellectual ability, another because of the sheer strength of his drive, and a
third because of his ability to generate friendly relationships.

The only conclusion to be drawn from the weight of the evidence that
has already been accumulated is that managerial assessment programs administered by most organizations have to be restructured to eliminate the
successive-hurdle system. Instead of using a naive empirical strategy by
which the applicant undertakes one test at a time, a global or analytical
strategy must be substituted. This is the procedure that is being followed
in the development of assessment centers in some of the larger corporations
in the country.

Generality vs. Specificity

Then there is the question whether to assess men for particular positions
or for managerial assignments in general. The particular strategy employed
depends upon whether the way the manager behaves in one managerial situation is likely to predict the way he will behave in a different situation.
Early psychological research tended to support the specificity position; but,

more recently, modern statistical techniques have offered support for the generality of managerial behavior.

On the other hand, there is evidence to indicate that the level of managerial behavior requires considerably different characteristics for effective performance. The supervision of subordinates, for example, is not a significant dimension of top-level managerial positions as it is of first-line managerial roles, but planning and exercising broad power are more significant at the upper rather than the lower levels of management.

The argument that there is likely to be a single universal formula for identifying managerial talent is especially applicable to companies where mobility and job rotation are practical and where there is not a great technological overlay. But, in large, highly compartmentalized organizations that have little opportunity for cross-pollination, it is less applicable.

Statistical vs. Clinical Prediction

Still another assessment issue concerns the question whether prediction is more accurate when made globally by a skilled clinician or on the basis of a statistical formula by a computer or a clerk. In the statistical or actuarial method, a clerk can figure the odds of success for any given assessee on the basis of an empirically derived equation. This procedure is said to be objective and is highly favored by many textbook psychologists. In the clinical procedure, on the other hand, the experience, special insights, and knowledge of the assessor have an important influence on the final prediction. This procedure is said to be subjective and is viewed more skeptically by the behavioral science establishment.

The issue is rather critical, but the odds would seem to favor the clinical approach simply because managerial jobs are so unique and therefore so underpopulated that statistical analysis is almost ruled out. While a few companies, referred to in Chapter 6, have been able to make extensive use of the statistical technique, most organizations use consulting firms, university professors, or in-company psychologists to make clinical assessments. The question is, how do the two techniques compare in predicting managerial success? Most of the comparative studies favor the actuarial over the clinical method, but there is some doubt that the clinical approach has been adequately represented, because many of the studies relied upon the measurement model of selection.

The Measurement Model of Assessment

The discussion of assessment issues can become quite technical and can quickly reach a level beyond the comprehension of most lay managers. Therefore, it is desirable here to examine the fundamental principles of the measurement model of assessment.

Elementary Measurement Concepts

First of all, to appreciate the assessment process, certain elementary measurement concepts must be understood. While assessment encompasses more than measurement, it is apparent that the process consists generally of the assignment of a class of numbers to a class of objects or characteristics. If we stick with such adjectives as "intelligent," "aggressive," or "sincere," we become involved immediately in problems of clarification and of interpretation. But, when we reduce these adjectives to numbers, we can achieve a clearer and more universal understanding of the ideas we are trying to convey. For example, to describe a person's weight I may use the term "heavy" or "light." But I can be more precise, and therefore better understood, if I state that a person weighs 170 pounds.

Measures can also be misleading, however, and are often prone to error. The temperature on a particular day in a particular city, for example, will vary according to the location, the time of the day, and the thermometer used. The faith that one can place in a measurement is determined by *reliability* and *validity*. To appreciate assessment issues and to evaluate assessment instruments and procedures, it is essential that we understand these terms.

Reliability

A measurement will always contain a degree of error, no matter how infinitesimal, as in measuring the distance between two continents. Two sets of measures of the same features of the same person will never duplicate each other exactly, but repeated measures of the same person under the same circumstances will ordinarily show some consistency. This tendency toward consistency is referred to technically as *reliability*. If a person achieves a test score of 50 on one day and a score of 100 on the next day, the test results will be inconsistent and, therefore, unreliable. Putting it another way, we can say that reliability is the extent to which a measurement is free of error.

Reliability is a primary characteristic of a measure. If the measure is unreliable, it has little merit because it is undependable and prone to error. An unreliable watch is useless, worse than no watch at all. The first quality of an assessment tool, therefore, is its reliability; that is, its consistency from one situation to another and from one day to another.

VALIDITY

When a tool such as a ruler, a micrometer, or an aptitude test measures what it is intended to measure, it is *valid*. But validity implies more than this. It depends on the answers to three legitimate questions that can be asked of any assessment measure:

1. Does it really measure the personal trait it purports to measure?
2. Is the trait it measures possessed by effective job performers?
3. Does the trait it measures predict future performance?

An affirmative answer to the first question is called *construct validity,* which indicates the extent to which the measurement factor defines the performance in question. An affirmative answer to the second question is referred to as *concurrent validity,* which indicates the extent to which the measurement factor represents effective *present* job performance. An affirmative answer to the third question is called *predictive validity,* which indicates the extent to which the measurement factor predicts *future* job performance.

For example, suppose a company is offered a test by a publisher who asserts that it is a measure of salesmanship and will help select and promote effective salesmen. Before purchasing and using this test, the company must determine whether it is reliable and valid. Ideally, the test must meet four distinct criteria.

Step 1. The publisher must prove that the test consistently yields the same results with the same people. This he does by showing that each applicant obtains the same score each time he takes it and that the test score is independent of the person administering or scoring it. There are many ways of demonstrating test reliability, and these are usually provided in the test manual that the author puts together in the process of constructing and standardizing it. A prospective test user should study this manual carefully before adopting any test.

Step 2. The next step is to determine the *construct validity* of the test by finding out whether it really measures salesmanship rather than intelligence or social skill or verbal fluency. The author must define what he means by salesmanship in terms of human behavior and human characteristics. In other words, he must present a theory of selling on which he bases his instrument. Then he must show that people who have the trait of salesmanship score higher on his test than people who lack it.

If the author gets this far with his instrument he is definitely in business because his test is now useful for descriptive purposes at least. Many competent authorities would say that his job is done, because all a test constructor must do is establish construct validity.

Determining construct validity is very difficult, however, because of the problem of defining a trait clearly and of identifying people who possess it and people who do not. (Remember, for example, two of the traits that we have already considered: intelligence and leadership.) That is why other competent authorities say that a test author can skip construct validity as long as his test is concurrently and predictively valid. Knowing what it measures is of little consequence, they declare.

Step 3. The next step is to determine *concurrent validity* by administering the test to a group—in this case, of salesmen, some of whom have been evaluated as excellent and some as average or below average. If the excellent salesmen obtain high scores on the test and the below-average salesmen obtain low scores, the test is concurrently valid. We now know that the test discriminates not only between salesmen and nonsalesmen but between good and poor salesmen, and we can properly conclude that the test is useful as an evaluative instrument.

Step 4. The final step in the measurement model is to determine the *predictive validity* of the test. The test must be administered to a number of applicants for sales positions who are hired without regard to their test scores. After a suitable period of time has elapsed, the salesmen's performance is compared to their test scores. If the successful salesmen turn out to be high scorers and the ineffective salesmen low scorers, the test can be said to be predictively valid.

Although in practice it is much more complicated, the procedure we have just described constitutes the essence of the measurement model of assessment. In other words, any user of an assessment instrument must address himself to the four questions we have enunciated; he must prove the test's reliability and validity for a specific role in his own organizational milieu. For, unlike the thermometer or the micrometer, a psychological measure depends on the environment and the circumstances in which it is used. While we know that a thermometer measures nothing more or less than the degree of heat in an object, we are never really sure what a psychological instrument is measuring, because its constructors rely on concurrent and predictive validity to demonstrate its usefulness.

Consequently, an instrument that is valid in one company may not be valid in another. This gives rise to the measurement problems that plague those who approach the assessment process with a blueprint based solely on the measurement model.

Measurement Problems

Despite its almost universal acceptance as the norm for the evaluation of the effectiveness of assessment tools, there are many difficulties with the measurement model of assessment. We shall mention six, some of which we have already alluded to in previous pages.

Numbers. Proper statistical validation requires a rather large number of subjects, particularly if the method of cross-validation is to be used. Cross-validation refers to the projection of a previously validated test on a completely different group of subjects in the same job. This is not easy in small companies, and even in larger ones it becomes impractical in the less populated positions that occur at the higher levels. Therefore, it is quite difficult, and sometimes impossible, to meet one of the major requirements of the measurement model.

The criterion problem. We have already discussed certain aspects of the criterion problem, which can be summed up as follows: Criteria of managerial effectiveness usually lack clear specifications; and, even when they are clear, their traditional indicator—supervisory judgment—reflects them inadequately. So-called objective measures, when examined closely, can be demonstrated to be neither objective nor relevant. A frequently used criterion, salary, can easily be demonstrated to be no more than a function of time, prejudice, or some other subjective assessment that renders it at least nonobjective. And subjective measures, when examined closely, are often shown to be biased or unreliable.[3]

The definition of managerial effectiveness is more bothersome than any other aspect of managerial assessment. Numerous criteria of managerial success have been used or proposed, ranging all the way from the completely

[3] See Felix M. Lopez, op. cit., Chs. 9, 10.

objective (salary data, number of promotions, pretax earnings, sales volume, production data) to the completely subjective (supervisors' appraisals, rankings) and from global, overall ratings of effectiveness to very specific measures such as the number of subordinates promoted. Each criterion has its strengths and its weaknesses, and it may not be possible to utilize very many of them in an organization without interfering with the accomplishment of goals.

Situational effects. Another reason why assessment instruments may be poor predictors—and, in fact, one of the underlying theses of this book—is simply that they do not measure those personality dimensions that are significant for performance in a specific job and environment. People exhibit different traits in different situations; the same person may be aggressive in one situation and quite reserved in another. The very characteristics that make the manager successful in a sales-oriented organization may be fatal in a research laboratory.

An individual's performance is affected by the task and the climate. Most validation studies based on the measurement model do not account for the interaction of task and climate on personality variables.

Moderator variables. Certain assessment instruments differentiate more accurately among those persons who are preselected by means of some other measuring instrument. The trait measured by the latter test is referred to as a "moderator" variable because it determines how well the first test will predict.

For example, a number of men were given a mental ability test to determine their potential for a particular job. The correlation of the test scores with the success criterion turned out to be rather low. The investigator felt that the job might have been too simple for a number of the applicants; so he gave all of them a questionnaire to complete which indicated how appropriate the level of the job was for them. With the results of the second instrument, the applicants were divided into two groups: those for whom the job seemed to be appropriate and those for whom it was deemed inappropriate. It was found that the predictive validity of the mental ability test was greatly increased when it was used only with those men for whom the job level was appropriate. The predictive efficiency of the mental ability test was negligible for those for whom the occupational level was too low, but the latter were unlikely to be successful on the job anyway because they really had no interest in it. Level of interest in the job, therefore, constituted a moderator variable that affected the predictive efficiency of the first test. A more effective assessment procedure was established by which those who were poor prospects because of lack of interest or suitability for the job were screened out and the rest were given the mental ability test.

Often the predictive efficiency of a test is either enhanced or attenuated by moderator variables that are not readily apparent.

Contamination. Contamination is a practical, not a theoretical problem that besets some of the most well-publicized research studies. Frequently the results of an assessment become a matter of general knowledge to those who are involved in making promotion and salary decisions and even performance evaluations. A young manager, because of a favorable assessment rating, becomes identified throughout the organization as having high potential. He is then given more favorable opportunities to distinguish himself than others who have been rated as having less potential. The "anointed" manager then tends to get promoted more often and to receive greater salary increases.

In some companies, for example, a person's score on a mental-ability test is considered when promotion decisions are made. Later, predictive-validity studies will show a very positive relationship between the assessment result and the criterion of number of promotions. In reality, the high correlation is spurious, representing a confirmation of the self-fulfilling prophecy.

Assessment results, therefore, must be maintained in the strictest confidence and made available only to top-level managers. Even here, contamination can creep in and render any subsequent validity study suspect. On the other hand, it is impractical and fruitless to put assessment results in a vault to be opened 20 years later. Times will change and make the obtained results valueless. Assessment results have to be used in making personnel decisions to justify their costs. In fact, the contamination problem can never really be resolved and the measurement model never actually implemented.

Prediction. The most serious difficulty with the measurement model of assessment lies in the fact that while its purpose is oriented toward the future, its procedures are oriented toward the past. It is like rowing a boat; as soon as you look to see where you are going, you have to stop rowing. The idea of predictive validity is an impossibility, a logical contradiction in terms.

When any instrument is administered to a person, we can never know for sure that it will predict success for him. All we can know is that in the past, for people like him, it did predict successfully. There is always a degree of uncertainty in assessment that the measurement model can only reduce, not eliminate. Those respected but tough-minded psychologists who would ban the use of all assessment instruments until their predictive validities are fully established are completely wrong.

The practical aspects of this assertion are far-reaching. As we have stressed throughout these pages, change is the only certainty in organizational life. People change, jobs change, organizations change, and society changes. What was valid in the past may be seriously invalid now. For example, one study of managerial success isolated self-reliance, manifested by behavior in late adolescence, as a valid predictor of managerial effectiveness. Self-reliance was measured by such life-history items as the age at which the young man made his first long-distance telephone call, drove a car, or went on a trip of over 100 miles. But these were indications of youthful self-reliance only at a specific period of time in the late 1930s; they no longer were indications of this trait in the late 1960s when the measurement instrument was validated.

This is not to say that validation studies are a complete waste of time. It says only that, no matter how valid an instrument may be, it must be updated continuously and that no one can tell for sure whether the judgments made by means of it today will be predictively valid for the future.

What may we conclude from our discussion of these six problems? One certain conclusion is that a company must be careful in its choice of instruments to use in its assessment process. A second is that the techniques and the logic that are so effective in the physical sciences and are based on a mathematical-mechanical concept of reality are simply not transferable to the social sciences.

We must look for other approaches. Even if the measurement model were applicable, it would not always be possible to conduct the rigorous research required before an assessment procedure is put into operation for real-life decision making. Some psychologists have suggested "synthetic" or "borrowed" validity in lieu of strict adherence to a predictive-validity design. But even the notion of synthetic validity is cumbersome, requiring almost as much time as the predictive-validity design and offering results that are no better. The answer seems to lie in the development of a broader concept of the evaluation of assessment instruments.

We prefer the concept provided by decision theory. By adopting a decision-making approach, the pitfall of trying to reduce assessment procedures to a series of equations, usually based on a host of very tentative assumptions, is avoided. Not the least of the assumptions—and the one that represents the greatest stumbling block to the solution of the problem—is the assumption that the future is best predicted by what has determined the past.

In a dynamic society, with the applicant population changing constantly, an employer simply cannot afford to take for granted that his validated instruments will hold up indefinitely. He must realize that there are many ways in which job success can be achieved and that there are many combinations of human traits to predict it. Instruments that worked well for one group at one point in time can be utterly useless for another group at another time.

These are such far-reaching conclusions that we must not accept them at face value. We must confirm them by investigations involving various groups and various assessment instruments. These studies must stress the broader construct of relevancy which includes many variables important to the quality and the effectiveness of the overall decision—administrative feasibility, cost, recruitment attractiveness, community and employee relations, *and* statistical validity.

The results of this approach will lead to a rather different concept of assessment than has appeared so far in the literature. The new emphasis will be upon construct validation in which job performance is viewed as an evolving process, a function of the interaction of the person not only with his superiors but with the situation and the passage of time.

The Decision-Making Model of Assessment

The concepts just outlined underlie the decision-making model of assessment. Every business firm, government agency, university, public school system, or religious congregation maintains some kind of assessment model consisting of the policies, programs and practices that determine how its members are recruited, selected, and promoted. Most models are quite informal, inherently contradictory, and basically dysfunctional because they are based upon intuition, personal judgment, incomplete and inaccurate information, and dubious traditions.

The solution to the problem does not lie in an attempt to lay down a rigorous statistical procedure based on the notion of predictive validity, nor does it lie in the direction of the random choice implied in the political and career personnel systems. Selection and assessment must be considered as representing important managerial responsibilities; they are, after all, particular applications of the manager's basic function of making decisions.

A decision-making model of assessment has the advantage not only of being logical and sensible but of offering a way out of the complexity that surrounds the process. An important asset of this approach is that it can be utilized in small as well as in large organizations. The only difference will be in the nature of the information-gathering, storage, and retrieval processes, which, for the larger companies, will require more formal communication techniques and more elaborate computer hardware. The characteristics of the model are the same for all organizations of human beings.

In subsequent chapters, we shall unfold the main features of this model as it applies, in particular, to the assessment of managers, but a roughly similar program can be adapted to other occupational classes.

Assessment-Decision Making

Since selection involves a decision, it necessarily implies a commitment to action made in the face of complexity and uncertainty. Since it is basically an organization decision, it must contribute to the fulfillment of the organization's purpose, the dimensions of which are illustrated by Exhibit 3.

EXHIBIT 3
The Dimensions of the Decision-making Assessment Model

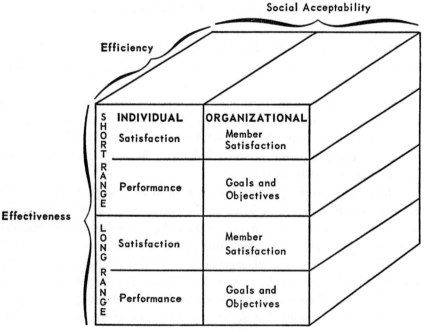

As in any management program, an assessment strategy must meet three broad standards: effectiveness, efficiency, and social acceptability. *Effectiveness* refers to how much it contributes to the achievement of individual and organizational goals, *efficiency* to the ratio between input and output, and *social acceptability* to the degree to which it meets the values and the needs of the society and the community in which it operates.

Effectiveness. Effectiveness, as shown in Exhibit 3, can be viewed as an eight-celled matrix formed by the dimensions of individual and organizational needs and time. The first objective of assessment is to select individuals who can contribute to organization performance and satisfy their own needs. We looked at this model in Exhibit 2 in Chapter 3. The second objective of assessment is to contribute to organization performance and to satisfy the needs of its three member groups: investors, employees, and customers. And, finally, these four subgoals have short-range and long-range implications.

It becomes obvious that no assessment program can meet all of these eight criteria of effectiveness simultaneously. Once again, we confront the problem of suboptimization, which automatically rules out the possibility that assessment can be treated purely actuarially; that is, computerized and handed over to clerks with a table of expectancies. Final selection decisions can be made only by managers, who must choose at any one time those effectiveness criteria they are interested in at this particular point: individual or organizational, short-range or long-range.

Efficiency. Assessment must be efficient; that is, the gains achieved must be greater than the resources and the effort put into it. Theoretically, it is possible to develop a perfect predictor of job success, but the cost of such an instrument might be twice that of another instrument that was wrong 30 percent of the time. To determine whether the perfect instrument should be used, a manager would have to weigh its cost against the cost of a 30 percent error. This is difficult, because determining the cost of inefficient selection is hampered by the inadequacies of the accounting system.

The development of a manpower-information system is basic to the decision-making assessment model. What such a system would probably show, however, is the startlingly high costs, financial and human, of present informal assessment techniques.

Social acceptability. Assessment decisions are viewed today as more than a private contract between an employer and an employee or a prospective employee. The public has a definite interest in the assessment programs of its institutions. It is therefore insufficient for an employer to point to the predictive validity of an instrument and shrug his shoulders about the fact that it excludes certain groups from being considered seriously for employment. The issues of invasion of privacy, equal employment opportunity, and employee confidence are as vital a part of an assessment program as its costs and its effectiveness.

There is a practical aspect to this consideration. Often a selection instrument that seemingly bears no relationship to the prediction of job success can be so very impressive to applicants that it plays an important role in the attraction of high-caliber applicants. To this extent, then, its acceptability makes an important contribution to the success of the assessment program even though, statistically speaking, it is useless.

Assessment Strategy

These three considerations present the decision maker with a three-dimensional matrix of choices from which he must select the right combination to insure the success of the organization. It is a decision situation with magnitudes and complexities that can tax the resources and the wisdom of even the best-run organizations. The task is to reduce the magnitude and to make the complexity manageable by developing a suitable assessment strategy.

A proper assessment strategy can be developed and followed only within the framework of what we have described as the human-resources personnel system. This strategy has to be based on a sound manpower-information system, as described earlier, and a program of sequential decision making.

The manpower-information system. The basic difficulty with most assessment programs is that they operate on a starvation diet of information within inadequate time frames. They then lead to faulty decisions which create more problems and to a cycle of assessment crises that is hard to break. The antidote to this situation is information of the type generated by a well-run manpower-information system. The information gathered will consist of rates and trends plus data on costs, profits, productivity, employee morale, and personnel stability. The idea is to determine whether the organization is growing. If it *is* growing, if its employee members possess a high degree of morale, if it is living up to its community and social obligations within the limits of its resources, then its assessment program can be considered highly effective, even though it is impossible to produce one statistically significant validity coefficient.

A key to the determination of these criteria is the establishment of a managerial accountability for personnel resources similar to the accountability for operating results. The head of each unit—department, division, or major corporate affiliate—should be asked to review annually, with higher management levels, the quality of the members of his unit. This accountability will generate a great deal of management interest in the whole assessment strategy.

Sequential decision making. The manpower-information system, however, is designed to furnish data about how well the assessment program is operating. What is needed is a way of handling the very complexity and the magnitude of the decision situations imposed on management.

Complexity and magnitude are reduced by a process of sequential decision making in which considerable relevant information is accumulated about each assessee in sufficient time to make a sound decision. This is not another method of successive hurdles but, rather, the development of specific time-oriented alternatives for the decision process. The sequence is based on three selection principles, requires four instruments to obtain the information, and involves five stages.

The first principle, that of the selection ratio, holds that—all other conditions being equal—the larger the number of applicants from which to select, the better the chances of making a sound selection decision. Thus an assessment strategy always seeks somehow to broaden the field of candidates. This principle rules out the notion of crown princes and backup men inherent in some managerial manpower plans.

The second principle, that of individual differences, simply states that to maximize selection decisions one has to take into account all the ways in which people differ—in particular, those differences that refer to intellectual and motivational characteristics. This principle implies, therefore, that effective selection requires the assessment of the whole man in relation to the total job situation.

The third principle, that of prediction, states that the purpose of assessment is to predict how a person will behave in a specific role and organizational milieu. Whatever contributes either directly or indirectly to this prediction is relevant; what does not is irrelevant or erroneous.

There are four instruments that are available to obtain information about a candidate: biographical questionnaires, interviews, tests, and verification procedures. Each of these, like any tool, has its uses and its limitations. In any assessment program *all* are needed because each, in its own way, elicits unique information essential to the prediction of job success.

There is a sequence to assessment that provides for an orderly approach to decision making in sufficient time. The first phase is recruitment, which is designed to insure a satisfactory supply of quality candidates. The other phases deal with the tasks of screening and sifting the information in a logical sequence leading to a final decision. This sequence is of two types, short- and long-range. The short run concerns the selection of a person for an immediate opening, and this is largely the problem of procurement. The long run concerns the selection of a person for a career, and this is the problem of progression.

In the remaining chapters, we shall develop a decision-making model of assessment by considering the uses and limitations of assessment instruments and the mechanics of a managerial procurement and progression program.

9

Interviewing Managers

GETTING adequate and relevant information about an applicant is the heart of the assessment process. Two recent but quite unrelated incidents illustrate how ineffective or incomplete information can cause serious problems.

A woman entered a Los Angeles bank one morning. Suddenly she screamed and pointed an accusing finger at one of the bank's assistant managers. "That man is a crook!" she cried. The astounded bank officials, who had hired the manager after what they assumed was a thorough check, decided to investigate further. They called in a former FBI agent, who made inquiries across the nation. Within 24 hours, he had the answer. In a midwest city where the woman had known him, the bank's assistant manager had headed up an investment firm that had closed amid threats to prosecute him. The casual verification by the bank had shown that the man had no criminal record, but that was because he had paid the $10,000 he was accused of misappropriating. It took many months for the bank to live down the embarrassment. What it cost in dollars and cents is incalculable.

The other incident has to do with job requirements. An executive search firm was given the assignment to find a new president for a division of a very large company. Several other executive search firms, which had been engaged previously by this company, had been trying to fill the position for over a year without success. The salary bracket the company put on this opening was in the $60,000-to-$70,000 range. The new recruiting firm decided to disregard the salary tag and look for a man who could meet the company's requirements, a man with a proven record of accomplishment in this particular field. It found such a man with a price tag of $125,000. The client bought him without hesitation, but the company had wasted a year and a half and untold sums of money in lost production by looking for the wrong man at the wrong salary level.

Incomplete and inadequate information plagues assessment efforts, and yet the tools are there if the assessors know how to use them. To understand the nature of these tools, it is useful to digress momentarily to examine the functions of a physician with respect to his patient.

When a patient visits a physician to ascertain the current status of his health, he naturally expects to furnish the physician with sufficient information for an accurate diagnosis. The more certain he wishes his physician to be, the more information he is prepared to give him by completing a medical-history questionnaire, by conversing with the doctor, and by submitting to a series of tests. To make his diagnosis, the physician uses two sources of information: the patient's *life history* with respect to the number and extent of childhood diseases, the quality of parental and sibling health, and the patient's present life style and dietary practices; and, second, *samples* of the patient's physical condition and bodily functioning obtained through a series of X rays and laboratory tests ranging from simple measures of height and weight to elaborate analyses of the blood and tissue. The physician synthesizes the life-history facts with test results to arrive at an evaluation of the patient's health. He compares the results with standards established for people of similar age and sex and then advises the patient as to the best course to follow in order to maintain his health, if he is healthy, or to remedy his condition if he is ill.

When conducted properly, the assessment process follows the same pattern. The information needed to assess properly comes from two sources: the life history of the applicant and behavioral samples obtained through tests. Life-history information is obtained primarily through the interview augmented by a well-designed biographical questionnaire and a careful verification process. Behavioral samples of an applicant's psychological characteristics are obtained through intellectual and motivational tests.

In this chapter, we shall consider the life history and, in the following chapter, tests.

The Assessment-Information Process

Before reviewing either source of information, it is appropriate to review the assessment-information process itself. For, to use information accurately in making assessment decisions, three problems must be dealt with. First, one has to know what information is relevant to effective job performance. Second, one must have adequate man specifications. Third, one has to obtain accurate and complete information from the candidate and be able to interpret that information properly.

Most of the failures in the assessment process can be traced to the inability to solve one or all of these problems. For example, there are interviewers who place a lot of importance on a quality, observed in an interview, which is referred to as "eye contact"; that is, the extent to which an interviewee looks directly into the interviewer's eyes as he speaks to him. Lack of eye contact has been interpreted as an indication of anxiety, lack of self-confidence, or even evasiveness, all three of which would appear to be serious handicaps to effective managerial performance.

However, to accept the conclusion that an applicant who fails to maintain eye contact with the interviewer lacks managerial ability, we would have to answer three questions:

1. What evidence have we that anxiety, shyness, or evasiveness predicts failure in a managerial position?
2. What evidence have we that lack of eye contact in an interview indicates anxiety, shyness, or evasiveness?
3. What other conditions, such as a strong light behind the interviewer, can cause lack of eye contact during an interview?

Obviously, there is little specific information to answer any of these questions. Consequently, the quality of eye contact in an interview gives the interviewer little solid information on which to make an assessment.

The Nature of Information

The best way to process information obtained in an assessment procedure is to understand clearly what information really is and how it may legitimately be interpreted. We have defined information as the reduction of uncertainty. The more we have of it, the greater the possibility of making an accurate assessment if it is relevant.

Relevancy. In a factory assembler's position, for example, the information required to predict success is relatively simple, although not nearly as simple as is usually imagined. Most employers concentrate on the applicant's ability to do the relatively simple tasks required. They ignore a more significant bit of information: whether the applicant is willing to do this task day after day for a number of years. The first bit of information predicts whether he *can* do it; the second, whether he *will* do it long enough to make his employment and training pay off.

Take another example, that of a bus driver. Most bus companies concentrate on an applicant's driving skill and his ability to do simple arithmetic sums. But a bus driver's success really lies in his ability to tolerate the frustrations of manipulating an unwieldy vehicle in congested traffic while coping with querulous, demanding passengers.

The information obtained has to be relevant to the position under consideration. Facts about a person that do not affect job performance constitute no information at all because they do not reduce the uncertainty surrounding his ability to do the job. Knowing that an applicant's father is a member of a social club, for example, is of no information because it is unrelated to the applicant's employability.

Usability. Relevancy is only part of the information problem; it is necessary to get usable information. Getting a piece of information leads only to error unless we appreciate clearly what we are getting.

Suppose that belief in a product is a clear index of sales success. In assessing a sales applicant, then, we try to find out whether he believes in the product he is being asked to sell. We ask him how he feels about it. If he answers that he believes it is an important and vital product that belongs in every home, he has told us nothing except that he knows what answer we expect. At best, he has given us an opinion in a highly prejudiced situation.

A better question would have been to ask the prospective salesman whether he owns or uses the product. Since ownership or use of a product is a verifiable fact reflecting a positive attitude toward it, an affirmative answer would be a strong indication of his feeling.

Types of Information

The ability to discriminate among types of information is essential in assessment. Information ranges from objective and reliable to subjective and unreliable. There are *factual* data on the objective, reliable side, *psychological* data on the subjective, less reliable side, and *logical* data in between. There is no clear-cut dividing line separating one type of data from the others; each blends into the rest like the colors of a spectrum.

It is the responsibility of the assessor to recognize the differences in the type of data he collects. Factual data such as a person's height, weight, and birth date represent sensible events that are verifiable through other sources of information. Logical data consisting of ideas, conclusions, feelings, opinions, and beliefs lie within the observer and are not susceptible to direct verification by other persons. (If a person says he has a headache, you have to take his word for it.) Logical information may approximate factual data—as when two facts, height and weight, are joined to form a conclusion that a given person is under- or overweight. The conclusion, while based on facts, is not a fact in itself.

Psychological data are even more subjective, simply because they are not accessible even to the person who possesses them.

The assessor who seeks information of an applicant must be able to discriminate carefully among the three types of data. He must recognize when he is collecting facts, when he is noting feelings, opinions, or beliefs, and when he is attributing values or attitudes to an applicant. Statements about another's attitudes must be treated with particular caution. The first rule in assessing a person for a position is to base your judgment on facts wherever possible and to use opinions, beliefs, values, and attitudes as tentatively as you can.

Getting relevant and useful information is important, but it is also necessary to get *all* the information required. Even a young adult who is 21 years of age has accumulated close to 200,000 hours of living experience. By age 21 he is already a complex person with a rich and varied history. For most occupations and certainly for managerial positions, it is necessary to sample that rich background adequately to make accurate predictions about the applicant's future behavior. This requires more than a 20-minute meeting with him, but what the assessor often does is to use the few gleanings of information he obtains to sketch a flimsy outline of the person which he then fills in from the memory core of stereotypes and caricatures formed by his own attitudes and experiences. In the process he completes a grossly erroneous description of the applicant that provides no basis at all for comparing it to the requirements of the job. And, to know what information about a person is relevant, usable, and adequate, we must know what the job requires.

Man Specifications

It is quite logical to expect that before we can find someone we must know whom we are looking for. Yet top-flight recruiters and executive search firms report that one of the principal reasons for their failure is the fact that managers who engage their services and pay them handsomely do not know what sort of person they want.

The first task, then, that must be undertaken in managerial assessment is to establish a set of man specifications. These specifications (which differ greatly from position specifications) call for a description of the personal characteristics of a successful incumbent. They specify, not what he has to do, but rather what he has to have to do it. Managerial-manpower specifications contain two types of requirements, general and specific. General requirements refer to those qualifications that all managers share; specific requirements, to those that are necessary for a particular function, organization, or industry.

There are a number of ways of presenting man specifications. One way is to follow the outline presented in Chapter 2 and list the intellectual requirements, the attitudes, the drives, and the expressive trends of the motivational system that define the high points of the profile specified by Holland's typology. This may, however, be a difficult task unless it is performed by a competent psychologist. Another way that is equally helpful is to list the *general requirements* in a series of statements in the following areas: [1]

1. Initiative. This category describes the degree of originality, inventiveness, imagination, resourcefulness, energy, and willingness to accept responsibility required of the incumbent.
2. Intellectual competence. This category describes the incumbent's intellectual, analytical, and problem-solving abilities and his skill in speaking and writing.
3. Interpersonal competence. This category describes the incumbent's ability to establish effective relationships with superior, peers, subordinates, and customers.
4. Dependability and stability. This category describes the qualities of dependability, responsibility, emotional stability, and perseverance required of the incumbent.

[1] For a model man specification constructed along these lines see Felix M. Lopez, *Personnel Interviewing* (New York: McGraw-Hill, 1965), pp. 249–250.

5. Work habits. This category describes the loyalty, the self-discipline, and the adherence to established order required of the incumbent.

The *specific requirements* will refer to the incumbent's personal qualifications—desirable age range, marital status, physical ability, and personal appearance. They will also include the educational qualifications necessary—college degrees, professional licenses, and affiliations. And, finally, the specific requirements will describe the quality, level, and duration of the work experience necessary to perform the job effectively.

Last of all, a statement in the man specifications might describe the potential for growth desired of the incumbent.

Naturally, all of this information must be based upon verifiable facts, on evidence accumulated from an analysis of successful managers in the organization and not on someone's hopes or prejudices. The position description studies listed in Chapter 6 and the occupational dictionary described in Chapter 7 could well be used as tools to build the available data into the required specifications. In preparing them, several points must be kept in mind:

1. Overqualification is as undesirable as underqualification. Sometimes an excess of virtue is a vice. The ideal manager often falls in the middle with respect to such qualifications as aggressiveness, perseverance, and initiative. And for some organizations there can be such a thing as too much intelligence, energy, or drive.
2. In managerial positions, technical qualifications can easily be over-evaluated. When companies make technical qualifications their major requirement, they can fall into a serious trap and wind up with a group of technicians and no managers.
3. Man specifications should be present- and future-oriented. They should be oriented, first, to the situation now existing in the company and in the outside managerial market. They should also be oriented toward the future, toward the corporation's long-range goals, toward the likelihood of change in managerial needs and attitudes. By all means they should ignore the past—and failure to do so is a fault that most companies are addicted to. The fact that the company president was born in a log cabin is no justification for requiring all future presidents to be born in log cabins. We are exaggerating, of course, to emphasize the futility of hiring what has been successful in the past. Data from research should be evaluated only in terms of what they portend for the future.

Obtaining and Interpreting Life-History Information

Overall, there should be a clear delineation of what the organization requires with respect to its present and future managerial needs. Starting an assessment program without a clear idea of these requirements is like starting on a long journey with no idea of where you want to go. With this information strongly rooted in clear, unassailable facts, it is fruitful to get on with the task of obtaining information about the people who present themselves as candidates. But, even after we have accumulated this information, it has to be assembled in a coherent, logical, and meaningful pattern that describes the person accurately when compared to the man specifications and predicts his future behavior. This is the most difficult task of all, because people's life patterns are not so obviously logical and coherent or amenable to interpretation.

The tools we use in the assessment process are designed merely to generate information. In and of itself, information is sterile. What is done with the information is the heart of the matter.

Most managers have difficulty in interpreting information because they make two common mistakes: (1) They draw invalid conclusions from the facts; and (2) they fail to recognize that there are several equally plausible explanations of the same fact. Or, to put it in another way, managers tend to draw conclusions from bits of information, then accept them as being valid rather than treating them merely as hypotheses that must be tested against other evidence. The art of interpretation consists of the ability to resist leaping to erroneous conclusions.

Interpretation is essentially a logical process. The assessor must elicit information about a person, put it together to posit a hypothesis that explains the information, seek confirmation in other information about the person, and apply the whole to determining the probability of success in performing the job. Basically, interpretation is a process of continuous generation of hypotheses from the applicant's life history, his self-reports, and his test scores and their confirmation or rejection on the basis of other evidence.

This approach is either reinforced or deterred by the attitudes of the assessor. Most assessors follow the traditionally cautious course of seeking the applicant's weaknesses; they wish to avoid at all costs what we call the Type 1 assessment error. For there are two types of error an assessor can make: Type 1 involves recommending an unqualified applicant for employment, whereas Type 2 involves the rejection of a qualified applicant. Type 2 errors are encouraged by the fact that, when an assessor makes an accurate prediction about an applicant, he rarely is commended by his clients; but, if he recommends an unqualified candidate (as even the best assessors must occasionally do), he will have it brought to his attention in one unpleasant way or another.

Each person has his strengths and his limitations. The most satisfactory assessment approach is to concentrate on an applicant's strengths and then compare them with his limitations to determine which strengths compensate for them. This is the applicant-centered approach that is a basic feature of the human-resources personnel system. We shall return to it later. Now we must look at the tools of assessment that help to obtain adequate, relevant, and useful life-history information.

Biographical Questionnaires

Completion of a biographical questionnaire is usually the first step in the assessment process. There are two purposes to a biographical questionnaire (or application blank, as it is popularly called): to enable the candidate to record the relevant facts about his life history in a systematic manner and to give him an impression of the efficiency, objectivity, and courtesy of the prospective employer.

There is an art to designing a useful application blank, an art that is usually beyond the competence of systems analysts and forms designers. An application blank should be designed solely with the assessment process and its purposes in mind. Attempts to make it double as a future personnel record or as an input to the data bank or to the payroll record are misguided. An application blank is just what its name implies—a selection tool that is usually completed by 10 to 50 times more people than are employed. It must be designed from the viewpoint of the applicant who will never become a company employee, keeping in mind the significance of factual information, the requirements of the law, and the purposes of the assessment process.

The application blank is absolutely essential to the assessment process. Résumés and *curricula vitae* furnished by applicants are interesting but generally biased statements that an employer should note and ignore. Their weaknesses have been amply documented in the literature.

Properly used, the application blank or biographical questionnaire is a powerful tool with a significance that extends beyond its appearance as a personnel record. Predictions of job success can be computed from it as accurately as from test data and just as objectively. It may take either of two forms: the weighted application form or the biographical information blank.

The *weighted application form* generally appears as a fairly conventional application blank which contains items that can be scored to arrive at a numerical index of success in a given occupation. These blanks have been used for positions such as sales clerks, air crews, seasonal workers, toll collectors, police officers, and management personnel. Usually, they are developed by relating information on the form to various criteria of performance.

The *biographical information blank,* in contrast, consists of a number of multiple-choice items that permit the applicant to describe his background and early life history.

Typical BIB items. Here are two examples of typical items on such a biographical information blank:

1. How old were you when you were (first) married?
   a. Less than 20 years old.
   b. 20 to 23 years old.
   c. 24 to 25 years old.
   d. 26 to 30 years old.
   e. Over 30 years old.
   f. Have not been married.
2. During your grammar and/or high school days, in which type of activity did you participate the most? (*Check one.*)
   a. Sandlot games.
   b. Boy Scouts, 4-H clubs, FFA, YMCA.
   c. Student government, school politics.
   d. Student paper, science clubs.
   e. I worked or studied most of the time and did not participate.
   f. None of the above apply to me.

Many so-called biographical instruments are heavily loaded with items usually found in personality, temperament, or interest inventories. For example, this is a typical item:

1. Which of the following best describes you?
   a. Socially introverted, not a joiner.
   b. A dreamer; would rather speculate than plunge into action.
   c. Unconventional, not much influenced by precedence.

d. Physically lazy, intrigued with all labor-saving devices and techniques.

e. Dislike routine or detailed work.

Labeling these items as "biographical data" improves their acceptability but removes them from the category of genuine biographical questionnaire items, which should concentrate on such life facts as number of brothers and sisters, class standing, and parents' occupation.

Effectiveness of the BIB. Biographical data lend themselves to conventional psychometrical measurements, evaluation, and interpretation. A biographical information blank has several advantages:

1. Being essentially an extension of an ordinary employment application blank, it is accepted readily by applicants.
2. Since it is really a pencil-and-paper interview, it augments the effectiveness of the regular interview that usually accompanies it.
3. The information furnished in a biographical questionnaire can be validated to provide indices of managerial success.

The Humble Oil and Refining Company has made the most notable use of the biographical information blank to identify managerial potential.[2] This firm has developed a 48-page, 292-item blank that focuses upon the early-life behavior it has found to be predictive of later success as a manager. In developing this instrument, Humble administered it to many of its present managers and compared their responses to later success as determined by position, salary, and peer judgment. The relationship between the questionnaire responses and executive performance gave the company a way of scoring it and establishing standards of success. As management candidates complete the blank, their answers are compared to these standards to help predict the likelihood of their success.

Humble avoids labeling the specific kinds of personalities identified by the questionnaire. Its major premise is that different types of managers with different backgrounds can be successful at Humble. The results to date indicate that such early signs of self-confidence and assertion as wide-ranging interests and willingness to step forward to take risks are the principal behavioral predictors of executive suitability.

The most attractive feature of the biographical information blank is that a number of factors that underlie responses to its individual items have

[2] Harry Laurent, *Early Identification of Management Potential* [Social Science Research Div., Employee Relations Dept., Standard Oil Company (N.J.), Aug. 1961].

been identified. Analysis of one questionnaire, whose total score was highly related to managerial effectiveness, isolated the following factors:

1. Upward mobility through educational achievement.
2. Realistic self-description and self-perception of personal abilities and achievement.
3. Positive attitudes toward family.
4. Satisfactory interpersonal relations in social activities.
5. Positive attitudes toward work.
6. Self-sufficiency and a capacity to take care of oneself.
7. Adequate physical and mental health.

Research with biographical questionnaires has demonstrated fairly conclusively that very early life-history antecedents shape later motivational forces that determine a person's style of life and predict future behavior. What is more interesting, studies show that successful managers in different cultures have the same general life-history patterns.

In summary, it appears that the biographical information blank is a useful device for discriminating among individuals who are likely to become successful managers because it is a concrete manifestation of the person's intellectual and motivational systems as they have operated throughout his life. The biographical questionnaire, however, must be interpreted in conjunction with other information obtained about the applicant.

Assessment Interviews

The interview is one of man's oldest communication tools, the medium by which a good store of his knowledge was handed down by father to son for thousands of years before the invention of writing. Although it simulates mere conversation and dialog, it is, in fact, a highly technical tool, skill in whose use is not mastered easily. The person who proposes to conduct an interview must understand from the outset that he is not engaging in a conversation, that he is trying to communicate for a purpose. He must be aware that when two people talk to each other many psychosocial factors distort and contaminate the ideas that pass between them. This contamination makes it quite possible for two people to hold a conversation and come away with completely different understandings of what passed between them.

The Indispensable Tool

But the purpose of the assessment interview is much more than the exchange of information; it is a preliminary to a selection decision. It is a most indispensable tool of assessment, not merely for its informational potential, which is considerable, but primarily for its distinctly human and personal qualities.

Few applicants would want to be judged without the opportunity to discuss their qualifications in a face-to-face meeting with their assessor. As Alan Harrington has noted, it is the only vehicle in the assessment process where *"I* talk to *you."* [3]

An interview gives an applicant the feeling that he matters, that he is being considered by a real human being and not by a computer. No junior manager, for example, will be impressed by a promotion system that is based exclusively on a computer-activated skills inventory and retrieval system. The fact that his qualifications are reviewed in detail and then matched with the job specifications by an electronic reader in microseconds will never convince him that he has had his day in court. A personal interview gives him the feeling that he was considered fairly.

The interview also gives him a chance to ask questions about the job and, in the case of an outsider, about the company and its benefits. It gives the interviewer an opportunity to do some selling if that is necessary—and it often is in campus interviewing. Finally, because it can give an applicant a chance to feel that he is the one who is doing the deciding, it enables him to maintain his dignity in what can be a very impersonal process.

The difficulty is that judgments based upon the interview material have been repeatedly shown to be highly fallible. Perhaps the chief lessons that have emerged from interview research are that the interviewer's attitudes and opinions strongly influence the selection of the "facts" he will perceive and remember from the interview, that his own attitudes and opinions may be picked up by the person being interviewed and fed back to him, and that he may make judgments based upon his recollections of "facts" that never came out in the interview.

These lessons suggest, however, that the source of error lies not so much in the interview as in the interviewer. He is, more often than not, untrained; he does not appreciate the interview's purposes, processes, and pitfalls and, therefore, is likely to conduct an unreliable and an unsystematic interview.

[3] Alan Harrington, "The Personnel Interview," *The Atlantic* (Aug. 1959), pp. 51-54.

Interviewer Problems

The interview is, of course, the most widely used method of evaluating candidates for employment or promotion, including candidates for managerial positions. It is also the most widely abused technique. As early as 1922, an investigator noted that when 57 applicants for positions as salesmen were interviewed and appraised separately by 12 sales managers, the results showed very little agreement and some astonishing discrepancies. Years later, another comprehensive review of the literature on interviewing revealed that very little evidence had been obtained testifying to its effectiveness. And, ten years after that, another pair of investigators surveyed the state of the art and concluded that a moratorium on interviewing books and articles should be declared.

The most recent review, covering 300 articles, concluded that the situation was still the same: The interview was highly suspect as an assessment tool.[4] Yet this review and all its predecessors, written approximately ten years apart over a 40-year period, ended with a plea for "more research," recognizing that abandonment of the interview was completely out of the question.

Problems with the assessment interview fall into seven categories:

1. As normally conducted in a selection situation, the interview is of little value because of its low reliability. The interviewing of the salesmen just referred to is a good example. The same men, when interviewed by different sales managers, received widely different ratings of their qualifications.
2. The interview subject matter is inconsistently covered since each interviewer discusses only material that is of interest to him.
3. Even when they obtain the same information, interviewers are likely to interpret or weight it differently. One researcher found that interviewers differed widely on how certain items affected their impressions of the applicant. The same items gave some interviewers an extremely unfavorable impression and others as extremely favorable impression.
4. The form of the questions asked by the interviewer often affects the answers obtained. The interviewee is often placed in the position of trying to determine what answer the interviewer would like rather than giving the correct response.
5. An untrained interviewer will do most of the talking rather than most of the listening. If the interviewer does the talking, he gets little infor-

    [4] Eugene C. Mayfield, "The Selection Interview—A Re-evaluation of Published Research," *Personnel Psychology*, Vol. 17, No. 3 (Autumn 1964), pp. 239–260.

mation from the interviewee. After the interview, he will then have such a sketchy impression of the applicant's qualifications that he will fill it in from his own store of stereotypes without realizing what he is doing.

6. The interviewer's attitudes affect his interpretation of what the interviewee says. He is influenced more by unfavorable information than by favorable information. He sometimes overestimates the value of previous experience and neglects less visible factors associated with high potential. One researcher, finding that an interviewer's impressions were more likely to change from favorable to unfavorable than vice versa, concluded that the interview was chiefly a search for negative information. This conclusion is reinforced by the policies of many professional assessors who feel that the interview's purpose is to probe for the applicant's weaknesses.

7. The interviewer tends to make his decision early in the interview and look only for information to support this decision. The initial appraisal of information derived from an application blank or from the applicant's personal appearance appears to be decisive for the final outcome. The often-stated assertion—"The minute he walked into the office I sized him up"—only verifies the notion that the interviewer's decision is based more upon the interviewee's manner, facial expressions, and personal appearance than upon his life facts.

Interview Effectiveness

Despite these problems, interviews are more effective than most studies show. Unfortunately, however, most research studies on interview effectiveness have been quite limited because they have measured imperfectly and incompletely both the objectives and the consequences of interviewing.

For example, most interview studies do not include rejected applicants in their data. If they did, it is probable that the power of the interview would be better demonstrated, because an interviewer does his most important job in screening out the unfit or the uninterested applicants. Among those deemed qualified, there is likely to be much less differentiation. In other words, research has to concentrate on the extent to which the Type 1 error occurs—that is, how often an unqualified person is employed. The Type 2 error, which is probably easier to avoid, is never considered.

Many studies have demonstrated that the interview can make a contribution to the assessment of management potential. The long-term

AT&T management-progress study indicates that information from interview reports definitely contributes to assessment-center evaluations, that extensive and reliable information on many personal characteristics can be obtained from an interview. In addition, several of the interview variables, especially those affecting career motivation, dependency needs, work motivation, and interpersonal skills, are directly related to management progress. The findings of this study clearly demonstrate that relevant information on personal characteristics important to managerial success can be obtained from the interview reports.[5]

Certain Sears, Roebuck studies and others also confirm the fact that the assessment interview can make an important contribution to the prediction of job effectiveness. One of the most respected authorities, Professor Edwin E. Ghiselli, concludes that the validity of ordinary personnel interviews may be at least equal to if not greater than the validity of tests. Interviewers today, he says, unlike those of 20 or 30 years ago, are better educated, have greater experience, and have more knowledge of individual differences.[6]

Conducting the Assessment Interview

To be useful, an interview must be conducted properly. But this aspect of interviewing is so well covered in the literature that we need only make a few generalizations here.[7]

To begin with, there are three types of assessment interview, each having different purposes, requiring different techniques, and demanding different levels of interviewer skill.

1. The *primary* interview, the initial interview, focuses upon facts, is employed at the beginning of the selection sequence, and results only in a preliminary decision. The campus interview is a good example of an initial interview; it should never result in a hiring decision.
2. The *secondary* interview, the evaluation interview, focuses upon a combination of factual and logical information, is usually conducted later in the selection sequence, and can lead to a final selection decision. In most instances, this interview is conducted at the end of the assessment pro-

---

[5] Donald L. Grant and Douglas W. Bray, "Contributions of the Interview to Assessment of Management Potential," *Journal of Applied Psychology,* Vol. 53, No. 1 (Feb. 1969), pp. 24–34.

[6] Edwin E. Ghiselli, "The Validity of a Personnel Interview," *Personnel Psychology,* Vol. 19, No. 4 (Winter 1966), pp. 389–394.

[7] See, for example, Felix M. Lopez, op. cit.; Richard A. Fear, *The Evaluation Interview* (New York: McGraw-Hill, 1958).

gram after test scores, biographical data, and verification information have been collected.

3. The *tertiary* interview, known as the "depth" interview, is normally conducted only by those with extensive training in professional assessment. This type of interview focuses upon psychological data, on a person's attitudinal and expressive system. It is required only in assessment programs for highly sensitive positions.

Knowing how and why and when to conduct each type of interview is part of the overall assessment strategy. Like any tool, an interview breaks down when it is overloaded—that is, when it is used to obtain more information than its format will permit—or when it is put in the hands of a person untrained in its use or incapable of learning how to use it. You don't carve a turkey with a scalpel, and you don't try to make a ballet dancer out of a middle line backer.

Who should interview? The selection of interviewers is very important. Not everyone is emotionally predisposed to engage in this rather delicate and sensitive task. A common company practice is to designate line managers to interview candidates for jobs in their departments. But, even though they have the ability to judge technical competence, they may have little aptitude for or personal skill in interviewing and assessing other human beings. The evidence strongly suggests that the practice results in so many differences in approach used and information obtained that the net effect is absolute zero in terms of usefulness.

Although most managers feel that they have a right and an obligation to participate in selection for their units, often they only hamper the process. Apart from the evaluation of technical competence, the only other question that a manager is qualified to answer about an applicant is "How would you like to have him around?" Of course, in most cases, good managers can be taught to interview properly, but they must be willing to put in the time and the effort to do so.

Sears' success with assessment interviews is due to the training it gives each interviewer and the way it structures the actual interview to obtain factual information. After the interviewers are selected to participate in the college recruiting program, they are required to spend a full day in interview training. They are furnished with a detailed interviewer manual that covers interviewing skills, Sears' personnel policies, and the company's college-manpower requirements. The manual also contains interview questions to be asked and the inferences that may be fairly drawn from the responses to them. During the training day, the men role-play and tape-record interviews with other students, and these are then critiqued. In addition, the trainees observe a model interview and practice completing interview reports which are compared to skilled-interviewer reports. Finally, they practice live interviews with college students who are paid to work with them. After the training, they are prepared to conduct highly structured interviews according to the techniques described in the manual. And all this is only to prepare them to conduct initial interviews, in which the basic decision is whether to refer for further assessment.

The interview plan. After the selection and training of interviewers, the next input variable is the interview plan. The interview plan includes consideration of the subjects to be discussed, the length of time to be spent, the types of questions to be asked, and the area in which the interview will be conducted. There are basically two interview plans, structured and unstructured.

The *structured* or *patterned interview* follows a predetermined outline of questions because it is designed to minimize variability in the form of the information obtained. The information supplied by the interviewee is recorded on a preprinted report form during the progress of the interview. Later, these data are reclassified, tabulated, and used to build standards with which the responses of various applicants are compared. The drawback of this type of interview is its very standardization, which results in a loss of flexibility and a curtailment of interpersonal rapport that inhibits the flow of information. It is usually possible to obtain only information that previous research has shown to be significant. The structured interview is an excellent format for the initial or screening interview.

Professional interviewers prefer to use the *unstructured interview* in which more open-ended and nondirective techniques are permitted. The interviewer uses comprehensive questions and permits and encourages the interviewee to take the lead in covering the information desired. In this way, unexpectedly significant data are more likely to be uncovered. The unstructured interview, in the hands of a highly trained interviewer skilled in the art of listening, is quite effective. But it also requires a good deal of know-how, not only in eliciting the information but in interpreting it properly.

Background Verification

In the assessment interview, the hypothesis approach is vital. The assessment interview functions best when hypotheses about the person that can be confirmed or rejected by other information obtained are generated. The most powerful test of any hypothesis about a person, however, lies in its verification by events that occurred in his background.

The case for not only verifying but adding to the information obtained during the assessment process is unassailable. A few years ago, a large national employer, proud of its carefully selected crop of young managers, offered them to a behavioral science research group for study because it felt that they were typical of the top-level college-educated youth of America. After studying these young, recent college hirees, the researchers were so unimpressed that the company decided to check their backgrounds. They had assumed on the basis of information obtained at the time of hiring that these young people had all graduated in the upper quarter of their classes. A check with their respective universities revealed the dismaying fact that nearly all of them were in the bottom half of their classes.

This not-unusual situation should cast no aspersions on the integrity of these young men. A study of the validity of work-history information obtained by interview has demonstrated that it is not very high.[8] While it varies from item to item, it is least high in the case of pay items. Information on job title, duties, and length of job duration are valid about two-thirds of the time. Time is the factor that seems to effect validity most. The more recent the information, the more reliable and accurate it is likely to be. In most instances, the inaccurate information is the result of an upgrading process; the person states he earned more money or higher grades than he actually did.

Verification Purpose and Procedure

There is a good deal more to verification than simply getting the record straight. Not long ago, a major employer was embarrassed by the disclosure that its financial vice-president, who had been hired a year before, was in fact a rank impostor. He had come so highly recommended by important members of the financial community that no one had bothered to check his background. Only when the auditors noted serious discrepancies in his accounts did they take the trouble to investigate his university credentials, his CPA status, and his previous employment. By the time they discovered that he had not graduated from high school, he was living in South America.

---

[8] *Validity of Work Histories Obtained by Interview,* Bull. 34 (Industrial Relations Center, Univ. of Minnesota, Sept. 1961).

U.S. industry plays an increasingly desperate game of cops and robbers with its own employees. In an attempt to reduce losses from employee and managerial thefts of money and merchandise (losses that are now estimated at over $2 billion a year), employers in stores, factories, and financial institutions and in government are resorting to a battery of crime-prevention and detection techniques. The best technique is a careful preemployment investigation.

A company must be prepared to verify its assessment of an individual by factual information about his past performance. The best indication of what a man will do is what he has done in the past, and an important way to evaluate him is to find out what others who know him think about him.

It is true that in some quarters the value and the propriety of verification are questioned. There is, indeed, a legitimate concern for the right of privacy, and some of the techniques employed are far from perfect and often remain unformulated. But real though this concern may be, the case for verification remains impressive. Systematic verification and skillful analysis of the information obtained are important tools in assessing a manager's qualifications. They can contribute strongly to appropriate placement and to the full use of the manager's abilities. In addition, as the word gets around that a company is in the habit of careful verification, job applicants will be less inclined to give erroneous information.

MEDICAL EXAMINATION

The first step in the process is a thorough medical examination. Such an examination should include the following:

1. A careful medical history, with questions as to personal habits and present living style.
2. A complete physical examination of the whole body with clothing removed.
3. Laboratory tests, including X rays of heart and lungs, cancer-detection, and electrocardiogram.
4. A check on draft status, military discharge, and previous hospitalizations.

Such an extensive medical check-up for managerial candidates is not unjustifiable, nor is it expensive in terms of results. One study of 500 men showed that over half had major medical conditions. One-third of these were discovered for the first time, and one-half were asymptomatic—that is, the patient was not aware of any symptoms. In another study of 481 men and 19 women, 78 percent had one or more physical defects that required treatment. The vast majority of these defects were suggested by the patients' personal history, and only 12 percent were detected by laboratory techniques.

Background Investigation

Background investigation should include fingerprinting and a police check, where possible, to obtain information about previous criminal record. It should also include a full field investigation of the most recent 15 years of the applicant's life or the period from his eighteenth birthday on, whichever is shorter. This should cover name check; verification of vital statistics, military service, and education; a review of credit records; and neighborhood investigations for the past three years.

To neutralize the problem of invasion of privacy, inquiries should be limited to matters that are relevant to a determination of fitness for the position. Inquiries about race, religion, national origin, fraternal affiliations, and political preference should be excluded unless they arise from bona fide requirements—as, for example, when a manager is being sought for a religious organization.

A word about personal references: Many employers require the applicant to furnish these on his biographical questionnaire. This is a complete waste of time. A study of the references of 120 persons on whom unfavorable reports had been submitted by an independent investigator revealed that only 34 of the 341 individuals contacted replied with even the slightest hint of anything unfavorable. Seventy-nine persons, well established as undesirable because of such problems as criminal background, alcoholism, very poor work history, and the like, received complete approval from their references. While it is desirable to speak to people who know the applicant, it is better for the investigator to find them on his own. Verification procedures in general follow three basic courses.

Letters and cards. One way of verifying personal history is by sending letters and postcards with self-addressed return envelopes to former employers and references. While the response to this approach is generally acceptable, its value is questionable. In most instances, the replies will be innocuous and nonspecific.

Telephone calls. An excellent and by far the most popular method is to phone past employers and people who know the applicant. The telephone inquiry should be carefully structured and conducted by a trained interviewer who knows what to ask for.

Dr. John Drake, president of Behavioral Sciences Technology, Inc., has found it helpful to be open and frank about the candidate with those on the other end of the phone. For example, the inquirer may say something like this: "We are considering John Doe for the position of manager in our production department. We plan to start him at a salary of about $25,000 per year. He will have to supervise about 5 people directly but, overall, a plant employing 750 people." This approach brings the other person "in" on the situation and encourages him to be more informative.

It is also useful, says Dr. Drake, to state some negative aspects of the candidate's record or personality that you have observed in order to get the other's reactions to them. For example, you may say, "In my interview I felt that this man may walk around with a bit of a chip on his shoulder and perhaps does not react too well to criticism. I wonder if you have noticed anything like this in your work with him?"

The chief value of the telephone inquiry, when conducted by a skillful interviewer, obviously, lies in the tendency of people to speak candidly and to mention observations and reactions that they would not put in writing.

Personal visits. The most complete way of obtaining essential information on an applicant is by personal visits to the people and places listed on his application blank. This, of course, is a most expensive method, but it is the most valid. It is usually employed by hiring outside agencies that specialize in this work and can produce fairly complete and accurate reports as necessary.

The polygraph and other covert investigations. It is generally considered to be an invasion of privacy to use such covert or surreptitious means of investigation as mail covers, inspection of trash, paid informers, telephone or wire taps, or the polygraph.

By far the most widely used of the covert methods is the polygraph. One source estimates that between 200,000 and 300,000 polygraph tests are made annually by American industry. Some employers consider the polygraph to be the most effective weapon for combating employee theft. However, there is increasing suspicion of its reliability and validity. It is now considered to be useful only as a psychological blackjack. It can be effective if people believe it is a real lie detector and confess their guilt when confronted by it.

Personnel experts usually warn against using pseudoscientific substitutes for managerial judgment. Indeed, one polygraph operator found that, after learning how to interview properly, he could obtain better results without his machine. This suggests that users and would-be users of lie-detector tests might well reexamine this simple solution to their problems. The U.S.

Civil Service Commission has banned the use of the polygraph for all positions except those in agencies that have intelligence or counterintelligence missions directly affecting national security and approaching in sensitivity the mission of the Central Intelligence Agency.

Despite the rising crime rate, it is probably safer for a corporation to avoid altogether the use of surreptitious investigative techniques and stick to the more traditional methods. Generally speaking, the telephone interview, when carried out properly, is much more reliable and effective.

Biographical questionnaires, interviews, and background investigations can provide a complete dossier on an applicant's life history and behavioral patterns. But, to obtain a completely synthesized view of his life style, one needs to tap another source of information: actual behavioral samples that are provided by psychological tests.

10

Testing Managers

Ever since the first tests were introduced into personnel selection 50 years ago, their usefulness has been debated heatedly, and in recent years even the Congress of the United States has been drawn into the argument. William H. Whyte, Jr. expressed the apprehensions of many in a *Fortune* magazine article in 1954, alleging that the behavioral norms used to evaluate test results were actually abnormal and that, in any event, the investigation of a person's psyche was an invasion of his constitutional right to privacy.[1] Since the appearance of this article many other writers, informed and uninformed, have taken up the cudgels against testing.

The case against testing was apparently clinched by Professor Ross Stagner's experiment, which was said to expose the gullibility of personnel managers. Professor Stagner, chairman of the Department of Psychology at Wayne State University, administered a "personality" test to a group of personnel managers, submitted a common "personality" description to each, and then asked him to gauge its accuracy. Each man assumed that the description he received was a personalized report, although Dr. Stagner carefully refrained from saying so. Fifty percent saw the report as being "amazingly accurate," and another 40 percent reported it as being "rather good." The results of this experiment have been repeatedly cited by test critics as an example of the misuse of personality tests as selection devices, even though

[1] William H. Whyte, Jr., "The Fallacies of 'Personality' Testing," *Fortune* (Sept. 1954), pp. 117–208.

Dr. Stagner's intent was to demonstrate the difference between glittering generalities and a quantitative set of scores used to describe human traits.[2]

We would expect that these intense and highly articulate protests would lead to a steady decline in the use of tests as selection devices. The facts, however, point to the reverse. In a 1948 National Industrial Conference Board survey, 16 percent of nearly 3,500 companies reported that they were then using employment tests. Less than 10 percent had initiated their programs before 1930, and only 25 percent before 1940. Six years later, a 1954 National Industrial Conference Board survey reported that 40 percent of the responding companies made substantial use of personnel tests.

In 1956, the U.S. Employment Service reported that its more than 1,200 local offices were testing more than a million applicants a year, that 1,400 multistate employers (double the 1948 figure) regularly requested test-selected applicants from state employment services. In 1960, Harvard Business School Professor Lewis Ward reported that over 60 percent of the companies he surveyed were using tests as part of the selection process and that 85 percent of the responding executives reported personal experiences with some type of psychological test. Professor Ward summed it up this way: "Psychological tests seem here to stay. The majority of companies are using tests, and the great bulk of executives have been favorably exposed to them." By mid-1965, it was estimated that over 20 million Americans were taking 60 million tests a year.

How can we account for both the increasing protest against testing and its steady growth as a major selection tool? By simply looking at the way tests are used and the purposes for which they are used.

The Pros and Cons of Testing

To a personnel administrator charged with the responsibility of making important decisions about people, tests offer a promising source of help. The critics of testing, on the other hand, are properly concerned with the amateurs and the naive managers who misuse this admittedly complex tool. It is, therefore, necessary to examine carefully the pros and cons of testing to identify the ways in which it can be used most effectively in the assessment process and to point out the weaknesses that detract from its value.

It is well to keep in mind that a test is an actual sample of a person's

[2] Edith Goodman, "Professor Gulls Personnel Men with Phony Psychological Test," *American Business* (Dec. 1959), pp. 6–8.

behavior in response to stimuli obtained under standardized conditions with his full knowledge and cooperation. There are instruments called "tests" (some of which we shall describe later) that do not meet this specification. There are other instruments, not called tests, that do.

When we consider a *true* test, therefore, it is obvious that if employed properly it represents a tool that can contribute important information to the assessment process.

Test Advantages

We must keep in mind the fact that managers have to make selection decisions, that people must be hired and promoted. There are not many information sources available to managers to help them to do this job. Biographical data and interview material can be unreliable or misleading even when they are carefully verified and interpreted. The need for test data, for actual behavioral samples, is felt keenly everywhere, even in Socialist countries. Soviet leaders in education, science, and management have urged that their schools and employer institutes adopt aptitude tests on a wide scale to insure the proper allocation of manpower in their increasingly complex national economy.

And an American Psychological Association task force stated recently that "decisions regarding the selection and promotion of personnel inevitably involve a degree of subjectivity. . . . Because of their relative objectivity, psychological tests, properly designed and used, are potentially less discriminatory than other personnel assessment techniques, but it is apparent that no single step in the sequence can properly be adjudged the primary source of unfair distinction." [3]

Besides being more objective and prone to greater reliability, the preemployment test can be the most economical screening device. If certain critical requirements are to be evaluated, such as numerical skill or typing ability, it is possible to test, score, and evaluate hundreds of applicants in a matter of a few hours. To evaluate a similar number by interview would require 15 to 20 times as much staff and applicant time.

A test can furnish an employer with information not obtainable with any degree of precision by other techniques. The most accurate representation of mental ability can be obtained by tests. Decision making, for example,

[3] "Job Testing and the Disadvantaged," *The American Psychologist*, Vol. 24, No. 7 (July 1969), p. 639.

so important to managerial competence, can really be measured only by a carefully designed situational test.

Moreover, and despite the many published criticisms to the contrary, employment applicants are more willing to accept selection decisions based on test results than on those based on biographical or interview data, particularly if they understand the relevancy of the tests to job performance. In a study of the attitudes of workers in eight organizations toward employment tests, a group of researchers found that a majority were favorably disposed toward all types of tests and experienced greater job satisfaction and security after having been selected and placed by tests. And, in a study conducted in another organization, an overwhelming number of employees expressed a preference for promotion by competitive tests rather than by any other means.

Tests, therefore, are more objective, more economical. They can tap more areas of a person's intellectual and motivational systems and appear to be more acceptable to applicants.

Test Criticisms

Like an ordinary carving knife, any selection tool—no matter how useful— is dangerous if it is abused or misused. Thus the criticisms of testing are directed at its misuses or abuses.

An *abuse* is the wrongful treatment of an instrument, such as improper administration, scoring, or interpretation of the results. When a test is administered, for example, under conditions other than those specified in the test manual, it is abused and the results distorted. The "blind analysis" technique of interpreting test results and making selection decisions without reference to other information about the person tested is also an abuse.

Misuse of a test refers to its inappropriate use. A test designed, for example, to diagnose emotional disorders in a clinical setting should not be used in a selection situation except under carefully controlled experimental conditions. Nor may a test designed to predict academic success be applied to an industrial situation without careful and thorough research and the development of new norms for it. But the most flagrant and the most common misuse of testing is the practice of furnishing test results to managers with no competence to interpret them.

The severest objections to test misuses and abuses can be found in the responsible personnel and psychological literature. They boil down to five areas.

The problem of test confidentiality. Almost all professional psychologists agree that test scores should *not* be made available directly to managers. Test data must be interpreted by professionally trained personnel before their significance can be determined. Most managers, however, feel that they have a right to test data, and they will not permit the use of such data unless they themselves have access to all the available material. This leads to the second problem.

The invasion of privacy. Many persons believe that no one has the legal or ethical right to ask the types of questions that are included in some personality inventories. Some even question the right to measure a person's intellectual ability. As employed by responsible industrial psychologists, however, tests probe into private matters only insofar as they are related to employment stability, attitudes toward work, and job performance. This information is frequently indispensable if the best interests of the individual as well as the organization are to be served.

And, for management positions, a prospective employer has not only the right but the obligation to explore the personality of an applicant to determine his fitness for the position. No applicant who chooses to assume responsibility for the direction and the control of other people's working careers should be unwilling to undergo an intensive personal appraisal by a qualified assessor. In short, when one aspires to high private or public office, one necessarily yields his right to privacy. No one can really argue with this position. The problem is that, after the appraisal is made, it is not very private. Although psychologists may assure those taking tests that the results will be held in the strictest confidence, there are many instances where this assurance has not been kept.

Use throughout career. Use of test results obtained during the early stages of a young manager's career to determine all future educational and career opportunities does not give adequate consideration to the changes that result from development and maturation. There is evidence to show that intelligence viewed as knowledge and wisdom, rather than as genetically determined ability, increases throughout life. Thus test results should not mark a person for life. Yet many persons who commit themselves on personality, attitude, or aptitude tests find that the results follow them throughout their careers.

The conformity issue. Testing can often breed conformity and the organization man. But this is, as we have indicated in Chapter 5, a possibility only when tests are used in an extremely naive fashion to select only specific types—that is, to bring to the surface those personality characteristics that conform to the organization's role and climate.

Discrimination against minority groups. Minority-group discrimination has been the most recent criticism of testing. It is contended that intelligence tests in particular are biased against the underprivileged and that they are used consciously or unconsciously to discriminate against them. That there is a basis for this criticism is attested to by evidence showing that the differences in the scores of certain ethnic groups are not reflected in subsequent performance on the jobs for which the tests were designed. However, if a test differentiates between those who will succeed and those who will fail, it is measuring what it is supposed to measure and is, therefore, unbiased no matter what the effect is ethnically.

Using Tests Properly

When tests are used properly, they can help substantially in selection, particularly and most especially in selection for managerial positions. The question is how best to use this instrument. There are many excellent texts, numerous pamphlets, and magazine articles to aid the user.[4] Here we shall present only a few considerations that are of significance for the selection of managers by managers.

All tests do is provide clues about an applicant which, when confirmed by other information, enable the assessor to make fairly accurate predictions of job effectiveness. They suggest hypotheses about the applicant's intellectual capacities, aptitudes, vocational attitudes, or personality dynamics, each of which must be confirmed or rejected by data drawn from other areas of the applicant's background.

Suppose, for example, that a mental-ability test score places an applicant in the highest quarter of a college-educated population. Before we can say that the applicant is "bright," we must confirm his brightness by evidence such as high academic standing or other intellectual achievement. If we find no evidence to support the high test score, we must reject the hypothesis.

But, even before we get that far, we must have a degree of confidence in the hypothesis itself. And confidence in a test score depends upon the test itself: how it was administered, scored, and interpreted.

[4] See, for example, Robert M. Guion, *Personnel Testing* (New York: McGraw-Hill, 1965) or Marvin D. Dunnette, *Personnel Selection and Placement* (Belmont, Calif.: Wadsworth, 1966).

Selecting a Test

The first step in selecting a test or, for that matter, any selection instrument is job analysis to gain a thorough understanding of what is to be done and the patterns of behavior required to do it. This is why we discussed the role of the manager in so much detail in Chapter 4.

Each organization must conduct a job analysis, taking into account not merely the specific functions of the job but the role demands and the milieu in which the role must be performed. Each instrument used to assess individuals must be associated positively with one of these factors.

A company can make or buy tests. There are a great many first-rate examples that are commercially purchasable. Textbooks describe these tests in detail, and there are certain other specific sources that evaluate published tests. Before purchasing a test, a prospective user should consult such sources.

It is also important to recognize that tests are subject to the same "caveat emptor" precaution as any other product. There are many major test-publishing concerns that are reputable and unquestionably ethical. Unfortunately, there are others whose practices and products range from questionable to outright fraudulent.

In purchasing a test, there are a few simple rules to follow. First, tests developed by responsible authors are made available to the psychological community for research and evaluation. The test author is also bound by his scientific obligations to do his own research on the instrument and to publish the results before he makes any claims for it. This information will be contained in the test manual that always accompanies a test. Therefore, always read this manual carefully. It will include the names of the authors, their professional backgrounds, and the nature and purpose of the test. Beware of titles that are deliberately designed to disguise a test's nature. Watch out for instruments with names like "Test of Executive Potential" or "Test of Creative Capacity." Find out what the author defines as "executive potential" or "creative capacity." Be on guard, also, against highly abstract and impressive titles that mean little—such as "behavior-dynamics analysis."

The test manual will likewise contain information concerning the groups for which the test is designed, the selection of test situations, item-analysis procedures, the length of the test, directions for administration, and evidence concerning reliability and validity. In addition, it should list references to reviews of the test in the literature. We are unable to elaborate on these technical matters here, but they should be carefully studied before a test is adopted in a situation where it will have an impact upon people's careers.

Custom-built tests are, of course, much more desirable—for many obvious reasons—than those purchased commercially. The construction of a test, however, is a difficult, complex, and expensive process requiring the assistance of a professional psychologist. Only the largest organizations can afford to build their own tests.

It is in fact desirable, and virtually mandatory under current federal and state regulations, to choose or to construct tests with the help of a competent psychologist. The reliable industrial psychologist is more likely to underestimate rather than to guarantee results. He will never make extravagant promises of overnight miracles or short-cut cures. As a matter of course, from the very outset he will be reluctant to commit himself at all before he has had time to make his own appraisal of the company's problem. He will want to have his own look at the situation, usually on company premises. His preliminary inquiries will tell how much time will be involved on his part and on the part of his staff before any test program is recommended.

The psychologist will also want to check over the results of his program and he will plan follow-up procedures as well.

Implementing a Test Program

It is quite important to make certain that a test is administered properly by a person trained in its administration. Such matters as clarity of instructions, good physical test conditions, and strict adherence to time limits are so obvious to satisfactory test administration that they should hardly require discussion. But apparently they do.

Employers should monitor their programs closely to make certain they are being administered as specified in the test manual. Any change in time limits affects the results drastically. One unfortunate practice adopted in the interest of efficiency is to load the test administrator with many duties: test scoring, filing, typing, and even fingerprinting. Under such circumstances, adequate test administration is improbable. Firms with limited resources for proper test administration can take advantage of the recent trend toward cassettes and other recorded instructions.

Another often-violated requirement of good test administration is the provision for guaranteeing the security of test materials. Test materials are highly confidential documents that should be made accessible only to a restricted few within the personnel department. All test materials, booklets, answer sheets, manuals, and results should be kept under lock and key, and—to repeat—they should never be released to line managers.

Test Review and Research

As with any management activity, we continually need to know how our assessment program is doing and how we can improve it. When testing is part of the process, its control aspect becomes even more critical. The testing program must be audited constantly to make sure that tests are being administered properly, standards are being adhered to, and the results mean the same as when the tests were first introduced.

In addition to these control features that look to the past, a continuous program of research oriented toward the future is essential. It is impossible to begin a testing program with a battery of completely validated tests. Tests often have to be selected on the basis of *a priori* judgments, but these can still be valuable if data are collected looking toward ultimate evaluation within the meaning of the decision-making model described in Chapter 8. There is nothing more useless than the administration of tests with no knowledge of how effective they are.

Test data can be collected in many ways and related to actual job success through the manpower-information system described earlier. But a research program should also provide for the development of more effective techniques and for the adaptation of existing techniques to the changing requirements of the environment. For, even when a test program is placed on a sound professional basis, caution has to be taken to guard against certain pitfalls.

It is advisable to approach the whole assessment program with large doses of old-fashioned common sense. There are certain hazards even in an effective program. For one thing, by its very objectivity testing may be viewed by people as a serious threat. An impersonal numerical index of a person's intellectual ability is not something that can be explained away easily, particularly if that index places its owner at an organizational disadvantage. Failing to be selected or promoted on the basis of favoritism or personality conflict can be understood in a socially acceptable way. Failure to be selected or promoted because of a low score on an intelligence test is extremely embarrassing. Management must therefore expect criticism of its testing program and alleviate the anxiety that will be aroused by interpreting the results with considerable caution.

It is advisable, also, to remember that no test result is ever 100 percent accurate. Human error does enter into the situation. There are people, not many, who suffer from test anxiety to such an extent that they are ineffective test takers; their results will not represent their true skills. Similarly, the built-in speed factor in some tests causes individuals to score lower than their true ability would warrant. Therefore, judicious test interpretation always requires that the error factor be considered as a distinct possibility.

A test score can mislead a naive manager into treating it as an absolute number. There is something so appealingly simple about it that the temptation is strong to draw sweeping conclusions from it and overlook the very complex questions of human ability that are involved. A billion-dollar corporation, for example, classifies each manager by the score he achieves on a 12-minute mental-ability test designed originally to select employees for semiskilled occupations. Applicants of otherwise high caliber for top executive positions have been turned down by this company solely because of an insufficiently high score on this test. This is the kind of nonsense that management must avoid.

Tests, then, can be a means of obtaining objective, reliable, and accurate information about a person for the purpose of making predictions about his future job behavior. They are, and will continue to be, used extensively in government and in industry to select employees in positions where they can make sound and effective contributions to overall organizational goals and from which they can obtain large measures of personal satisfaction. They are not, however, a simple panacea for every assessment problem that troubles and besets managers. Testing is not an easy tool to master. Misuses and abuses will creep into even the best and most soundly administered programs. Constant vigilance is an absolute must.

Test Typology

With these preliminary thoughts we can approach now the subject of test typology. We have been using the term "test" in a generic sense, which is really improper because there are so many types that in any discussion of tests it makes considerable difference to specify the type referred to.

Although there are thousands of tests in use by employers and educators, they can be classified into two very broad categories: trait tests and situational tests. *Trait tests* are, for the most part, the traditional tests that have been developed to facilitate the process of psychological measurement in academic and clinical settings. *Situational tests,* which are both older and younger than trait tests, represent a response to the need of industry and government for measurement instruments more representative of job performance.

Trait Tests

Most trait tests are designed to measure some characteristic of the personality that describes or gives rise to an individual's typical behavior and distinguishes it from that of others. These characteristics can refer to a *style of behavior* (such as "aggressiveness"), to a *process* (such as "ability to learn"), or to the *content* of his information (such as "accounting theory").

The object of a trait test is to isolate certain clusters of characteristics in an individual for the purposes of description and prediction. Trait tests are, therefore, analytical in nature because they break a person's behavior up into components in order to obtain a simpler, clearer view of them. Traits can be highly specific (as, for example, "spelling ability") or very general (like "intelligence"). The more general the trait measure, the wider its applicability to a variety of life situations but the greater its possibility of error.

Trait tests can be and are usually classified along the lines of the personality taxonomy described in Chapter 2. These are tests of the *intellectual system* and tests of the *motivational system.*

Tests of the Intellectual System

The intellectual system—or, as it is more often called, the cognitive system—includes not only the processes of the intellect but the special aptitudes, skills, and knowledge that go into the performance of any human activity. Cognitive tests are usually subdivided into three types: *intelligence, aptitude,* and *achievement.* Since this classification is artificial, it can be quite confusing and even misleading.

Every cognitive test measures the learning an individual has achieved and, at the same time, requires the use of his intelligence and his aptitudes.

A cognitive test score, therefore, is made up in varying degrees of what has been learned and what is presumably the effects of his intelligence. What justification there is for the classification lies only in the purpose for which the test is used, but since most traditional textbooks have adopted this classification we shall use it here.

Failure to appreciate the importance of the lack of distinction among intelligence, aptitude, and achievement has caused wide misrepresentation of test results and, in many companies, has led to the unfortunate practice of erroneously labeling individuals as very bright or mediocre. Because of this, we must examine intelligence tests in more detail than the other two types of tests.

Intelligence tests. It is well to keep in mind that it is really impossible to measure intelligence. All that we can do is measure its supposed effects, which are necessarily interwoven with the binding effects of the motivational system and of previous experience and learning.

The nature of intelligence constitutes one of those mysteries of life about which there is no more agreement among psychologists today than there was 50 years ago. The fact that the most widely accepted definition of intelligence is "that which is measured by intelligence tests" is of great significance. It means that every intelligence test score must be treated with caution and by no means accepted as a precise measure of a person's mental capacity. There are many problems with intelligence tests, three of which we shall mention here: the origin of intelligence tests and the possible effects of age and culture on their scores.

Intelligence tests were originally designed to identify children who could not profit from the regular course of instruction in primary school. They were designed to predict academic performance, which consists largely of reading, writing, and rote memory skills. In addition, success in school from the primary grades to graduate institutions is a function of one's ability to perform well on tests. Therefore, traditional intelligence tests measure, in part, simply the ability to take tests.

Nearly every intelligence test in use in the occupational world today is, by content and process, a direct descendant of tests designed for use in an academic setting. We should expect, therefore, much lower correlations between test scores and criteria of managerial success because of the preselection that goes on in the schooling process and in prior jobs and that limits the range of scores obtained by managers. But, even if there were no preselection, it is probable that the intellectual processes required to be a successful manager are different from those necessary to excel in school. This may be one reason why many studies seem to demonstrate that managers as a group are not extremely bright—or, to put it another way, that very intelligent people do not make good managers. As a matter of fact, the probability is quite high that excellent managers are exceptionally intelligent. They just don't seem to get particularly high scores on academically oriented intelligence tests.

The problem is that many intellectual factors are not yet represented by tests. In 1942 Raymond B. Cattell summed the situation up in this way: A considerable proportion of intelligence tests used in adult testing show every evidence in their difficulty, style, and educational presuppositions of being designed for college students, so that they are of uncertain validity and even inadequate standardization when applied to the general population.[5]

More recently, as we have already noted, Professor Cattell has subdivided general intelligence into two broad types: crystallized and fluid.[6] *Crystallized* ability appears as a related circle of abilities—verbal, numerical, and reasoning—that normally are taught in school. *Fluid* ability, on the other hand, involves culture-fair perceptual judgments. People high on this ability excel at the strategies of games because this type of intelligence leads to the perception of complex relationships and new environments, a key ability in handling the complexities and the magnitudes of decision making. One would expect, therefore, that fluid intelligence would be an important predictor of managerial performance and that tests that are heavily crystallized in content would not.

Professor Cattell flatly states that to regard the test scores of traditional intelligence tests administered to people over the age of 20 as measures of their intelligence is pure delusion. This leads to an important question:

How representative are the test scores of mature managers?

Most intelligence tests are timed tests; that is, the examinee is required to complete them within a specific period of time, measured usually in small segments of three to six minutes. Speed tests, as they are called, place great emphasis on reaction time, an emphasis that is largely absent from the intellectual tasks faced by a manager.

Psychologists have concluded from many studies of a cross-sectional na-

[5] Raymond B. Cattell, "General Review and Summary: The Measurement of Adult Intelligence," *Psychological Bulletin* (March 1943).

[6] Raymond B. Cattell, "Are I.Q. Tests Intelligent?" in *Readings in Psychology Today* (Del Mar, Calif.: CRM Books, 1969).

ture that intelligence-test scores decline with age, beginning at age 20. This decline, which proceeds at the rate of about one percent per year and closely approximates such physical deterioration curves as that of visual acuity, has led many psychologists to conclude that there is a general decline in mental efficiency from about the age of 20. But other psychologists, such as the late Irving Lorge, have argued that the decline indicated on speed tests for older people is due to the fact that they are slower physically, are more careful, and work at a different tempo. His data indicate that the scores achieved by individuals on intelligence tests may be adversely influenced by speed, education, or culture and therefore represent declines in performance rather than in ability.

The evidence also indicates that mental ability of the *crystallized* sort increases over time, so that it may be useful to assess a man periodically if his early showing is not impressive. Studies have shown, moreover, that motivation can play an important role in test performance in older adults. Adult managers tested over a seven-year span, for example, under conditions where the outcome was important to them, where they had practiced taking tests and believed in them as a fair way to make promotion decisions, showed significant increases in score. And other researchers using longitudinal methods have also noted this uniform growth in ability. The exact amount of such improvement that can be attributed to such factors as test wiseness, memory, and attitudinal changes is of course difficult to determine.

But perhaps the most heated controversy over intelligence tests concerns the effect or possible effect of culture on test results. People who are members of socioeconomic groups generally referred to as "disadvantaged" do not perform as well on intelligence tests as majority groups. The importance of this fact has led to the rather stringent governmental requirements concerning the development and use of tests in the selection process. While these requirements do not apply to managerial positions, the test user should, as a matter of policy, comply with them until further information is obtained in this complex area.

The only question that matters is whether the differences in intelligence-test scores predict differences in job effectiveness. As we have indicated, it is doubtful whether this question can even be answered adequately by the measurement model of assessment, but that is what the law requires. And, even when the question is answered affirmatively, the results of future tests must be treated with reservations. The validation of a test becomes unanchored from its normative group from the moment it is validated because of the rapid changes occurring in the environment.

What seems to be indicated is that the development of tests of fluid intelligence may offer a solution to the problem. Cattell argues for the measurement of this ability through culture-fair tests that measure perceptual forms and figures that are equally familiar or strange to all cultures. Since crystallized intelligence is all that is measured by traditional intelligence tests and is affected strongly by scholastic achievement and social status, it would be expected that lower socioeconomic groups would have less of it. Cattell, however, has demonstrated that culture-fair tests show no difference in scores between groups where there are profound differences in culture but where no differences in real ability are expected to exist. Whenever there is reason to believe that there will be real differences in ability due to differences in background, they do show up even on these tests.

Despite these reservations, intelligence tests form one of the major components of nearly every assessment battery designed for the selection of managers. Studies consistently show that intelligence is a primary factor in the prediction of managerial success. The correlations are by no means perfect—probably because of the problems cited. But the fact is that a positive relationship does exist between intellectual ability and managerial effectiveness.

Aptitude tests. Aptitude tests measure an individual's ability to acquire, with training, some particular skill. It is important to recognize that this skill is not already possessed by the subject. In administering aptitude tests, an employer tries to determine whether it is worth his while to put the examinee through a specific training course. Aptitude tests, therefore, are of value chiefly in situations involving potential for growth and learning.

There are many aptitude tests available with proven validity for measuring success in clerical and mechanical training programs. Incidentally, it is important to recognize that while a test may be called a *"mechanical-*aptitude test" there is, in fact, no such aptitude. The trait is really a combination of motor skills, prior exposure to mechanical devices and tools, interest in mechanical objects, and cultural approval of the interest. The reason why most women do poorly on mechanical-aptitude tests is that in our culture mechanical aptitude is a masculine trait. For the same reason the disadvantaged may appear to lack mechanical aptitudes; their fathers could not afford a home workshop, and they were never required to repair a vacuum cleaner or an electric toaster.

There are aptitude tests that purport to measure managerial, leadership, or creative aptitudes. What has just been said about mechanical aptitude applies here. For the most part, these tests measure achievement, knowledge, or experience. Tests of supervisory practices or judgment, for example, measure an individual's exposure to certain accepted principles of effective supervision. They do not predict how well he will perform as a supervisor or as a manager. A low test score on one of these instruments simply means that with respect to commonly accepted supervisory practices the testee is rather uninformed. It does not prove that he cannot be taught to be an effective supervisor. Nor does a high test score indicate that the person will be an effective supervisor. Effectiveness as a supervisor is a function of the individual's total personality as modified by training and experience.

Creativity tests suffer from the same weaknesses as intelligence tests. Authorities are unable to agree on a definition of creativity. All that is possible at present is to recognize a highly creative person after he has demonstrated his possession of this trait by actual accomplishment. It is almost useless to attempt to measure a person's aptitude for creativity. Regardless of the situation, a creative person will act creatively, and an uncreative person will not.

Proficiency tests. Proficiency tests measure the amount of information or the level of skill an individual has already acquired by learning and practice. Such tests include those administered at the end of a college semester or course of instruction, civil service examinations, typing and stenographic tests, CPA and bar examinations, and even the driver's test required to obtain a motor-vehicle license. Since these tests usually cover a specific area of knowledge or skill, they are not difficult to construct, can be easily standardized, have an intrinsic construct validity, and are the safest to interpret.

Tests of the Motivational System

Undoubtedly, most of the controversy surrounding testing centers about tests of the motivational system. Motivational tests are designed to predict whether a person who has certain abilities will utilize them to perform the tasks involved. To put it simply, ability tests measure *can do* factors; motivational tests measure *will do* factors.

The probability that a person will behave in a specific fashion depends on many subtle and obscure factors that are inextricably interwoven in the dynamics of his motivational system. In the personality model presented in Chapter 2, this system included a person's attitudes, his drives, and his expressive choices. Fathoming a person's motives requires deep probes into the inner workings of his psyche, into regions of the personality that are quite intimate and very sensitive.

The invasion-of-privacy argument, therefore, is generally aimed at these tests which are commonly but mistakenly called either *psychological* or *personality* tests. And, once again, the main difficulty with tests of the motivational system is their ancestry. The antecedents of most personality tests have been developed in clinical settings and standardized on emotionally disturbed people or in academic settings on immature people. There are very few instruments that have been developed on normal adult populations in occupational settings.

As a matter of fact, most authors and researchers in this area are rather unfamiliar with the demands of the everyday occupational world. Therefore, it would be expected that validities for this type of test are not overwhelmingly positive. One recent survey of articles appearing in psychological journals over a 12-year span concluded that it is difficult to advocate with a clear conscience the use of personality tests as a basis for making employment decisions. This opinion is concurred in by many other psychologists, particularly those wedded to the measurement model of assessment.

To be sure, not every researcher who has explored this area is quite so negative about personality tests. But all agree that, even where personality tests are valid, the validities are low. And no personality-test author is justified in making the claims for his instrument contained in the advertising literature that has accompanied some of these tests.

The companies that are making the most intensive research effort, on the other hand, find some measures of the motivational system to be among the more powerful predictors of managerial success when used correctly—that is, when all the ethical and legal implications are taken into account. We have referred to these studies in Chapter 6.

There are two major types of motivational-system tests: interest and personality tests.

Interest tests. Interest tests measure people's attitudes toward certain vocational or occupational fields. When administered to young people for purposes of career guidance and interpreted by competent counselors, these tests have a great deal to offer in pointing out the best career path to follow. Attitudes, as we have demonstrated, are among the most enduring aspects of personality, tending to remain stable from early adolescence to late adult years. The rationale behind interest tests is that a person is more likely to succeed in an occupation toward which he has the most favorable attitude because he is more willing to apply himself and because of the satisfaction he obtains from such efforts.

Little can be said, however, for these instruments as predictors of job success. There is little solid evidence for or against them unless we include the work of Dr. John Holland cited in Chapter 5, and his work is usually classified under the heading of personality testing rather than interest testing. The fact that an individual has a strong interest in a field is no assurance that he will be successful in it. Ability and the opportunity to acquire formal training are necessary concomitants of interest as prerequisites of success. Nevertheless, interest tests are effective tools in placing people in occupational and organizational situations with value systems and climates similar to their own.

Personality tests. Tests of an individual's temperament, values, and self-concepts are generally referred to as personality tests although, in the strictest sense, they do not measure personality and many are not tests. Personality tests are either *objective* or *projective* in format.

Objective tests are generally self-report inventories administered by paper and pencil. The individual, by responding to a large number of questions about his feelings, his personal habits, and his approach to a wide assortment of life situations, submits a "report" about himself from which inferences are drawn about his general motivational patterns.

The most serious objection to these instruments is the relative ease with which they can be faked. Questionnaire items, to a large extent, are transparent. A person applying for a managerial position would certainly know whether to answer yes or no to the following item: "I like to take charge of things." But conscious faking is not the only problem. It has been demonstrated that a person is not always the most accurate reporter of his own feelings and behavior. Most of us have the habit of describing our behavior in the most flattering way.

Despite these reservations, there is considerable evidence for the usefulness of these instruments in assessment situations. They form an important part of the executive-selection batteries of many companies and professional psychologists.

A projective test permits the subject to *project* his personal feelings and attitudes and approach to life through responses to a set of ambiguous stimuli such as ink blots, pictures, incomplete sentences, or drawings. Projective tests were originally developed to diagnose emotional disorders and are still used widely in clinical situations.

Dr. David C. McClelland, of Harvard's Department of Social Relations, is a leader in a group of psychologists at Harvard and M.I.T. who have been studying the achievement motive in managers for a period of nearly 20 years. Dr. McClelland's principal measurement tool is a projective test involving a series of pictures which the subject looks at, afterwards telling a story about what he sees. For example, the test administrator will show a picture of a man sitting at a desk. If the subject says, "He is a man who is working very late at night and is very tired," it might suggest that the man's achievement motive was not very salient. On the other hand, if the man says, "It's a guy working very hard on a new contract for a bridge. He knows it's very important for promotion," Professor McClelland might say that this individual was achievement-motivated and probably a good bet for management.[7]

Dr. Donald L. Grant, of the American Telephone & Telegraph Company, has found that the contribution of projective techniques to his company's assessment of managerial candidates clearly indicates that relevant information on managerial motivation has been obtained. Analysis of the data shows that the projective reports have particularly influenced the assessment staff in rating such characteristics as work motivation, passivity, and dependency. In addition, several of the projective variables have been reliably related to progress in management, especially those pertaining to leadership and achievement motivation.[8]

Projective tests can get at the more subtle areas of the personality and are not so easy to fake. Because they actually do sample behavior, they fit the definition of a test. But the main objection to projective tests is that the results depend more on the skill of the administrator than on the subject's responses.

Graphology. Essentially, graphology works by examining how an applicant's handwriting deviates from the way he was taught. In Europe this technique is widely used as a personality measure, but in the United States there are so many amateurs and charlatans in the field that few business corporations make use of it. Only one college teaches the subject, and according to Daniel S. Anthony there are only 10 or 12 expert graphologists in the United States today.[9]

Anthony is employed by a number of corporations to analyze the handwritings of applicants for positions. He asserts that he has an accuracy record of 93 percent and has reduced employee turnover well below the industry average.

---

[7] David C. McClelland, "As I See It," *Forbes* (June 1, 1969), pp. 53–57.

[8] Donald Grant, et al., "Contributions of Projective Techniques to Assessment of Management Potential," *Journal of Applied Psychology,* Vol. 51, No. 3 (1967), pp. 226–232.

[9] Daniel S. Anthony," Is Graphology Valid?" *Psychology Today,* Vol. 1, No. 4 (Aug. 1967), pp. 30–35.

It may be very true that graphology has an important contribution to make to the selection of managers, but so few studies have been reported that it is difficult to make any statement about its effectiveness. The only conclusion to be drawn is that the relationship between handwriting and character is still no more than an interesting theory.

To summarize trait testing, we can say that tests are only as good as the persons who administer, score, and interpret them. Crude tests in the hands of skilled professionals are far more effective than highly validated, quantitative results in the hands of naive managers. The basic problems of the apparent irrelevancy of most trait tests for job performance, together with the sensitive nature of their content, has led to the revival of an older but more appealing managerial assessment technique, the situational test.

Situational Tests

Situational tests are essentially samples of job performance. Popularized by experiences of the Office of Strategic Services in selecting agents during World War II, they have appeared in many forms in government and in private industry. Their appeal lies in their face validity; they simulate real life much more closely than any other assessment technique. Unmindful of the difficulties of assuring scoring reliability and objectivity, a job candidate recognizes a test's logic and its relevancy to the job for which he is being considered.

The value of the situational test, however, rests on its basically *synthetic* format. The subject combines his intellectual powers, motivational traits, prior learning, experience, and physical abilities in his own unique way to produce an observable pattern of behavior under a given set of circumstances that closely matches those of the role for which he is a candidate. The assessor obtains a range of information about the applicant's ability to use his intellectual, motivational, and social characteristics in a detail not possible through biographical questionnaires, interviews, or traditional trait tests.

Essentially, the situational test is a device by which a person is placed in a situation designed to elicit the behavior in a form similar to that required in the activity for which he is being evaluated. In other words, to find out how a person will actually do a job or to find out how he will react under a given set of circumstances, we design a sample situation having all or most of the aspects of the actual situation and then place him in it. The situation test, then, has three aspects:

1. A situation structured to elicit the behavior to be evaluated.
2. A role that will enable the examinee to provide a sample of his behavior in the situation.
3. A system of classifying and interpreting the behavior manifested in a standardized fashion that permits comparsion with other persons placed in identical situations.

The major disadvantage of situational tests is the lack of scoring economy, but this is offset by the substantial gains made in acquiring a deeper and more realistic assessment of the subject's abilities and his application of them. There are many variations of the situational test, but the principal ones in use in industry today are the *in-basket* and the *leaderless group discussion*.

THE IN-BASKET TEST

The in-basket test takes its name from the in-basket or tray on a manager's desk that is used to keep incoming correspondence in order and to provide a place to deposit incoming documents for his attention and action. Many of the problems a manager or an administrator faces on his job are presented to him in this manner. In fact, studies have shown that a majority of the inputs that a manager deals with daily come to him via this receptacle or by telephone.

The in-basket thereby simulates the problems of a specific management role and requires the examinee to handle them as if he were actually on the job. Usually, he is instructed that his predecessor has suddenly left for other parts and that he must now deal with what is left in the in-basket on the basis of his own managerial judgment.

The particular documents in the in-basket constitute the test items, and the actions which the participant takes with respect to them constitute the test. He makes his responses as though he were actually on the job, and whatever he produces represents his answers to the test problems. The participant's work requires the display of such complex skills as the ability to organize discrete pieces of information, to analyze the problems implicit in a situation, to consider the effects of alternative courses of action, and to make decisions on a variety of matters involving people and money.

Use and advantages. The in-basket exercise is used in several ways: for instruction, for research, or for assessment. When it is used for assessment, it must be carefully constructed and tailor-made to the situation. At present, there are no ready-made, standardized in-basket tests with objectively scorable answer sheets and a test manual describing norms and standardization and validation procedures. Only one, so far as is known, is now in preparation and experimentation. Nevertheless, many organizations—among them, Sears, Roebuck, AT&T, IBM, General Electric, The Port of New York Authority, and the cities of New York and Philadelphia—have used in-basket tests for selection and promotion purposes. They have found these tests to be efficient predictors of managerial performance, and the implications of the results have been so interesting as to warrant further research.

On the basis of work with over 8,000 managers, it may be said that the in-basket test has a number of advantages over ordinary assessment tests:

1. Unlike most standardized tests, it measures recall, insight, judgment, and organizing ability rather than mere recognition and speed of reaction.
2. It requires the assessee to use the higher mental processes of the fluid intelligence: analytical, critical, and strategic thinking and problem solving.
3. It provides an opportunity for an individual to demonstrate his creativity.
4. It tests an individual's ability to judge a situation correctly and to appreciate the social and interpersonal subtleties that always complicate a management problem.
5. Perhaps most importantly, it measures the subject's ability and willingness to make decisions.
6. Unlike most simulations and situational tests that are group-focused, the assessee's performance is not affected by the actions or the feedback of others.

While, in form, the in-basket test meets the psychologist's definition of a test as a systematic procedure for comparing the behavior of two or more persons, in substance it calls for the knowledge, skill, and personality that seem to constitute the managerial mind.

Application to assessment situations. There are many difficulties that have to be dealt with if the in-basket technique is to be utilized in assessment situations. The major problem is to evaluate the subject's performance, both systematically and quantitatively. In some usages, as in the Bell System, in-basket performance is not evaluated quantitatively; instead, the participant is interviewed by an assessor who determines what the subject has done and why. The Educational Testing Service uses specially trained scorers to evaluate the results of its in-basket exercises. And a specially constructed action report will enable the examinee to record his performance with the in-basket objectively, thus permitting scoring via mechanical means.

After repeated administration of in-basket exercises in a variety of settings to both public and private managers, the following conclusions seem to be in order:

1. The in-basket exercise simulates the functions of the managerial type of position most accurately.
2. The specific behavior elicited by the in-basket exercise that differentiates one participant from another in a unique manner is decision making in an organizational context.
3. The decision-making behavior displayed in an in-basket exercise is quite representative of the participant's real-life decision making in his own organization.
4. The decision-making behavior of the typical manager reflects his personal traits, his unique organizational experiences, and the perceptions he has of the organization milieu in which he must make his decisions.
5. The maximum potential of the in-basket as an administrative technique lies in its use as an assessment instrument.

THE LEADERLESS GROUP DISCUSSION

Another situational test that is in wide use in industry is the leaderless group discussion known by such names as the "group oral performance test" and the "group interaction test." The idea of this test is to assess an applicant's social skills by observing them in a typical group situation calling for a display of his interpersonal behavior. Essentially, the technique involves asking a group of candidates to act as a committee to discuss and to solve a problem under the observation of several raters. The problem can be structured or unstructured; the group can range in size from five to nine members.

In the highly structured version, the group is required not only to discuss the problem but to come up with a specific solution. Each member may be assigned a position to defend or a specific point of view which conflicts with that of another, thus insuring considerable debate among the participants.

One version of this test, for example, is the "draft board" game. Each applicant is instructed that he is a member of a local draft board and is assigned a "draftee" whom he is to persuade the five other draft-board members to exempt from military service. Since each "board member" has similar instructions and the board is required to draft at least five of the six potential draftees, a lively debate ensues.

In the unstructured version of the leaderless group discussion, the participants are merely given a topic—such as the merits and demerits of college-entrance examinations or the right of public employees to strike. Each participant may take any position on the matter that he wishes. There is likely to be less heated discussion in this unstructured type of test.

The advantages of the leaderless group discussion as a test are these:

1. It permits greater concentration on the part of the observer because he does not have to devote his attention to asking questions or motivating the assessee to interact with him.
2. It affords a longer period of observation. One can continue the discussion for three hours if required.
3. Candidates can be rated more uniformly and compared more readily with one another.
4. The candidates accept it with great enthusiasm.

The behavior displayed in this test appears to be small-group leadership skill. Since the crucial aspect of the test is the accuracy of the observations and of the evaluations drawn from them, the rating techniques become a major target for control. A number of rating forms have been developed that have yielded high degrees of validity.

Situational tests undoubtedly offer a very promising way of assessing managerial candidates. The logic behind them is as compelling as the evaluation of a person's driving skill by a road test. But this does not necessarily obviate the necessity of traditional trait tests. To fill out the dimensions of the managerial life-space, we need a combination of assessment techniques: traditional tests, administrative-ability tests, group-interaction tests, and performance evaluations. Each has a contribution to make, and the skillful administrator will put them all together over a period of time to develop a mosaic of information about the present, past, and future performance of the managerial group. And, with such an assessment strategy, he is ready to implement a program for the procurement and progression of managerial talent.

11

Finding Managerial Talent

A FEW years ago a large manufacturer of electrical goods undertook a no-holds-barred study of its successful plant managers. The researchers discovered that the characteristics of the engineers who had been promoted to managerial positions closely resembled those of the young men who had left the company in the first few years of their employment. Both groups had expressed strong interest in fields other than engineering and had aspired to positions with broad administrative responsibilities. Those engineers who stayed and were not promoted to managerial positions showed much greater interest in engineering work and aspired only to higher-level specialized jobs in engineering.

This finding illustrates a major problem of managerial progression. It has been estimated that only 2 out of 10 college recruits have the ability to become successful managers, that one out of 150 has the potential for a high-level decision-making post, and that only one out of 1,000 has the potential to make it all the way to the top. Yet young men with the broad interests, abilities, and ambitions to become managers are less likely to find their early assignments in a company challenging; they are therefore the most likely to leave. Nearly 95 percent of college recruits, whose average recruitment costs amount to over $3,000 per man, leave their first employer within ten years; and 50 percent do so in the first year. This high mortality rate in young talent is due for the most part to an inadequate managerial progression program that results in mobility not only in the lower ranks but at the top, too.

To find unusually dynamic, tough-minded, aggressive men to fill top posts, many corporations have to go outside to get them ready-made. This solution has stimulated a feverish hunt for managerial talent. Well over half of the 250 largest industrial corporations have used an executive-recruitment firm in the past five years.

American managers seem to have caught the message. To move up, you have to move out. It is no longer considered a mark of insecurity or disloyalty to keep in your desk an up-to-date and well-prepared résumé. A recent survey of nearly 1,600 managers shows how unwise it is for a company to believe its executives are so happy and secure that they would not consider a job change. Of the managers questioned, 22 percent said immediately that they would leave for a better opportunity, and 55 percent indicated that they would consider an offer seriously. And one executive register, which charges its clients $75 every six months to keep them informed of managerial job openings, maintains in its files over 13,000 clients, almost half of whom earn over $30,000 per year.

This situation places a heavy onus upon boards of directors, chief executives, and their counterparts in government and nonprofit institutions to undertake a program of management procurement and progression as an integral aspect of their short- and long-range planning responsibilities. Among the questions these men must answer are "Where will our future managers come from?" and "How shall we find and select them?" For, as we have just noted, turnover in the executive suite is not lost on the recently hired college trainee.

There is another effect, however, that goes beyond this young manager. Recruiting for top-level managers does not seem to upset middle managers to any great extent. They tend to stay on—a fact which accounts for the finding that nearly 90 percent of managerial positions are filled from within. They are filled within the middle management ranks.

But turnover at the bottom and recruitment at the top constitute a form of negative selection that makes its mark on middle management. This level of the management hierarchy becomes populated by men without the ability to inspire life, spirit, and a sense of direction in their subordinates. Young managers leave because they are exposed only to the thinking and the style of these middle managers. They rarely get a glimpse of what is happening and what is being said and thought at the summit.

What follows, then, is a steady erosion of management talent which represents an irreplaceable loss to the organization that is unable to challenge its new recruits—a loss, perhaps, to society as a whole because many of these young men may never get another opportunity to develop the talent necessary for success at the top. One more dimension of the managerial crisis thus becomes clear, and so does a solution.

In this and the following two chapters, we shall try to put all the models and ideas we have discussed together to develop this solution. Using as building blocks all our notions of human and organizational behavior, of the role of the manager as a decision maker, of the organizational milieu, of the human-resources personnel system, and of the decision-making model of assessment, we shall describe a strategy designed to—

1. Identify at an early stage men with the skills and abilities to move up to higher-level management positions.
2. Provide them with the challenge they need to stay with the organization.
3. Make sure they are ready when their time has come.

The Recruitment Process

The process begins by finding them, which is called *recruiting*. This is a little-understood management activity that has more than its share of discontinuities and contradictions, stemming largely from the uneven, helter-skelter, free-wheeling approach of our society to its manpower problems. Before we develop the managerial progression plan, we must first explore this business of prospecting for the crude ore.

Recruiting, then, is a process by which people in the labor market are induced to apply for employment in a specific organization. It is the first step in the selection and placement sequence; and, as the first step, it determines the effectiveness of all the others. If a company attracts only mediocre applicants, it can hire only mediocre employees.

The process is so obvious that few organizations have given much thought to it. There are comparatively few publications treating it in depth, and the few seminars that have been conducted usually devote more time to selection techniques than to recruiting. This is a serious omission that badly needs remedying. For most company problems stem from recruiting ineptitude rather than from poor selection procedures.

Recruiting, in short, is a science and an art involving a strategy, objectives, sources, and techniques. The corporate recruiting strategy consists of the plan it follows to generate a sufficient number of quality applicants to insure the selection of effective employees. The plan may be quite haphazard and ill-considered, or it may be deliberately designed and put into writing. But it requires a choice of the most fruitful sources to cultivate likely applicants and the adoption of appropriate techniques to identify the most qualified.

The Selection Ratio

Earlier we referred to one of the basic principles on which the decision-making assessment model was based: the selection ratio which holds that the more candidates the selector has to choose from, the more likely he is to make a good selection. Providing an adequate selection ratio is the primary goal of the recruiting effort.

Naturally, mere numbers do not guarantee a successful selection outcome. The attraction of a hundred mediocre candidates leads only to the selection of a mediocre employee, but by increasing the number of applicants the chooser increases the probability that in the group will be at least a few high-quality candidates. Thus a recruiting strategy consists of the identification of appropriate sources and then, through effective techniques, of generating a sufficiently high number of applicants from these sources.

RECRUITMENT SOURCES

The logical source for positions in the higher levels of a company is its own employees. Particularly in the case of managerial positions, the reason for this is not a matter of increased morale but, more importantly, one of selecting from among those about whom the company knows a good deal and who know a good deal about the company. Promoted candidates need less time to adjust to a new job and to perform effectively.

Eventually, however, people must be brought in from the outside—preferably at the entrance level, when the promotional system is functioning effectively, or occasionally (and for very good reasons) in higher-level positions. Knowledge of the best outside sources of managerial talent is a major advantage to a company. Drawing its new blood from fruitful sources is often more important than using appropriate assessment techniques.

Company referrals. The best outside recruitment source consists of the large pool of applicants who are attracted to the company by its reputation, products, or services; who are referred by customers, employees, or friends of the company; or who are recruited at professional meetings and conventions. These people share a significant characteristic: They submitted their applications to the company voluntarily because of their interest in it.

This pool can be a very productive reservoir of potential management if it is handled properly. The trouble is that it usually is not. The steady stream of applicants who visit the firm annually, even those who are given the "red carpet" treatment, are usually lost in the shuffle because their applications or inquiries arrive at a time when there is no suitable opening and their applications are then misfiled or destroyed. If a company lacks a way of processing applications so that they can be stored for effective retrieval when a vacancy opens up, it wastes a valuable recruitment asset. It is not uncommon for a manager who has been hired after a costly search to mention that he had filed an application with the company a few months earlier but had heard nothing from it.

Every company should establish an applicant-information storage-and-retrieval system as a matter of course. The particular system utilized will depend upon the size of the organization and the volume of applicants. A number of corporations are now developing computer-based recruitment-information systems. IBM, for example, utilizing a 1410 computer, has designed a system it calls "IRIS," which is utilized for prospective engineers and scientists. It works this way.

When a location needs a person, it lists the requirements on a requisition which is filed with all the current openings sent in from other locations. An applicant who answers an advertisement is sent a "Data-Pak" that asks for the number of years and the last year he worked in a specific occupational area. There is also space for him to list his academic honors, patents, professional societies, and job preferences. The information from the Data-Pak goes into a master file in the computer which matches applicants to job openings. The computer prints out the experience of all applicants who meet the job specifications. The printout and the résumé are then sent to the appropriate IBM location, where the file is reviewed and, if it seems desirable, the applicant is contacted.

Several professional consulting firms have developed electronic data-processing equipment to do much the same thing on a broader basis. Career-Ways Systems, for example, is aimed at the middle-management market. It feeds names and backgrounds onto a magnetic tape. When a client company sends in job specifications, the system cranks out of its computer the candidates who match those specifications and sends each a notification of the opening.

A New York firm, Employment Systems Inc., owns a data bank in Detroit and leases it to such other clients as the 89 offices of Management Recruiters International; university placement officers; some community service agencies, individual employees, and national manpower registries; and its own subsidiaries Compujob and Eurojob, student placement services. College students, of course, are the primary input to this data bank.

Whether highly sophisticated equipment is needed depends upon the volume of applicants. But the principle is the same in large or small installations. Company referrals represent a surprisingly good source of applicant material if they are processed through an effective storage-and-retrieval system.

Agencies and consultants. At times, management will need the services of special agencies and consultants to find managerial candidates. There are two distinct types of these firms: commercial employment agencies and executive search firms. Neither is to be confused with another type of consulting firm, the executive counseling agency. The counseling firm tries to help managerial candidates pursue their own job-hunting activities in a more systematic way by giving them deeper knowledge of their own capabilities and the way in which jobs are landed. The methods of some of these firms have been open to question, and a potential client should understand clearly that they are not in the business of executive recruiting.

There are important differences between the employment agency and the executive-search firm. Essentially, the employment agency, which is regulated by state law, represents the job seeker. It is engaged by him, and he (or his eventual employer) is obligated to pay the agency's fee. Usually, employment agencies work on jobs in the lower salary ranges.

The executive-search firm, which is not regulated except in one or two states, is engaged by a company seeking executive talent. It pays all fees and expenses. The search firm generally deals with vacancies above the $15,000-per-year class, with the largest cluster in the $30,000 range.

Anyone can walk into an employment agency and file his résumé with it, but most executive search firms discourage this practice. Both, however, operate on an individual-search basis and are interested, for the most part, in candidates to fill specific vacancies on hand. They do not engage in the practice of counseling applicants or storing applications against future openings. It is pretty much a waste of time for a job hunter to scatter his résumé among a host of employment agencies and executive-search firms, for they have no facilities for storage and retrieval.

Both types of recruiting firms have advantages and disadvantages. The employment agency can attract many job candidates quickly because of its wide variety of company clients and its accessibility. And, since it often knows where to find the most qualified candidates, it can save a company a good deal of time. The name of the company can be kept confidential for as long as is necessary. On the debit side, employment agencies have come in for a good deal of criticism (and not just from those outside the field), primarily because of the unprofessional conduct of some of its representatives. In any case, employment agencies by and large are geared to fill clerical, sales, and lower middle-management positions—areas in which they can operate on a high-volume basis. They are fairly ineffective in terms of top managerial recruitment.

Public employment services also handle managerial placements and, in some sections of the country, do an excellent job. But, on the whole, neither public nor commercial employment agencies are very productive sources of managerial talent.

Some professional societies maintain placement services which many companies deliberately ignore in the mistaken belief that the job seekers who use them are not the better candidates. Actually, these services represent a good recruitment source if they are cultivated properly and if the employer is willing to spend the time necessary to work with the professional society. The best way to utilize this source is through the regular company referral program and applicant-data bank.

All things considered, however, the two most popular sources of managerial candidates outside the organization are the *colleges* for junior managers and the *executive-search firms* for higher-level positions. Because each is so important, we shall explore them in more detail later.

Recruiting Techniques

Recruiting techniques refer to the steps taken by the company to induce candidates to apply for a job. There is quite a bit of literature on this aspect of recruiting; so we need only make a few general points here.

The corporate image. The organization's reputation is its most powerful recruitment aid. All its public relations and corporate advertising activities should reflect an awareness of this fact. If the company projects the image of a dynamic, progressive employer, there will never be a dearth of applicants.

But a handsome profile is not enough. The way in which applicants, their application blanks, or their letters of inquiry are processed also is a key element in recruitment. If an applicant is received courteously and efficiently, if his application receives prompt action, he will be favorably disposed toward the corporation.

A company that acts pleased to receive employment applicants and knows how to handle them when they get them will find its recruitment problems eased considerably.

Advertising. We live in the age of advertising, an industry that has contributed greatly to the postindustrial society. But, however valuable it is in selling toothpaste and cigarettes, advertising is often nearly a complete failure when it comes to recruiting. This may be because most employers do not know how to use employment advertising effectively and—what seems to be worse—neither do advertising agencies.

A curious investigator once undertook to answer over 200 advertisements placed in the Sunday business section of a large metropolitan newspaper. He mailed a résumé that fitted precisely the requirements specified in each advertisement. Within a week's time, he received replies from less than 10 percent of the advertisers. He received no reply at all from over 50 percent.

Newspaper advertising is largely ineffective because it attracts the person who is either out of work or dissatisfied with his present position. Besides, in today's labor market an advertisement can be literally buried in the thousands of ads surrounding it in the help-wanted section of the paper. The more highly qualified an applicant is, the less he is inclined to answer an advertisement, especially one requiring him to write in to a "blind" box number or to contact somebody at a local hotel. Well-qualified applicants will often hesitate to present their personal histories to an unknown inquirer.

Magazines, particularly the professional journals, are probably a better medium than the daily newspapers. But, whatever medium is used, the advertisement must have attention-getting appeal for someone idly leafing through the journal. Radio and TV advertising is better suited to high-volume recruitment. The only kind of newspaper or magazine advertising that is at all effective in managerial recruitment would seem to be the institutional advertising that appears in college publications.

Brochures, pamphlets, and films. An essential adjunct of the recruiting effort is an array of brochures, pamphlets, films, and filmstrips describing company employment and selection policies. Unfortunately, recruitment brochures are usually prepared by graphic specialists who are quite artistic

but have a limited knowledge of recruiting. Expensive paper, dramatic illus-
trations, and sharp copy have little impact on most employment candidates.

This is not to say that a well-designed brochure, interestingly laid out
and concisely written, is not without its value. However, recruiting literature
should be designed as simply and as tastefully as possible to fulfill its primary
purpose: to transmit information. The content is vastly more important than
the context. A brochure should describe the organization, its products, its
personnel policies and programs, typical career patterns, and existing benefit programs; and it should describe the employment process in detail. It can
be the employer's best friend or worst enemy, because it is the first and
last item an applicant checks in the employment process.

Nevertheless, employers continue to turn out large quantities of elaborate
and expensive brochures that are little read and are quickly "filed" in the
wastebasket. A better way of communicating with young people would be
through *their* medium—the motion picture. Although expensive to produce,
there is no quicker way to get inside a person, provided the film is made
with color, directness, and imagination. This, in particular, appears to be
the best technique to use for today's major recruiting effort, which is among
college students.

College Recruiting

It is not surprising that business, starving for high-talent personnel during the years following World War II, waded upstream to their spawning
grounds in the nation's colleges and proceeded to fish these waters with the
passion of a dry-fly angler. Out of this activity emerged what we shall refer
to as the college recruitment phenomenon.

Despite Nevitt Sanford's observation that "there is a remarkable discrep-
ancy between the wide public acceptance of the value of college education
and the paucity of demonstrated knowledge that it does some good,"[1] no
self-respecting business or government agency considers its personnel program satisfactory unless it includes an extended schedule of campus visits.
As with similar ventures that began as a worthwhile idea and evolved into
a national institution, the college recruitment phenomenon has turned out
to be a mixed blessing for both employers and college graduates.

By the end of the 1960s, college recruiting as a source of managerial talent had become a wasteful and inefficient process that serves mainly to push

[1] Nevitt Sanford, ed., *The American College* (New York: Wiley, 1962).

the salaries of graduating seniors to the point where they are pricing themselves out of the labor market.

The "Prehistoric" Period

Prior to World War II, very few major companies mantained what could be termed a college recruiting program. One recent survey indicated that over 80 percent of the companies visiting a midwestern college campus inaugurated their college recruiting programs after 1950. But the companies that did recruit in the prewar years, and in those years immediately after World War II, enjoyed a reception that was far different from that which has now emerged—one that was more in keeping with the true purposes of campus recruiting.

In the early days, when college recruiting techniques were subordinate to their purposes, a campus visit was a highly personal thing. Universities welcomed those companies that were interested in their graduating seniors. A company representative would arrange his visit directly with a departmental chairman or a dean. He would be met at the railroad station by a welcoming committee of faculty and students. After dinner with faculty members, he would meet in the faculty lounge with a group of interested seniors. The following day he might be invited to lecture to one of the classes, after which he would conduct a series of leisurely interviews with those seniors who had been recommended by their faculty advisers. Following the interviews, he would discuss each young man's qualifications with faculty members. He would leave the campus with a fairly clear idea of whom he should recommend for employment.

A National Institution

The year 1949 marked the end of this prehistoric period of college recruiting. In that year, such experts as the Bureau of Labor Statistics were actually expressing concern about the oversupply of engineers and college graduates in general. In the following year came the war in Korea, and with it the rapid buildup in the American economy, awakening management to the need to insure a continuous supply of high-talent personnel.

At that time industry's need for engineers, scientists, and nontechnical graduates—the accumulation of twenty years of neglect—was indeed very

great. But, as in the case of other wartime shortages, the demand was inten-
sified by the practice of stockpiling college graduates. It soon became apparent that to get one's share of high-talent manpower a firm had to go
directly to the campus. College recruiting became a national institution.

The professor who worked part-time as a contact with the few companies
that visited his campus gave way to a professional placement officer. The
small cubby-hole interviewing quarters were rapidly expanded into elaborate
placement offices with chrome trim and deep-pile carpeting. College recruiting meant hordes of company representatives swarming over the nation's
campuses, in many cases outnumbering the students whom they came to
hire.

The on-campus interview became nothing more than a rough screening
of men on a wholesale, assembly-line basis. Because of the large number of
company recruiters involved and the limited college placement facilities,
offers were made solely on the basis of a 20-minute interview and a 2-or-3-
minute review of a young man's personal data sheets.

As more management positions were allocated to graduating seniors as
part of the "management training" program, the social status of a college
education began to rise. Statistics were published widely, showing in dollars
and cents the increase in life earnings a college degree would bring.

The rise in earnings and status naturally motivated parents to make the
necessary sacrifices to send their sons and daughters to college. The supply
of high school graduates entering the labor market began to decline. Business was forced to restructure many higher-level clerical positions that were
normally filled by high school graduates to "staff and administrative assistant" positions more appropriate to a college graduate.

This process generated additional pressure to recruit college graduates
—which in turn created a demand for more colleges. In 1950, for example,
there were 2.2 million students enrolled in America's 1,800 colleges and universities. Now, in 1970, there are approximately 7 million students in 2,500
colleges, and we are told that by 1985 over 10 million Americans will be enrolled in "institutions of higher learning." Each year, 600,000 bachelor's,
160,000 master's, and 21,000 doctor's degrees are awarded by American universities. While only a minority of these degree holders go into private industry, it spends over $750 million per year to get its share of them.

The result has been a mad scramble, joined in by government, educational,
and nonprofit institutions, for the favor of the graduating senior who has
acquired a distorted idea of his own significance. The fact is that there is

probably little connection between college performance and success in business. A recent survey of executives indicated that although they were pleased with the college graduates they have recruited in the past few years, they had the following reservations:

1. The short-term expectations of graduates entering business are unrealistic.
2. Companies in general give graduates more than a fair day's pay for less than a fair day's work.
3. The starting salaries for college graduates are completely out of line.

For a More Realistic Program

The best way to deal with the present situation would be to abandon college recruiting altogether. In many companies this may not be possible for a variety of reasons, some excellent and some deplorable. The next best alternative is to adopt a realistic, low-pressure recruiting program.

This more effective approach to college recruiting should be based on two ideas: First, the employer should look for an educated man rather than a person with a degree. The educated man is one who, regardless of his exposure to formal education, has a cultivated intellect plus the breadth of vision and the discipline of mind to cope with real-life problems, to see the full implications of his actions, and to make decisions on the basis of facts rather than precedents. As Frederick R. Kappell pointed out as president of AT&T, the man himself is far more important than the school he went to, the grades he achieved, or the extracurricular activities in which he engaged. The fact that a young man is a graduate *cum laude* of one of America's most prestigious universities is insufficient basis for hiring him. A company has to find out through appropriate assessment techniques what manner of man he really is.

Second, the employer should select before rather than after hiring. Selecting one out of 30 or 50 applicants is neither time-consuming nor expensive if those who are offered employment accept it and if those who accept it stay with the company for a substantial period of time, grow, and advance.

A realistic college recruiting program, in any case, will encompass knowledge of where to recruit, how to recruit, and how to choose company recruiters.

WHERE TO RECRUIT

The first principle to follow in college recruiting is to recruit at as few schools as possible. The idea of visiting campuses for public relations or for prestige purposes is impractical, illusory, and unfair. After management determines its needs, it should carefully pick the colleges that are likely to provide the type of person it requires, and it should exclude all other colleges from its program.

The second principle concerns applicant quality. This has two aspects: the caliber of the college and the caliber of the student body. For business managers, it would be reasonable to assume that a business school would be the place at which to recruit. But, despite the supply of business-educated graduates, the evidence for the assumption is minimal.

Enrollment in collegiate schools of business and in college departments of business administration now approximates 600,000 students. A series of reports by the Committee of Economic Development, the Ford Foundation, and the Carnegie Corporation concerning the state of the nation's collegiate business schools all reached the same conclusions: They found these schools suffering from low-caliber students, inadequate faculties, and curricula that, to the neglect of liberal arts and science studies, are marked by excessive vocationalism and a proliferation of specialized courses that have no place at the college level. These surveys concluded that the business schools, though "restless giants in the halls of education," were not providing the kinds of education tomorrow's businessmen will need. In the Ford Study, Professors Gordon and Howell [2] summed up by saying that "it is practically impossible to do in the four undergraduate years what the undergraduate business schools try to do: to provide both a general and a professional education of satisfactory quality."

As an outcome of these studies, several attempts have been made to change the character of college business education. The ensuing revolution, however, has taken place in the graduate schools, where the emphasis is no longer on the standard marketing, accounting, or business-law courses but on such subjects as quantitative analysis, business policy, and organizational behavior.

It undoubtedly comes as a surprise to no one that thousands of today's outstanding managers entered business from the liberal arts colleges or from law and engineering schools and that thousands of tomorrow's managers

[2] Robert A. Gordon and James E. Howell, *Higher Education for Business* (New York: Columbia Univ. Press, 1959).

will undoubtedly possess similar educational backgrounds. The myth that liberal arts candidates are fit only for teaching or public administration is just that. There is evidence to indicate that, over the long run, the liberal arts graduate makes a superior manager if his education is supplemented by programs aimed at management-skills development.

But there is the matter of the quality of the school, too. Some colleges are little more than advanced child-care institutions providing places for young men and women to while away their time because, even though they are out of high school, they are not yet available for the labor market. Many of the recently founded community colleges are at this developmental stage; undoubtedly they will be upgraded, but they certainly are not now spawning grounds for potential managers.

But there is an opposite extreme. The high-quality college may be just as poor an incubator of managerial talent. The so-called high-prestige schools, for example, now enroll two types of students: the sons of upper- or upper-middle-class families who can afford to send them there, or of lower-middle- or lower-class families who are in the university on scholarships. The probability of either group's producing young men with managerial qualities is quite low for varying reasons: motivation, intellectual ability, social skill, positive emotional adjustment. Church-related schools, smaller liberal arts colleges, or even the larger urban universities are much more likely to turn out men with the toughness of mind, the intellect, the emotional disposition, and the ambition to become effective decision makers.

How to Recruit

An effective selection program must be carefully worked out from the initial contact with the school to the induction of the selected trainee into the company. The entire program should be supervised by a central staff unit, and it must be a year-round activity. A company cannot visit a college campus once or twice a year, shake a few hands, interview a few students, and hope to recruit high-level management trainees. The organization must establish rapport with the school and with those officials who can help it tell its story to the students.

Placement director and professors. The place to start is with the placement director, who is an administrator, not a teacher. He counsels students about companies and careers and can be quite helpful in giving the recruiter a picture of the college, its students' attitudes, its special programs, and its hiring salaries. The placement officer also announces the company's visit, schedules students' appointments, and catalogs company literature.

It will also be helpful to meet some of the faculty. Professors deal with students regularly, and in the students' minds they are the respected "pros" about business. If they speak well of a company, it is bound to impress the students.

The program is launched by calling the placement director for an appointment to see him. In this interview, the recruiter should establish specific dates for formal visits to the campus, setting up as many interviews per year as the school will permit and as far in advance as it will allow. It is best to obtain dates in the middle of the school's recruiting season because by that time the student will be aware of recruiting but will still be uncommitted. In selecting dates, too, it is desirable to find out which days of the week are better than others because of class scheduling or school work. It is also desirable to ask if posters may be sent to help publicize the recruiting dates.

After the initial call, the company should forward advance copies of its recruitment literature to the placement office. Two days before the actual interviewing day, it is well to check with the placement director to confirm the date and to get an idea of how many students have requested interviews. If a large number have signed up, it may be a good idea to send additional interviewers or to carry over the schedule to another day.

The campus interview. The recruiter should arrive on campus in sufficient time to meet his schedule. As far as possible, 30 minutes should be allocated to each interview. It is not necessary to ask a student to complete the company's application blank at this interview because most college placement offices require students to complete a standard form at the beginning of the year. The reproduced copies of this form which are made available to all visiting employers are usually adequate for initial screening purposes. But the interviewer should certainly complete his own interview report, recording his observations during the interview and his overall impression of the applicant.

He should assure the student that the purpose of the campus interview is to determine whether his interest and qualifications warrant further exploration at the company's offices. He should inform the student that the company will indicate its interest in him within three days of the interview.

The company visit. The company visit should consist of a full day of assessment, the main features of which will be described in the next chapter. The visit should also provide the student with an opportunity to get a clear idea of company operations and his prospects for advancement in it.

Within two weeks after the visit, a decision should be made and the student informed. Also, it is highly desirable to inform the faculty and other administrative officials, such as the placement director, of the outcome of the company's recruiting activities at the college.

THE COMPANY RECRUITER

The key man in the college recruiting effort is the recruiter who visits the campus to make the all-important initial contact with the college and the student body. One study concluded that he is a more important variable in the recruitment outcome than his company. Since, in the mind of the average student, he represents the company, his image is the company's image. Most of the problems colleges have with the recruiting process center on the recruiter himself.

Placement officers are critical of recruiters because they often fail to show up on time, they do not stay on schedule, they run off to catch a plane before the last man has been interviewed, they take up too much of the placement officer's time when they have light schedules, and they try to circumvent the placement office and work directly through the faculty. They also, it is claimed, make too many unreasonable demands on the placement staff, they promise more than they can deliver, they press students to accept unsuitable jobs, and—even though it may be early in the recruiting season, they urge them to accept offers immediately.

Many companies select line managers to do the campus interviewing. This, as we have said, is a mistake unless these men are very carefully trained. Line managers think in terms of their own unit needs, ignore the total company's requirements (which the student is more interested in) and are generally unfamiliar with the details of the personnel, fringe-benefit, and compensation schedules.

On the other hand, full-time professional recruiters, because they continuously visit many campuses, become fatigued by travel and the pressures of their work. Their interviews tend to become mechanical and stereotyped, their tempers short, and their judgments warped.

But the most damaging aspect of the college recruiter is the dubious quality of the results he obtains. A majority of recruiters, according to one study, harbor the illusion that they are excellent personality judges. Professor Stephen Carroll, of the University of Maryland, found that most recruiters are easily impressed by an applicant's performance if it matches their "image" of the man required for the job—good looks, prompt answers, and an easy going style.[3] In fact, says Carroll, looks and likability are the key criteria of college recruiters because they believe that, by hiring a handsome and pleasant person who is fun to work with, they're getting a cordial job companion for the manager.

The best strategy seems to call for using professional recruiters as a cadre and temporarily assigning line managers to this activity as supplements. Those selected must be intensively trained in interviewing, in campus etiquette, and in the requirements and the benefits of the positions they are recruiting for. Wherever possible, both a professional recruiter and a line manager should go together to a college and even interview jointly if the schedule makes it possible.

Problems with College Recruiting

As we have already indicated, college recruiting faces many difficulties today, difficulties that raise serious questions as to its practicality as a way of bringing new managers into an organization. These difficulties have to do with the intensity of the competition for graduating seniors, the attitudes of these seniors, and the inflationary salaries they demand.

The competition for college seniors. In a recent year, one large corporation interviewed 10,000 students at 300 colleges and hired 1,500; another, a large oil company with six full-time recruiters backed by 175 line-organizational people, conducted 15,000 interviews, made 1,800 offers, and hired 675 people. And over 300 recruiters descended upon one college of 65 seniors interested in entering business upon graduation.

Such practices represent considerable effort, time, and money, much of which is wasted. Obviously, with campaigns of these dimensions, a top-ranking college senior may get as many as 10 to 12 offers. But the problem is getting worse.

The number of college graduates going into the military service or on to postgraduate work is increasing sharply. At a top-flight college, as many as 80 percent will go to graduate school and thus become unavailable to industry. Those interested in going directly to work are generally in the lower sections of the graduating class academically, socially, and intellectually.

In fact, the graduate schools are vying keenly with business and industry to attract undergraduate seniors. One bank has indicated that the graduate

---

[3] "Handsome College Men Overimpress Recruiters," *Employee Relations Bulletin,* Rept. 1144 (May 14, 1969), pp. 1–5.

schools are its biggest competitors. In 1968, fewer than a third of the 600,000 graduating seniors were available for jobs in business according to government estimates, this figure being down roughly 50 percent from 1959.

Student attitudes toward business. In addition, at some of the better colleges there seems to be a substantial disaffection against business. As one student put it, "Business isn't where the action is." Consequently, company recruiters may hear so much antibusiness talk at these schools that they fail to return. The undergraduates, being somewhat dissatisfied with the whole society, simply do not show up for interviews. One large corporation, which, on the basis of past experience, would expect to schedule 50 interviews at a prestige college, now finds only four or five on its schedule. The picketing on many campuses against some companies and military organizations is not helping, either.

This is not to say that the antibusiness attitude prevails among college students. Far from it. Surveys indicate that most students respect business and see the American free-enterprise system as the main source of the country's strength. But vocal minorities, growing graduate-school enrollments, and the tight labor market have exacerbated college recruiting difficulties.

Inflated salaries. Spurred on by widely published surveys, the starting salaries of college graduates have increased at the rate of about 5 percent a year for the past 15 years. Consequently, an inexperienced young man now requests and usually gets a salary far beyond the value of his contribution to the organization. And the salaries of graduate students and technically trained people have accelerated even more, reaching levels that are forcing many employers out of the market altogether. From the standpoint of the national economy and the development of the young people concerned, this purely artificial situation is serious. Moreover, the problem is further complicated by the fact that in most instances those hired perform duties incommensurate with their salaries.

Most recently, there has developed what is referred to as the M.B.A. cult. There is no question that an M.B.A. is intensively trained and well prepared for taking his place in the modern corporation. But the M.B.A. is a unique individual—at least in his own view, if not in fact. He is likely to be very impatient with his early job assignments because in graduate school he was exposed to top-level decision making in computer simulations and business games. It may be difficult for him to make the cultural transition from a senior to a junior management role even though the former was purely fictitious.

The starting salaries of M.B.A.s are very high and almost never in line with their initial responsibilities. Therefore, before hiring an M.B.A. a company should weigh carefully, not only its managerial-manpower needs, but his probable salary and job expectations and the impact of the recruit on other managerial personnel. Hiring an M.B.A. is only the first step; the real challenge is keeping him. The extent of the challenge is indicated by the fact that many M.B.A.s are attracted to the consulting, financial analysis, and computer service fields where the action is faster and more exciting and the payoff is quicker.

Alternatives to College Recruiting

In the light of these problems, it is not a bad idea for a company to take a hard look at its college recruitment program and seriously question its bedrock necessity. For most employers, not only is it really unnecessary but there are more suitable alternatives to it.

Unless it is bound by a poor location or a poor competitive position, therefore, a company might very well discontinue college recruiting. The idea is not to abandon the procurement of college-trained young men, but rather to end or at least to limit the wasteful effort entailed in on-campus interviewing. It is wasteful both for the college that has to maintain facilities and staff badly needed elsewhere and for the company that has to support such a costly and elaborate effort. The money spent by the colleges for its placement activities can be used more effectively in counseling and in guidance and the company can put its funds to better use in a college-relations program.

A College-Relations Program

As the major beneficiaries of the products of the nation's colleges, employers have an obligation to take an active interest in their welfare. To pursue this interest, each employer should institute an intensive college-relations program, thus shifting the emphasis from "What can the colleges do for us?" to "What can we do for the colleges?"

A college-relations program continues to make the company's manpower needs known on the campus. Advertising in college newspapers and visits to the faculties proceed as before, and the company offers assistance to the university by furnishing educational help to needy students, by contributing to endowment funds, and by offering faculty members employment during the summer. This program enhances the corporate image on the campus much more than a mere recruitment effort.

The company must of course provide the means by which students can inquire about career opportunities. It also continues the practice of inviting interested young men to its plant or corporate office for further consideration. But the initiative and the enterprise are now up to the student. Instead of having the company seek him out, he has to seek the company out. This is a marvelous selection technique appreciated only by those companies whose human-resources policies and programs can really stand public scrutiny.

Recruiting thus is placed on a year-round basis that allows any college graduate interested to apply at his convenience. If all employers in the United States adopted this approach, the whole society would benefit because it permits the simultaneous cultivation of other sources of managerial talent.

Former Armed-Forces Officers

One alternative source, for example, is the pool of young men leaving the military services. Former junior officers of the armed forces are more mature and more realistic about their work goals than inexperienced college graduates. A young ex-officer is a man who is used to giving and taking orders. The company that hires him will get a lot more for its money than from even an M.B.A. fresh off the campus.

These undeniable facts are by no means being overlooked. Officers are increasingly the target of corporate recruiters who are turning away from the strife-torn college campuses and competing briskly for the best of the 8,000 officers being mustered out of the services each month. Military newspapers are accepting recruitment advertising, and several personnel agencies —or military departments in regular employment agencies—have grown up to handle this demand. One organization has placed more than 3,000 officers in jobs since it was formed in 1964, and it has staged conferences across the country for 10,000 officers and 500 companies. This agency boasts of a placement score of nearly 42 percent in contrast to campus recruiters, who normally expect 25 percent acceptance of their offers. There is a natural bond between today's junior officers and senior corporate managers, many of whom served as officers in World War II or in Korea.

The Insurance Community's Answer

Another approach has been developed in the insurance community, which has established its own college for training future managers. The reason for this development is simple: For the insurance industry in general, the annual safari to the college placement office had in recent years turned up very few trophies. Thus, in September 1962, the College of Insurance—a corporate program—made its debut in lower Manhattan. While it is still too early to evaluate this program, the fact that there are now 65 insurance organizations sponsoring it and sharing two-thirds of its tuition costs is testimony to its promise. Most of the sponsoring organizations have found that their total investment in this enterprise is far less than the cost involved in recruiting and training the green college student.

Executive Search

The best answer to the frenzied and often futile college recruitment effort is a properly implemented career-progression program, which we shall describe in the next chapter. But, before concluding this discussion of recruiting, we must look at the recruitment of mature managers through executive-search firms.

Executive search is, of course, that popular method of recruiting managerial talent by hiring it out of someone else's company. What is now known as the executive-search firm provides a way to do this without reproach. Such a firm is a consulting organization consisting of one or more persons involved in the business of helping companies to locate and hire executives. As we have already noted, it is always engaged by management, which pays for its services.

The exact number of executive-search firms in the United States is not known, but it has been estimated that there are approximately a thousand. Since there were fewer than 50 in 1958, their proliferation has been astonishing. A National Industrial Conference Board's survey in 1966 showed that the responding companies recruited outside for 257 appointments and that executive-search firms helped with 108 of these.

The standard fee charged by search firms ranges from 15 to 25 percent of the recruited manager's first year's compensation—plus search costs, which usually total 10 percent of the fee. Some recruiters engage in searches on an hourly or a daily basis, and nearly all guarantee the right man in that they will replace the appointee at no charge if he fails to make the grade in the first year.

Advantages over the Direct Approach

To begin with, most companies usually try the "find him ourselves" method; that is, they inquire about possible candidates in banks, advertising agencies, accounting firms, investment houses, or law firms where they have friends and associates. But in today's competitive managerial market these home-made recruiting efforts are expensive, time-consuming, and often unavailing. When the facts become obvious, the use of an executive-search firm is considered. It has the following advantages.

Experience. The recruiter has a wide acquaintance with men at all levels in a variety of businesses who are sources of qualified candidates or who may become candidates themselves. He maintains extensive personal contacts and records of successfully employed executives whose interest in exploring other opportunities can be probed quickly, accurately, and confidentially without embarrassing anyone.

Objectivity. The recruiter can communicate objectively with both client and candidate. His understanding of the client organization's needs allows him to assist in defining these needs precisely. He can accurately describe the company to the candidate and realistically apprise the company of the applicability of the candidate's qualifications to the job it wants to fill. There is a minimum of surprise when both eventually meet.

Anonymity. The recruiting firm can evaluate personnel in competitive companies without involving the client until it meets the candidate. And there are many reasons for keeping a search under cover:

1. The need for a new top manager may point up a weakness in the employer's ranks that competitors could exploit.
2. The recruiter's cloak is valuable where a firm wants a top manager from the outside without upsetting insiders who may be aiming at the job in question. In this way, an independent recruiter makes a diplomatic circumvention of the company's promotion policies when the hiring of an outsider is an obvious answer to a problem.
3. Anonymity can be useful when a company wants to put out feelers to a particular person who cannot be approached directly.

Expense. A recruiting firm can conclude a search in a relatively short time as compared to the company's own staff, which has many other responsibilities. It also saves the client's time by exposing him only to qualified candidates.

Professionalism. The recruiter can meet and establish rapport with potential candidates in an atmosphere of confidence, dignity, and self-respect.

Guides to Choosing a Firm

Whether or not the decision to rely upon an executive-search firm has been preceded by an attempt on the part of the company to do its own recruiting, successful use of outside help depends on the following factors:

1. The company should be sure it is taking the right position to the executive-search firm. Although the pressures may be considerable, the retention of a recruiting consultant may really only obscure a fundamental organizational flaw.
2. The company should develop realistic man specifications to cover the type of person it seeks and the position for which it seeks him.
3. The company should assign an appropriate salary to the position.

If these factors are considered carefully, the recruiter's task is greatly simplified. It is the bane of a managerial recruiter's existence to be asked to provide candidates for the wrong job at the wrong time and, further, to have an unrealistic salary level specified—not to mention personality characteristics that are not conducive to good working relationships with the other members of the management team.

As a rule, companies should choose recruiters by interviewing three or four of them, checking them out to insure ethical practices and professional competence. There are many shoestring operators in this business; therefore, it is important to ask an organization to show what it has done in particular job areas. Celanese Corporation's personnel director, James McCulloch, suggests the following guidelines in choosing an executive-search firm: [4]

1. Avoid firms that use high-pressure sales techniques, make overblown claims, and are indiscreet about their dealings with other companies.
2. Select the firm that can offer real help to key management people, that doesn't work with a system of long reports, and that appreciates the value of management time.

[4] "How to Select and Use an Executive Search Firm," *The Manager's Letter* (January 20, 1961), p. 4.

3. Give the search firm enough time to do a proper job; don't wait until the need is desperate. If given enough time (from 60 to 120 days), most searches are successful.
4. Furnish detailed and accurate information. Allow the search firm access to the organization and to its executives. Establish a relationship of real confidence by having the firm delegate one man to carry on all contacts with the company.

Not all searches are successful. In a speech delivered to a group of personnel professionals, Ward Howell, president of the executive-search firm, Ward Howell & Associates, lists these reasons for search failures:

1. Many searches are made for the purposes of comparison between an inside man and possible outside candidates.
2. The successful candidate shows up as a result of efforts made by the client before the search firm was engaged. In addition, some clients use more than one search firm at a time (a bad practice).
3. The job function is changed after the search is started; that is, the client changes his mind about his needs as the search progresses.
4. The search firm is unable to find suitable candidates. This happens because the client is unwilling to pay enough salary or because his requirements are so diverse that they cannot be found in one man.
5. The client is unable to interest suitable candidates.

With the great demand for experienced talent, it is gradually becoming obvious to the business manager that he is living in a golden age. And he is eager to take advantage of the situation. The number of top managers ready to consider offers from executive-search firms is astonishing; and, as we have pointed out, these are not necessarily disloyal employees. They are simply enjoying a seller's market—a market that reflects not only a new era of professional self-confidence and security in the executive suite, but the inadequacies of the managerial progression program. To keep a man happy on his job and resistant to the enticements of competitors it is necessary to build a solid career program for him.

12

Moving Managers Up

R ECENTLY another of those tongue-in-cheek books—*The Peter Principle*,[1] commenting on the manners and mores of the occupants of the executive suite—reached the best-seller lists. The authors of *The Peter Principle* state simply that in a hierarchy every employee tends to rise to his own level of incompetency because he will be repeatedly promoted until he reaches a job he cannot do. They conclude, therefore, that for every job there is a man somewhere who cannot do it and that sooner or later they will find each other.

As sly and amusing as it is, *The Peter Principle* is only one more in a long line of books, novels, and plays satirizing aspects of the managerial life-space. *Parkinson's Law*, *The Pyramid Climbers*, and *The Organization Man* are fairly recent examples of this literary genre, but the tradition goes back to Sinclair Lewis's *Babbitt* and to Frank Norris's *The Octopus* and *The Pit*. The resulting combination of fictional and nonfictional efforts depicts the manager as a status-seeking organization man lost in the lonely crowd of an affluent society, dwelling in a split-level trap in exurbia and commuting daily in his gray flannel suit to an executive suite in the crystal palace. What is interesting, however, is the fact that most of these artistic clichés focus on the manager's struggle to fulfill the American dream of reaching the top of the pyramid. That this struggle is interesting, entertaining, and even comical

[1] Laurence J. Peter and Raymond Hull, *The Peter Principle* (New York: Morrow, 1969).

to the general public is attested to by the financial success of the play and film *How to Succeed in Business Without Really Trying*.

Of course, these naive parodies written by men who probably never saw the inside of a manager's office aren't really so funny or so very accurate. The overall impression that they convey of the manager as an ulcer-ridden, unhappy adventurer, compulsively seeking advancement, is badly over-drawn. On the contrary, one survey of executive health found, for example, that the mortality rate of large-company executives is less than half that of the average American white male. And a national study of mental health showed that managers obtain greater satisfaction from their jobs because they are more ego-involved in them. They face greater problems, but these problems reflect not so much dissatisfaction as the greater expectations and demands of their jobs. Pyramid climbing, it would appear, is a healthy and happy activity.

The parodies of managerial life may, however, have a point that we do well to consider. Managers are by nature power-oriented; they possess high energy resources; they project strong drives and are ambitious and aggressive. They continually seek greater challenges and increased responsibility. All of which is to the good, for these are the traits of an effective manager. The most powerful motivational force for him, then, is career advancement. Moving up is not only the name of the game, it is the whole ball game.

To be sure, the restless striving that is the mark of the effective manager can also be an organization's Achilles' heel. If it does not provide constructive channels for legitimate managerial ambitions, a corporation will lose competent managers, fail to attract them in the first place, or exhaust its energies in internal political conflict.

In spite of current executive-search activity and the appearance of high managerial mobility, over 90 percent of all managerial positions are filled from within, and the trend is toward more of the same. In 1945, only one-quarter of company presidents had moved up from the executive vice-presidency of the same company; in 1960 over half of the presidents had done so. Earlier studies of the typical corporate president showed that he had joined his company before he was 30, after a short stint elsewhere, and had moved up to the presidency through the vice-presidency.

Some authorities view this stability as undesirable, a tribute to the power of the golden chains that bind men to their present companies. The fact is, however, that—for managers at least—the advantages of corporate mobility have yet to be demonstrated. It is true that corporations must oc-casionally bring new talent in if only for its cross-pollination effect. But most

high-level positions are handled best by men who have a firsthand appreciation of the problems faced by those in the lower echelons.

The difficulty is not so much with the American tendency to promote
from within as with the methods by which promotions are made.

Traditional Promotion Programs

As components of either the political or the career personnel system,
traditional promotion programs are based on one of two measures: seniority
or supervisory judgment, neither of which is really adequate. To illustrate
how the traditional promotion program operates, let us examine the purely
fictitious but unfortunately typical case of the American Buttonhook Company.

The president of this company is disturbed one morning by the letter of
resignation he receives from his marketing vice-president, who informs him
that he has accepted a position with a larger and more diversified competitor,
General Buttonhook Systems, Inc. Shocked and dismayed at losing a key
man, the president puts what he considers to be a well-designed promotion
plan into operation by calling his personnel vice-president into his office.
Together they review the multicolored "ABC Management Inventory
Chart" on the office wall. Since it lists three backup men for each key vice-
president, this chart includes the three candidates for the marketing vice-
presidency designated by the departing executive.

The president and his personnel vice-president next withdraw from the
files the folders containing the "track records" of the three candidates listed
on the replacement chart: White, Brown, and Green. White, the assistant
marketing vice-president, has been with the American Buttonhook Company
for the past 20 years, and both executives can cite his record from memory.
Competent, knowledgeable, steady, and reliable, he has been passed over
for promotion three previous times because he just doesn't have *it*. He is an
excellent No. 2 man who lacks the drive, the imagination, and the pzazz for
the top spot.

Next the two executives consider Brown, the market research manager,
who is radically different from White. He has drive and aggressiveness to
spare, but he can't get along with White or, for that matter, anyone but his
boss. He spends his time in organizational politics and conspiracies. Anyway,
White has forgotten more about buttonhooks than Brown will ever know.

Next they take a look at Green, who is just beginning to impress his associates as national accounts manager. He has been with the company four years, looks like a real comer, and could take over the top job within the next five years. But, shaking their heads, the two conclude that Green is not ready. Anyway, it would be impossible to promote him over White's head, and Brown would quit on the spot.

Reluctantly, they agree that there is no one inside the company to promote. The personnel vice-president then calls his favorite recruiting firm, which, after a two months' search, comes up with Edgar Beaver, a man with a strong buttonhook background, a master's degree in marketing, and an impressive record of steady progress in his previous four companies.

Beaver is hired. White accepts being passed over philosophically; it has happened to him before. Besides, what else can he do? He has a nice stake in the company stock-option plan and only eight years to go to retirement. Brown breathes a sigh of relief (because he hoped White would not get the job) and proceeds to put himself in right with Beaver. And Green? He registers the whole situation in silence, prepares his résumé, and six months later resigns to take a job with General Buttonhook Systems. Two years later, Beaver moves on to a bigger job with a buttonhook-consulting firm. And the president of American Buttonhook begins another search for a marketing vice-president wondering why there is so much turnover in this division of the company.

The answer here is fairly simple. What really was wrong at American Buttonhook was the lack of a promotion plan, a way of keeping the promotion channels open with good men moving up through them and a means of keeping everyone informed of what was happening and why. The ABC Management Inventory was beautiful to look at, but it was nothing but wallpaper covering a disorganized hit-or-miss system. The real basis of American Buttonhook's promotion system was seniority plus the uninformed opinions and biases of the president and his personnel vice-president. And, even if the decision to recruit had been correct, there was no way of explaining the reason for it to others and no plan to prevent it from occurring again.

Promotion by Seniority

Despite disclaimers to the contrary, the underlying criterion of many managerial promotion systems is length of service either in the job or in the company. Although quite destructive to management morale and to the retention of promising young managers, time, under most promotion systems, is the measure of all things. Its emergence as the ultimate criterion of advancement occurs simply because, in the absence of better ways of measuring promotability, it is the only yardstick available.

The trouble lies in the job and man specifications. The company builds additional years of experience into each succeeding level of management, so that it is impossible to move from one level to another without putting in one's time regardless of ability. The result is an organizational lockstep in which those with the greatest ability advance no faster than those less qualified. To move to a respectable level in an organization requires 15 to 20 years, putting a man in his middle years—at a period of life, psychologically speaking, when his willingness to innovate, to think flexibly and imaginatively, is somewhat diminished. And those who have reached this level naturally seek to protect themselves from the competition of younger and perhaps abler men.

One characteristic that sets the younger manager apart from his older counterpart is impatience with the seniority system. In response to a question in a recent survey—"Are young managers getting a break?"—65 percent of managers under age 35 stated that less than three years' experience was adequate to qualify them for higher positions in their career paths, whereas only 35 percent of the over-35 managers saw three years as adequate. In those organizations dominated by career personnel systems, top management tries with only limited success to change promotion programs that are essentially based on seniority. Continually, however, they clash with the professional corps of managers who rose high in the ranks by the slow climb up the age-and-length-of-service ladder.

Promotion by Supervisory Nomination

Seniority, however, is secondary as a problem to a more serious one—that of promotion by supervisory nomination.

It is a fundamental tenet of modern management that the manager has an almost divine right to select the members of his staff. Since it is argued that he can be held accountable for results only with this authority, he is as a matter of course given it by every personnel system: career, political, or competitive.

Two Kinds of Authority

The manager's authority in this area is of two kinds, says M.I.T.'s Theodore M. Alfred.[2]

Candidate authority. Candidate authority refers to the right of a manager to determine what candidates he will consider for promotion. In some programs, he may have absolute authority to promote anyone he wishes; in others, he may have to check with the central personnel staff and consider some candidates from other departments. But he is rarely compelled to select anyone in whom he is not interested.

Career authority. Career authority refers to the right of a manager to determine whether a subordinate may be considered for a promotion in another organization unit. This authority is twofold in the sense that the manager is free to refer subordinates to other managers or to turn down requests from other managers for his subordinates.

The Closed Labor Market

The unlimited use of these two authorities, Alfred declares, effectively closes the internal labor market. American management, in an effort to break out of this bind, has introduced two major tools into its promotion process: the computer-based skills inventory and the management-replacement chart. Both are usually incorporated under the misnomer "managerial manpower plan." Of the two, the management-replacement chart offers the most problems, but the skills inventory is scarcely more effective because neither limits the career and candidate authorities of the manager. And, unless these authorities are curtailed, the internal labor market remains closed. The way to get ahead is to move out.

When the internal labor market is closed, its capacity to match men and jobs correctly in terms of the objectives of both the individual and the organization is severely curtailed. This situation, then, creates four major selection weaknesses: biased selection, narrow selection, transitive selection, and secret selection.

Biased selection. A supervisor's selection of a person to promote often is either intentionally or unintentionally biased. Whether he realizes it or not, a manager will select the man he happens to like best. In a recent study of bias in promotion, supervisors asserted that they promoted on the basis of

[2] Theodore M. Alfred, "Checkers or Choice in Manpower Management," *Harvard Business Review*, Vol. 45, No. 1 (Jan.–Feb. 1967), pp. 157–167.

the technical, intellectual, and managerial skills of their subordinates. But, after the survey team had analyzed the actual bases for promotions, they found that three prominent nonability clusters of criteria emerged, one revolving around social connections and the other two around public-image considerations. In other words, managers deluded themselves into believing they selected on technical and ability grounds when, in reality, they selected on purely personal and emotional factors.

Narrow selection. Most corporate practices make it possible for a manager to promote from within his own department or from among his own acquaintances without considering others in the organization. Since he is rarely in a position to be familiar with all possible promotion candidates, his own men are bound to come to his attention more often than outsiders.

In addition, most systems make it possible for managers to hoard good people to the detriment of the total organization. The opportunity for the manager to narrow the selection ratio violates a fundamental principle of selection. It also limits the opportunity for individuals in the smaller departments to move up in the organization.

Transitive selection. "Transitive selection" is a term coined by M.I.T.'s Maison Haire to describe the situation in a corporation with, say, five levels of management: A, B, C, D, and E, none of which a person is permitted to skip in the climb up the ladder. It is necessary to pass successively through levels B, C, and D to proceed from A to E.

When we reflect on this widespread practice, we can see that lower-level managers exercise a disproportionate influence in determining who gets promoted to top management. Since the opportunity to move up to higher posts depends upon one's present supervisor's opinion and knowledge, a young man must receive a favorable report from him, particularly with respect to "promotion potential."

In short, as Lawrence L. Ferguson says, it is the managers at the lower levels who determine just which individuals higher-level managers will have the opportunity to consider for promotion.[3] Often, lower-level managers do not have the foggiest idea of what it takes to operate in the higher reaches of the corporation. That is why they have remained lower-level managers. They tend to give inferior ratings to the very subordinates who possess the traits demanded for effective functioning in top managerial roles, often terming them "misfits" and "smart alecs."

[3] Lawrence L. Ferguson, "Better Management of Manager's Careers," *Harvard Business Review,* Vol. 44, No. 2 (March–April 1966), pp. 139–152.

Secret selection. As noted in the American Buttonhook case, those who are not promoted do not really know whether they were considered and, if they were, why they were not selected. Their ignorance raises unfounded doubts about their future in the organization, an uncertainty that prompts them to leave for what appear to be greener pastures.

There is more confusion surrounding the notion of what it takes to advance in a company than is realized, says Ferguson. About half the managers in a 30-to-40-year age group who were viewed by their managers as outstanding candidates for future advancement said they did not know what the present promotion process was in their company (but, whatever it was, it was different from what they had been told), that it was not uniformly administered, that they could not aim for a particular job because of lack of knowledge beforehand about actual or probable opportunities, and that they could not discern any consistent pattern in the promotions made. Consequently, they remained in the dark as to how best to prepare themselves for advancement and were less effective in their present jobs than they would have been had they understood the true basis on which promotions are granted.

These problems point quite clearly to the necessity for the establishment of a promotion program that is more adaptable to the needs of new managers and that provides practical solutions to many of the difficulties inherent in this critical management responsibility. This new program must be based on all the principles that we have developed so far; indeed, our reason for going into so much detail concerning human and organizational behavior has been simply to lay the foundation for something better.

A Model Managerial
Progression Program

No personnel system will work successfully without an effective, efficient and an acceptable progression plan. This is the heart of the human-resources personnel system, which, as we have pointed out, focuses attention on all organization members as reservoirs of untapped resources. These include not only their physical skills and energies but their capacity for responsible, self-directed behavior. The rallying point of this system, therefore, is organizational purpose rather than loyalty to the service, the profession, or even the organization itself.

Basic Principles

As a subsystem of this overall system, the managerial progression program must be based on a set of principles that stem from the true characteristics of human and organizational behavior. The details of the program will not always be the same in every organization because they must be adapted to its history, environment, and purpose. But, since the basic structural members will be the same, we can present them to describe a model program and to show how the concepts we have developed in previous chapters can be incorporated into an operating program.

There are nine of these basic principles that underlie the development and operation of a sound managerial progression program.

1. Managerial progression is a major corporate concern critical to the survival and the continuity of the enterprise. As its major motivational force, it is the chief means by which managers become committed to the organization. When a promotion is earned and a person sees it as having been earned, it gives him nearly all the satisfactions that human beings look for in an occupation—recognition, self-respect, opportunity for challenge, experience of progress, increased social status, and material rewards.

2. Promotion is *not* a reward for excellent performance. It is, rather, recognition of individual growth and increased capacity. Excellence in one's present position is insufficient reason to move a person to a higher-level job involving abilities not present in the lower job. If men are promoted as a reward for loyalty and hard work into positions for which they are unqualified, they will clog up the promotion channels and reduce substantially the effectiveness of the entire personnel system.

3. The promotion program must be based upon the concept of an open market similar to that prevailing in the general community. The promotion program must involve the total managerial workforce. Everyone should have an opportunity to be considered for a vacancy if he meets its requirements.

4. The progression program must provide appropriate balance between specific organizational unit needs and overall organizational standards by centralizing the assessment of broader personal qualifications and leaving to each operating manager the evaluation of the specific skills necessary to perform a given job.

5. Since nearly all management positions have requirements that permit them to be grouped and to be treated uniformly in such matters as salary

administration and organizational planning, they can be included in a common system of procurement and progression.

6. The qualifications standards that nearly all management positions share are more critical than those that make them unique. In other words, managers are usually effective because of the quality of their intellectual and motivational systems rather than because of specific knowledge and experience in a particular field.

7. The starting point for a sound management-progression program is the early identification of managerial talent to enable men with the capacity for advancement to prepare early in their careers for higher-level responsibilities.

8. A realistic promotion program must also include arrangements by which some junior managers can move up along a "fast track" as warranted by their abilities. This feature involves not only an overall management-development program but a flexible position-classification plan to enable the more promising individuals to move in and out of various positions regardless of small differences in experience or educational requirements.

9. The keystone of an effective program of management progression is an up-to-date manpower-information system.

These nine assumptions point up the best approach to a management-progression program that combines centralized responsibility with substantial opportunity for divisional initiative.

Program Design

Exhibit 4 illustrates the major elements in the human-resources progression program. It is well to keep in mind that this plan is based upon the manpower-information system already described, which furnishes the necessary data for effective program operation—knowledge of the classification structure, qualifications of participants, and forecasts of manpower requirements. It is complemented by the other programs of this system: manpower procurement, progression, development, and rewards.

CREATION OF TALENT POOLS

Essentially, the progression program is based upon a two-way position-classification system—or a three-way system if the company is multidivisional

EXHIBIT 4
The Human Resources Managerial Progression Program

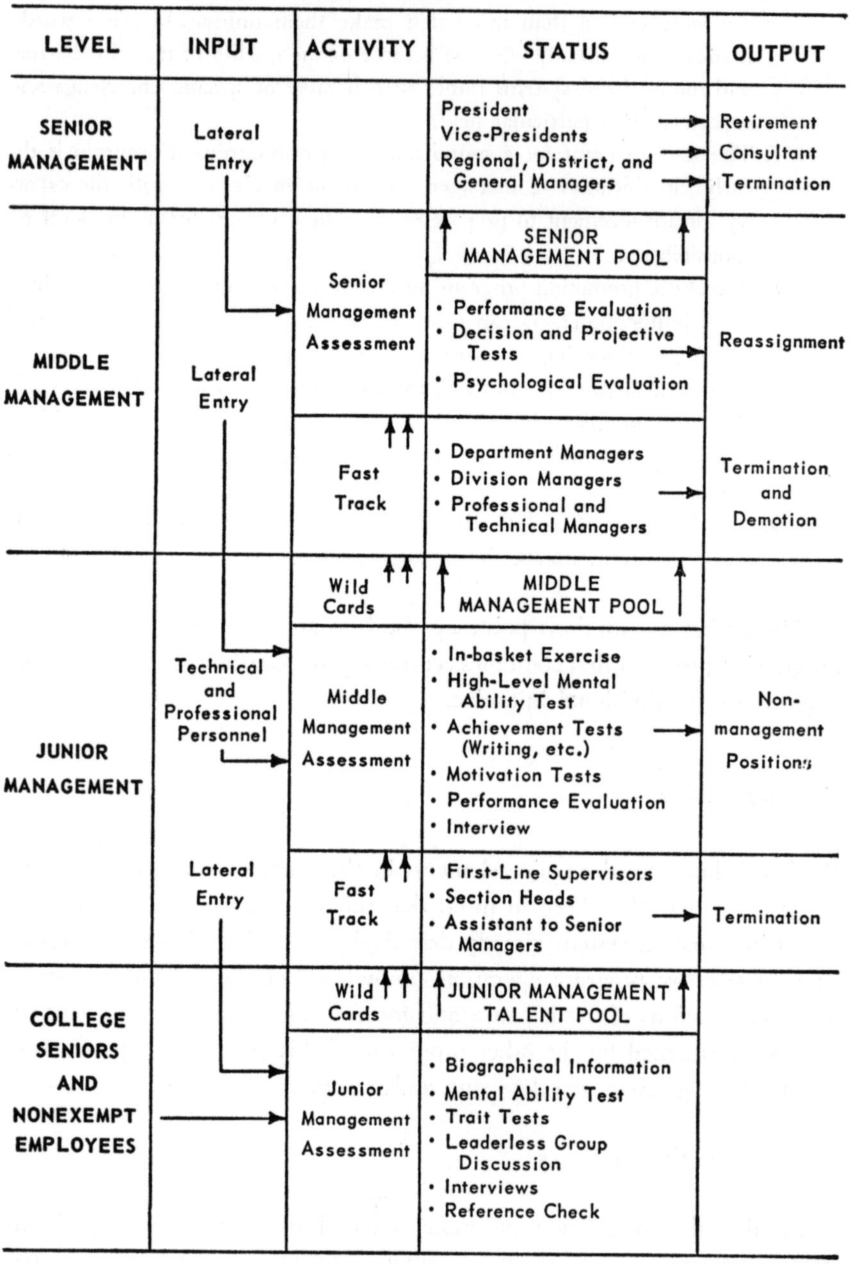

LEVEL	INPUT	ACTIVITY	STATUS	OUTPUT
SENIOR MANAGEMENT	Lateral Entry		President Vice-Presidents → Regional, District, and → General Managers →	Retirement Consultant Termination
MIDDLE MANAGEMENT	Lateral Entry	Senior Management Assessment	↑ SENIOR MANAGEMENT POOL ↑ • Performance Evaluation • Decision and Projective Tests • Psychological Evaluation →	Reassignment
		Fast Track ↑↑	• Department Managers • Division Managers • Professional and → Technical Managers	Termination and Demotion
JUNIOR MANAGEMENT	Technical and Professional Personnel	Wild ↑↑ Cards	↑ MIDDLE ↑ MANAGEMENT POOL	
		Middle Management Assessment	• In-basket Exercise • High-Level Mental Ability Test • Achievement Tests (Writing, etc.) → • Motivation Tests • Performance Evaluation • Interview	Non-management Positions
	Lateral Entry	Fast Track ↑↑	• First-Line Supervisors • Section Heads • Assistant to Senior → Managers	Termination
COLLEGE SENIORS AND NONEXEMPT EMPLOYEES		Wild ↑↑ Cards	↑ JUNIOR MANAGEMENT ↑ TALENT POOL	
		Junior Management Assessment	• Biographical Information • Mental Ability Test • Trait Tests • Leaderless Group Discussion • Interviews • Reference Check	

or multinational. This plan, described in Chapter 7, provides each manager with the coordinates of an organizational map to enable him to chart his own career course. To encourage each member of the management group to recognize that he is part of the plan and has an opportunity to progress upward in it on the basis of his ability and job performance, it must be drawn as broadly as possible, extending across departmental, divisional, company, and even national boundaries.

The objective of the plan is not to designate specific heirs apparent for each position in the organization but, rather, to provide *talent pools* from which to draw men as needed. Being a member of a talent pool is psychologically more motivating than being designated as the backup man for a specific position. Being designated as the heir apparent has a way of turning a person's developmental incentives off. Often, when a No. 2 man finally reaches the top, he is a dismal failure. Being only one member of a talent pool keeps a man on his toes, open and flexible, and it actually gives him more opportunity for promotion.

Using a sequential decision-making model of assessment, the aim of the program is to select men only for the next-higher talent pool. Since the career plan proposes the stratification of the management group into three levels—junior, middle, and senior—there will be three talent pools. There is nothing sacred about these three levels, of course. A company's requirements may make two, four, or even five levels more sensible. Three simply seems to be the most practical number.

Take, for example, a large retail organization. All the managerial positions below the level of store manager and even some smaller store-manager positions could be grouped at the junior management level. The store managers would constitute the middle level, and the district, regional, and corporate line managers could be grouped at the top or senior management level. Staff people—merchandisers, controllers, buyers, personnel administrators, catalog sales representatives, and so forth—would be allocated to functional, nonmanagement job families.

Individuals could move up either within the managerial family or within the functional families. Managers, as part of their development, could cross over into the functional families, but the reverse would not be likely to happen.

The junior management pool. The junior management-talent pool is formed by the college recruitment procedures described earlier and by a thorough canvass of nonexempt, time-card employees. All prospective candidates for junior management and functional positions can be selected on the basis of a careful assessment program consisting of interviews, tests, and proper verification. A typical assessment program at the junior level would include the initial interview at the college campus followed by a day-long administration on company premises of the following instruments: a biographical information blank, a measure of mental ability, a battery of trait tests, a leaderless group discussion test, two evaluation interviews, and a careful reference check.

The resulting profile should determine not only who should be hired but who may be an outstanding prospect. A custom-built development program can be designed for each newly hired employee to provide him with suitable exposures to company functions, processes, and products and so prepare him for promotion within a few years to the middle management-talent pool.

Some of the trainees will be designated as having management potential, and some will not, on the basis of their assessment profiles. It is not necessary to be too accurate at this point because the test of management potential comes from on-the-job experience and later assessments. All that is necessary here is to make reasonably sure that the input includes a fairly high proportion of potential managers. This will then constitute the lowest pool, the pool of junior managers, which will be larger than the corporation's need for middle managers over the next five years.

The middle management pool. After approximately three years—or earlier, if warranted, under some circumstances—each junior manager should be permitted to submit his name for assessment for promotion to middle management. It is important that *he* submit his name and not be nominated by his supervisor.

This assessment will emphasize achievement as well as potential. Supervisory evaluations and other performance data, as well as achievement tests, will be heavily weighted. A typical assessment battery might include an in-basket exercise, high-level measures of intellectual ability, achievement tests in functional areas, more penetrating motivation tests, a depth interview, and careful reviews of job performance.

If the young manager is evaluated as qualified for middle management, he becomes eligible for promotion to a position at this level by being placed in the higher-talent pool, which should also include more people than will be required over the next five years. (How people are picked out of this pool and what happens if they are not selected will be described presently.) No organization unit should be permitted to recruit from outside until a careful review of all qualified persons in this pool has been completed without success.

The senior management pool. After a period of five years, more or less, depending upon individual competence, a division may recommend a middle manager for assessment for top management—or the individual may submit his own name. At this point, he is reassessed again for performance capabilities at the top of the organization. Those whose assessments indicate they are indeed potential top managers are placed in the highest pool for further development and subsequent placement. Assessment at this level will ordinarily involve the services of a consulting psychologist, a review of job achievements, and the administration of decision-making and projective personality tests.

Program Operation

It would be impossible here to describe all the details of this program, but some should be mentioned to clarify its main outlines.

MODIFICATION OF SUPERVISOR'S STAFFING AUTHORITY

The chief characteristic of this progression program is its modification of the supervisor's staffing authority. While it encourages him to prepare his subordinates for promotion, it subjects his choices to central review to ascertain uniformity and quality throughout the organization. At the same time, no one is forced down a manager's throat.

None of the assessment information, of course, is ever made available to the line supervisor directly. It is all stored in the human-resources inventory of the data bank and is made available to him only in a general fashion. In filling vacancies, all he knows is the general caliber of an individual's performance and the fact that the individual is or is not in the talent pool. The central staffing unit maintains this information in the strictest confidence, primarily to facilitate manpower planning and to audit the operation of the plan as specified below.

Thus a line manager's career authority is limited by the role the central staff plays and the right of the subordinate to apply for openings as they occur. His candidate authority is limited by the requirement that he must review all qualified individuals in the pool who fit the specifications of a position and are interested in it.

When a vacancy occurs, a manager notifies the central staffing agency. He may send along with his requisition the name(s) of any subordinate(s) who he believes may be qualified for promotion. These nominees must meet the requirements of the job and must be in the appropriate talent pool. If the central staff approves, the preferred nominee can be promoted immediately. If the staff feels, however, that the recommended person is not as eligible for promotion as some others, it will require the opening to be advertised in a management bulletin circulated to all pool members. Interested individuals can then send their names to the central staff, who, after review, will pass them along to the unit manager for consideration and interview. In his final selection, the manager must justify the superiority of his candidate over all others who apply for the position.

An Open Labor Market

This program meets another requirement of a model progression plan: All members of the organization are continuously aware of the program's operations. First, they have an opportunity to apply for the middle and top management assessment programs. Second, they receive announcements of specific openings for which they may apply.

But there are two additional ways by which the whole scheme is thrown open to managerial scrutiny. First, promotions are announced throughout the company as they occur, citing where the promotees came from and where they are going. And, when it is necessary to recruit outside, this also is announced and the reasons why are given. Second, task forces and subcommittees composed of managers at all three levels can be appointed to work on problems that arise in the operation of the program and to establish ground rules for its operation.

In short, every manager has a good idea of what is happening in the program and how to prepare himself for promotion.

Career Counseling

To make the plan as productive as possible and to gain the support and confidence of those covered, a counseling program is imperative.

First of all, a vital part of the system is the prospective manager's assessment of himself. But there may be many men in junior and middle management who feel they have the qualifications for higher responsibility but who doubt their ability to stand the stresses of higher-level positions. They may hesitate to put their names forward and may never be considered by management unless they receive counseling and advice. Others may have unrealistic levels of aspiration; they will be hurt and chagrined by a negative assessment, feeling that they have been unfairly considered. Each individual manager should therefore have the opportunity to talk with a professional counselor to discuss his career objectives, progress, and opportunities for advancement—an encounter that will be quite different from the coaching undertaken by the supervisor in the performance-evaluation interview.

In addition, it must be recognized clearly and realistically that an open promotion system based on merit can be personally devastating to those who fail to get promoted. Frustration becomes deeper, and any sense of inadequacy is heightened. No one blames a man who fails to get promoted because he was overlooked, because he did not know "the right people," or because he lacks enough time on the job; but to be carefully assessed and refused a promotion is a traumatic experience. The organization has to cushion the effect of this shock by professional counseling.

Lateral Entry into Pools

To keep the system from becoming stagnant, there has to be some lateral entry into the higher-level pools from outside the organization. While it should not be necessary to recruit from outside frequently, there will be times when no one in the organization is sufficiently ready for a position. Before selection, however, an outside candidate should be given as much of the assessment program as is practical, and he must meet the same standards as promotion candidates. Wherever possible, he should be selected by joint decision of several managers and departments rather than just by the one in which the vacancy occurs. The justification for this approach is that a person hired from the outside is hired for the organization and not just for a specific location in it.

Special Progress Rates

To correct mistakes and to keep the program from degenerating into an elaborate competition, fast and slow tracks should be built into the model.

Fast tracks. At its simplest, a fast track means rapid promotion for exceptional men. What it really offers the individual is the challenge, the recognition, and the ego satisfaction that most men suited for top management positions seek. High-potential managers are identified through the assessment process. They are earmarked as "wild cards"; that is, young managers with unusually strong qualifications who are to be moved as far and as fast as they can go on the basis of their ability rather than on the basis of time. Top executives must participate directly in the designation of wild cards, who are then placed in a special program that telescopes the usual time requirements and gives them the opportunity for more intensive but more rapid exposure to managerial experiences.

The main element of this plan is a specific future job assignment with target dates for start and completion. The timetable should remain flexible so that progress can be as fast as the man's ability permits. There should be provision, too, for taking a man off a fast track if his performance does not justify the original evaluation. In any event, the fast-track idea should not be overworked, and the program should not commit itself to any rigid career pattern that will identify a young manager as a "crown prince." While much will be given him, certainly much must be expected of him.

Slow tracks. Assessment errors are inevitable. Some of the men placed in a talent pool may not live up to their original promise. If a person is running a slow track, provision must be made to help him or to remove him. Likewise, if a manager remains in a talent pool for three years without being promoted, his situation should be carefully reviewed. A career path, after all, is designed to be a promotion highway; anyone who performs as though it were a mud-filled bog should be pulled out. Clear, fast tracks are essential to a successful progression program; there can be no slow or clogged tracks in the organization, and men who are not making it should receive intensive counseling and development. Above all else, they should not be ignored or left to their own devices.

Some companies encourage an "up or out" philosophy. If a person who seems to have the potential does not progress, he is encouraged to leave. Unfortunately, this policy can have a vicious effect on good people who are not promoted as quickly as they think they should be—particularly in relation to some other manager whom they judge to be their equal but who moves ahead of them.

On the surface, the up-or-out philosophy seems to maintain a top-flight, highly viable, well-motivated group of young men. But the perception of how fast one should move can become grossly distorted. As a result, people leave after a short period of time even though the company may have great plans for them. What happens is that young managers come to feel they are not on a fast track if they do not move ahead at an inordinate rate of speed. And, once the up-or-out philosophy spreads, it is very difficult to root out. Hence General Foods has recently instituted a rule that all product managers will remain in their positions for 18 months before being promoted. And at Montgomery Ward there is a general policy that a young manager must remain in his job a sufficiently long period of time—two years—to "face his figures"; that is, to see the results of his decisions.

Program Administration

The program must be the direct and immediate responsibility of the organization's chief executive. He must take a personal interest in it. Moreover, to fulfill this important responsibility, he should appoint a top management advisory committee to direct the program and to report its operations to him.

The advisory committee. The advisory committee, consisting in sizable corporations of possibly ten key vice-presidents and a vice-president for organization and manpower utilization, will have the following functions:

1. Authorization of staff and money for program development and research.
2. Approval of the final details of the program.
3. Formulation of broad policies regarding the program's operation.
4. Resolution of intracompany conflicts over policies, procedures, or priorities.

Central staff. The program, as stated, should include a vice-president for organization and manpower utilization. He should report to the president, or at least to an executive vice-president, and he should be a member of the top-level advisory committee. It is he who will be responsible for the administrative direction of the program.

The person who fills this job is much more than a "personnel manager." He is responsible for insuring the adoption and full utilization of the manpower plan, including the manpower-procurement, progression, development, and rewards programs. Consequently, this position is a key one in the corporate structure and must be assigned to a person with broad competence in the field of manpower utilization and specific experience in manpower planning, personnel development, organizational analysis, and personnel administration.

The staff reporting to this vice-president will be the central agency that oversees the program's operations. It will be concerned with the program's design and with the development of the career plan and the human-resources inventory. It will also audit the program for operation according to plan and provide line management with advice and assistance.

Assessment Procedures

Fundamental to this progression program are the assessment procedures utilized to evaluate the abilities and the intellectual and motivational systems of the managerial candidates and to assign them to the appropriate talent pool. If these procedures are unreliable and biased, the end product is worthless. The particular assessment program adopted will depend upon the traditions and technical resources of each organization. It will naturally vary from company to company, but essentially there are three possible approaches: staff-administered assessment programs, assessment by outside psychologists, and the establishment of assessment centers.

Staff-Administered Programs

Most progression programs are administered by a centralized organizational unit such as the organizational and manpower utilization staff we have recommended. But, while the central staff will have overall responsibility for the program, the way in which it carries out this responsibility can vary. Although no organization has yet developed a model similar to that described in this chapter, several—such as Humble Oil, Sears, Roebuck, AT&T, The Port of New York Authority, and IBM—have programs that resemble it. Take Humble's for an example.

About 4,000 of Humble's 7,000 professional and managerial employees have been assessed since 1962. In 1966, the program was adopted throughout Humble, and most professional and technical employees are now invited to take the test battery about two years after they are hired. At age 30, each employee receives a follow-up set of tests.

A major premise of this program is that many different kinds of managers with widely varying early histories can be equally successful and effective in their work at Humble. The results of Humble's assessments are not allowed to override or to replace judgment based on actual performance. Testing is handled by the centralized employee relations department, which sends the results to line management—that is, two organization levels above the immediate superior of the employee being assessed. This practice of putting the test data midway between the employee's immediate supervisor and headquarters is a deliberate strategy to make sure that testing does not dominate management's decisions about a man but is permitted to be useful and valuable in reviews of his career.

At the highest levels of the company, these test data are almost never consulted when a man is being promoted. But, in the earlier years of his career, they can be important; and, if his test scores and his performance conflict, his record gets a thorough review by his superiors. Among those tested so far at Humble, half who scored in the top 10 percent had less than four years of service. Of these, only a fourth had been tagged by their superiors as having high potential.

Outside Psychologists

Many companies use evaluations by professionally trained psychologists to assess managerial prospects. These evaluations are most commonly conducted when a new person is being considered for selection from the outside. However, some companies have established regular psychological evaluations as part of their management-development and -progression programs. And other companies, when considering several candidates for promotion, refer the likely prospects to consultants for in-depth evaluations.

There is not much information as to the extent to which this method is used, but there are a considerable number of consultants in the field, some of whom specialize in managerial evaluations. Few companies use their own staff psychologists for this purpose because of the obvious internal relationships that might be affected by them.

One of the companies reported to use this method heavily is ITT, which is said to make its evaluations by means of its own psychological staff supplemented by consultants who are on retainer throughout the world. This company believes that each manager should be reevaluated once every five years. It feels that the procedures are most effective in predicting failure and somewhat less so in predicting success.

Every psychologist who makes such evaluations goes about the task somewhat differently. But the usual method is to administer a series of questionnaires, interviews, and psychological procedures. A wide variety of tests are used to provide for cross-checking and confirmation of the indications and the information obtained. A confidential report is then prepared for management in which it is strongly suggested that the content be disclosed to no one who is untrained in psychology and counseling and that it be treated like any other confidential management report.

The interpretation of the tests and the subsequent evaluation of the results are based upon the psychologist's training and experience with the tests, and the integration of the information to form a final evaluation requires a good deal of skill. Most reputable psychologists will caution management that a recommendation for or against hiring or promoting is based upon knowledge of the job specifications and the potential working environment. It is meant to be a supplement to management opinion, not a substitute. In practice, however, managers tend to follow the psychologist's recommendations quite closely.

A typical report may contain the following information:

1. A general summary of the strengths and weaknesses of the candidate.
2. A statement concerning his intellectual ability in terms of basic capacities and his effectiveness in applying them.
3. A statement of his special aptitudes, such as sales, mechanical, or managerial.
4. A description of his motivational patterns, including his drive, his expressive patterns, his goals, and his objectives.
5. A description of his personality adjustment, his relations with others, and his temperament.
6. A statement about his potential for advancement.

There are two considerations to be discussed with respect to psychological evaluations. The first concerns the person who makes the evaluation. There is evidence to suggest that the key to successful prediction of a psychological evaluation lies not so much in the techniques that are used as in the insight and the skill of the person making the evaluation. A psychological consultant is required to possess certain basic qualifications. To begin with, he should be a member of the American Psychological Association or eligible to become a member. He should also have a Ph.D. in psychology and should be a certified or licensed psychologist in his state. Assessment by individuals who do not meet these professional credentials should be treated with considerable caution. Moreover, many of the individuals in this field have been clinically trained. Where possible, an industrial psychologist is to be preferred because presumably he will have had experience in an industrial setting and can grasp the major problems of the organization. The clinician's training, for the most part, consists of work with emotionally disturbed people in a hospital setting that may make him less sensitive to the hierarchical aspects of the organization.

The second consideration has to do with the accuracy of the assessments and recommendations made. As we have already indicated, the research evidence is not clear-cut, but it does suggest that, while the overall assessments often meet the test of predictive validity, the various test scores and/or interview ratings the psychologist uses to reach this judgment correlate poorly with success criteria.

To judge the validity of the psychologist's predictions, one must attempt, not to predict individual components, but rather to make a judgment as to the final conclusion. One does not evaluate a surgeon on the basis of the type of instruments he uses; instead, one looks at the results he obtains when he uses those instruments. Firms engaging the services of psychological consultants are not likely to obtain a high degree of correlation between individual predictors and success because the process is still one of global judgment, insight—or "art," if you will. In other words, firms are really buying the talent of the psychologist doing the assessment, not the particular instruments he uses.

A good example of this is contained in a study completed by Dr. John Drake, president of Behavioral Sciences Technology, Inc. As the consequence of a program involving assessment and follow-up of 50 managers in an effort to help each man grow, Dr. Drake computed a gain of 320 percent in the company's investment, translated into dollar savings, in terms of successful promotion and decreased turnover.

Some companies, however, prefer a method of assessment that does not depend upon the expertise of a single man, that presumably affords an even greater penetration into the managerial mind. The result of this search has been *the assessment center.*

The Assessment Center

The assessment-center approach originated in the research studies conducted at Harvard in the 1930s under the direction of Professor Henry Murray, who is generally credited with being the first to use multiple methods of personality assessment. Essentially, this approach provides for the simultaneous assessment of a group of candidates by a team of evaluators. The assessees spend from one day to a week in residence at a center, where they go through a variety of assessment exercises. At the end of the assessment, the observers complete an evaluation report for higher-level management. This report is used to make promotion decisions.

The selection work used to select OSS agents in World War II gave the assessment center its distinctive characteristic. The techniques adopted in this program included ability tests of various kinds, detailed interviews, fantasy and projective materials, and situational tests. With the rapid expansion of management selection and development programs after World War II, the desire for realistic and valid assessment techniques led to the adoption of the OSS procedures by private industry and the public service. Thus, by 1950, multiple methods of assessment—including situational tests— were being used to select and to promote junior managers. At the same time, the emergence of operations research gave strong impetus to the adoption of simulation and games as developmental tools, so that ultimately they too were used in selection programs.

Fed by rapid innovation in game and decision theory, the creation of highly complex games expanded with astonishing celerity. The first formal assessment center was developed in the Bell System in 1959. Its program for the assessment of management potential grew out of a long-term study of the development of managers called the "Management Progress Study." Initiated to add to the store of psychological knowledge about the development of young adults, this study originated under the direction of Dr. Douglas Bray, now director of personnel research for AT&T. Over a period of years, 422 young men were checked annually in various ways in an effort to keep track of all the specifics in their lives, their reactions to these specifics, and their personal growth or lack of it.

As the research went forward, however, its promise as an adjunct to the normal appraisal process became apparent to the operating executives of the Michigan Bell Telephone Company, who asked that the method be utilized as a regular feature of their supervisory and managerial selection programs. In September 1959, the Michigan Bell set up the first assessment center in Detroit to assess the nonmanagement plant employees nominated by their supervisors as candidates for first-line foremen's positions. At least 50,000 people have been assessed since this first industrial application.

Since then, the assessment center has expanded in the Bell System to 60 installations which assess 8,000 employees per year. At this time there are ten companies that have assessment centers: AT&T, Standard Oil of Ohio, IBM, Caterpillar Tractor, General Electric, Sears, Roebuck, Olin Corporation, Wolverine Tube, Wick, and J. C. Penney. In addition, some government agencies—including the Peace Corps, the Internal Revenue

Service, the Oak Ridge Atomic Energy Facility, and The Port of New York Authority—administer variations of such assessment programs.

It is contended that assessment centers are more effective than normal employment procedures. Why? Because, it is claimed, all assessees have an equal opportunity to display their talents, they are seen under similar conditions in situations designed to bring out particular skills and abilities needed for the positions for which they are being considered, and they are evaluated by a team of trained assessors unbiased by past associations and intimately familiar with the positions' requirements.

By far the largest application of the assessment-center approach is to select applicants for management positions. In these situations, the company is primarily interested in estimating management potential, but centers have also produced training and development recommendations.

FEATURES COMMON TO ASSESSMENT-CENTER PROGRAMS

Most of the assessment centers utilize the original Bell System model, although there are programs—such as that of The Port of New York Authority—that differ from it considerably. The following features are common to most programs.

Assessors. Professional psychologists act as assessors in some programs, but in most the assessors consist of nonprofessional second- or third-level supervisors who undergo periods of professional training and are assigned to this work for six-month periods. There is evidence to indicate that these managers do as well as psychologists in controlled situations. However, the key to their use as assessors is the training they receive.

Assessment variables. In the assessment-center program, the major aim is to evaluate the candidate in terms of those variables that are relevant for managerial success. Emphasis is placed, therefore, on those traits that are not readily observable when the man works in his usual job (which often is nonmanagerial in content). Thus the assessment center is viewed as a supplement to the line-organization information and is just one more tool available in considering men in management for promotion.

Assessment techniques. The techniques by which various management skills are obtained can be grouped into three general classes:

1. Paper-and-pencil tests. These consist of tests of general mental ability, personality tests, and tests of the ability to organize and to write memoranda.

2. Group situations. These situation tests consist mainly of the in-basket exercise and the leaderless group discussion in its various forms.
3. Work situations. The assessment also includes depth interviews covering the background and the personal history of the candidate.

The participants in the assessment center are nominated by their supervisors. (As far as is known, no program except that of the Port Authority provides for self-nomination, which is a key concept in the progression program outlined in this chapter.) They spend from two and a half days to a full week at the center going through the various exercises under the supervision of assessors. There are, of course, variations of this approach; some companies use one-day and weekend centers, and others hold the sessions on company property and on company time. After assessment, the results are made known in a general way to line management, which then has the opportunity to accept or reject the recommendations of the assessment team. For the most part, these recommendations are taken seriously. Test results are played down so as not to influence the assessors unduly; they are generally communicated in broad categories such as "superior," "average," or "below average."

Some companies use the assessment-center experience as a valuable developmental experience for the assessors. Therefore, they may rotate assignment on a periodic basis.

EVALUATION OF THE ASSESSMENT-CENTER APPROACH

There is no question that the assessment center is a significant step forward in assessment techniques because it provides a decision maker with information that can be obtained in no other way. There are, however, some problems that need to be overcome.

First, most assessment centers omit job-performance data in the determination of the final assessment, an omission that is hard to justify. *Second,* the use of line managers as assessors leaves something to be desired, because, no matter how well prepared they are for the task, their training is necessarily limited. Therefore, they may lack the ability to evaluate the subtleties of the performance they observe. Their evaluations tend to be somewhat routine and mechanical; somehow, the real man does not come through the maze of evaluation variables.

Third, the assessment center is costly. While the costs are hard to define, they can approach $500 per man. (A recent notice from a psychological consulting firm describes an assessment center to which companies may send candidates at the price of $750 per man.) There is some question as to whether the information obtained from the assessment center cannot be collected at a much lower cost by individual assessments by professionally trained psychologists.

Fourth, most assessment centers appear to have adhered to the original model developed by the Bell System. While this model represents a significant advance in assessment techniques and offers a good deal of promise, it certainly ought not to preclude broader experimentation and innovation. And *fifth,* particularly when a center utilizes line managers as assessors, there is a suspicion that it may tend to produce nothing but conforming organization types. This accusation, of course, can be made against any assessment approach. It strongly argues for the introduction of outsiders into the assessment program to add a different perspective to the organizational view.

By and large, however, of all the techniques that have been developed it appears that the assessment center perhaps offers the most substantial promise for the future. It certainly fits in nicely with the decision-making model of assessment and the progression program that we have described in this chapter and with our overall concept of the human-resources personnel system.

13

Turning Managers On

THE president of an established, nationally known financial institution met not long ago with a consultant to discuss a perplexing personnel problem. He prided himself on the company's personnel program, which included such modern features as carefully executed college recruitment, a soundly based and competitive salary program, and a management-development approach that included sensitivity training and tuition-refund benefits. Yet the annual junior-manager turnover rate had exceeded 60 percent per year, a rate three times that of the clerical forces.

The president was disturbed, even annoyed. "What is wrong with young people today?" he asked the consultant. "How can they reject so frivolously the assured and dignified career which we, as one of the nation's most prestigious employers, can give them? What new personnel techniques do you suggest to hold these young men and women?"

Instead of answering these questions, the consultant asked three of his own. "What reasons did the trainees give for leaving?" "Lack of opportunity and challenge," was the reply given by the president. "How are promotions made in the company?" On the recommendation of the individual department manager, after consultation with the personnel director, on the basis of performance and experience. "What is the company's performance-evaluation program like?" The company, the president answered, had no formal performance-review program except that when a man was due for a salary increase, his supervisor justified it by references to his job performance.

When the consultant then suggested that the establishment of centralized progression and performance-evaluation programs might be the first step in an attack on the company's problem, the president bristled. There was no need for such programs, he declared emphatically. Company officers knew their subordinates well enough to be in the best position to judge who was eligible for promotion. And besides, he asserted, there was ample opportunity for young people to advance in his company through job rotation and training courses. Anyway, the company's record for promotion from within, he declared proudly, was outstanding—rarely was anyone hired from the outside. And, as for performance evaluation, many previous attempts in the company to establish such a program had demonstrated the ineffectiveness of the procedures used.

The meeting ended inconclusively. What the president was unable to recognize was the fact that, despite his good intentions, he was overlooking the motivating forces that turn young managers on. In essence, he was running a career personnel system that was like a beautiful crystal palace; development took precedence over selection, rewards over challenge, and security over growth. In such a milieu, the only human need engaged was *affiliation,* and this need is the least important to most of the younger generation.

The job-rotation and management-development practices in this company were nothing more than placebos. They contributed little to true personal growth.

The dilemma of this company is by no means atypical. It is, rather, the rule among many large employers who are sincerely interested in their employees' welfare. But the objective of the human-resources personnel system is not welfare but the optimization of talent.

To avoid the trap into which this company had fallen, it is necessary to view the personnel system as a four-legged table supporting the total organizational effort. The table top represents the manpower plan, the corporate strategy that is supported by the four legs: the procurement, progression, motivation, and development programs. Without these four, evenly balanced, the table will wobble or fall.

It has been our aim here to describe two of these legs, the procurement and progression programs. But, to complete our analysis of these programs, we must review briefly certain features of the other two legs insofar as they are related to the procurement and progression of managers.

The Managerial Motivation Program

The object of a managerial motivation program is to satisfy the manager's human needs by providing him with suitable incentives to perform to the limit of his capabilities. There are many incentives, of course, but all are related to a sound career-progression program. To demonstrate this assertion, let us examine two central questions: Why do managers stay with a company, and why do they leave?

Why Do Managers Stay?

By overdramatizing the shake-ups in the executive suite, the press has created the erroneous impression that American managers are continuously engaged in a national game of musical chairs. On the contrary, according to many thoughtful observers, there is really not enough managerial mobility. Whether there is or is not enough depends upon whether managers stay for the right reasons or the wrong reasons.

Staying for the Wrong Reasons

A manager stays in an organization for the wrong reasons when the job he is doing no longer stimulates him, when it becomes just a job. Performing the same duties routinely and mechanically month after month, year in and year out, can be a horrible drain on a man's physical and psychic energies. It saps his enthusiasm, dulls his intellect, and erodes his self-respect. Why would any educated man continue in such a situation without any change in procedures, responsibilities, or relationships? For three reasons.

False expectations. A manager stays because his company, considering promotion to be a reward for loyal and faithful service, raises false expectations in him. By constant observation he comes to believe that promotion boils down to company loyalty and length of service. The patient plodder will wait his turn to move into the big office on the top floor. Supported annually by "merit" salary increases that are thinly disguised cost-of-living increases, he is happy to wait hopefully for his ultimate reward.

Golden chains. Corporations weld golden chains around their managers' legs to keep them from straying. For some reason, companies have bought the idea that such benefits as deferred compensation, stock options, and pension plans will lock managers into the organization and deter them from leaving for greener pastures. Actually, the only manager locked in is the mediocrity who cannot obtain as much for his services elsewhere. To him, the golden chains become a badge of office and a lifeline to security. In due course he becomes the obsolete manager, and in spite of mobility and development programs he is joined by other obsolete managers. Together they then dominate the corporate hierarchy.

Lack of two-way selection. Obsolete managers stay because most organizations lack an effective two-way selection program; that is, one that operates both in and out. Selection-out programs, which are quite different from the up-or-out practices described earlier, have not been very successful so far because other personnel programs reduce the chances of identifying obsolete managers. What makes the Peter Principle work so well is the national error of confusing promotion with reward and tenure in office with social compassion. To place a man in a position beyond his competence is a mistake—an understandable mistake but still a mistake. But to keep him in that position is not only inexcusable but cruel.

A managerial demotion program is as essential as a promotion program. The difficulty, it is claimed, lies in the stigma of disgrace attached to a demotion. This is more apparent than real. The actual difficulty lies in the deep-seated guilt feelings of those who made the original error in selection and their reluctance to admit that error. Rather than demote an ineffective manager, they often prefer to compound it by moving him sideways or even "upstairs." Thus an organization gets cluttered with "special assistants to the president," "coordinators," and "consultants"—all representing sinecures that serve to erode further the victim's self-respect. Though painful at first, like pulling an aching tooth, a demotion can be a blessing to the man affected if it is handled with dignity.

STAYING FOR THE RIGHT REASON

Under our concept of the human-resources personnel system, the only reason a manager should have for staying with an organization is his commitment to its purposes and his deep involvement in achieving them. It follows, then, that the only reason for promoting a man is that the organization needs him and he is ready to take on greater responsibility. If the career-progression program is based on these two premises, it becomes a powerful motivating force for the individual. It will really turn him on. It must be clearly understood that the recognition, the greater security, and the higher status that accompany promotion are only byproducts of the fact that the person has grown in value to himself and to the organization. These by-products can never be the reasons for or the objectives of a promotion. If they are, it loses its motivating power.

There is increasing acceptance of this principle, but the old idea dies hard. The magazine *Business Management* asked 76 company presidents to describe the special privileges given executives and their own attitudes toward these status symbols.[1] Most appeared to believe that status symbols were practical devices for acquiring or holding capable managers because it seemed to be the "American way." Among the symbols they considered to be most valuable were larger and better-located offices, larger desks, special parking privileges, wall-to-wall carpeting, draperies, company cars, and larger expense accounts.

But psychologist Charles Hughes, of Texas Instruments, asserts that these status symbols hold more potential for dissatisfaction than satisfaction because they are incentives only when employees have been conditioned to respond to them. Since employees see these symbols as outward manifestations of the possession of power, their value is negative. If a company bases its motivational program on these, it will only invite trouble.

Arch Patton lists six factors which are in the forefront of the changes occurring in today's motivational patterns and will be important in tomorrow's motivational approaches: environment, excitement, a higher promotion rate, better use of performance appraisals, compensation, and job satisfaction.[2] It is interesting to compare these six factors with the dimensions of the human-resources personnel system that we have outlined.

1. Environment, both psychological and physical. Companies will increasingly strive to develop the subtle but potent strengths of a competitive, performance-oriented environment.
2. Excitement. This is simply the excitement generated by the purposeful pursuit of a demanding goal.
3. A high promotion rate. The company that provides this kind of motivation inevitably has an edge on its competitors.
4. Better use of performance appraisals. It is a well-known fact that men who are strongly achievement-oriented need feedback on their performance.

[1] "What Your Peers Think About Status Symbols," *Business Management*, Vol. 29, No. 7 (April 1966).

[2] Arch Patton, "Executive Motivation: How It Is Changing," *Management Review*, Vol. 57, No. 1 (Jan. 1968), pp. 4–20.

5. Compensation. It will play a crucial role in motivating managers. We shall have more to say about this factor.
6. Job satisfaction. We have already discussed this concept in an earlier chapter.

Why Do Managers Leave?

In considering why managers leave, it must be pointed out that, by far, managerial turnover occurs most frequently at the lower end of the hierarchy. One executive recruiter has noted that, with more and more companies turning to the practice of lifting talented young men into higher positions, the older, passed-over middle managers are becoming less notable because there are now so many of them. He estimates that only 15 percent of the passed-over men actively seek new jobs; the rest are content to stay put—hoping, perhaps, that in time they too will be promoted.

A passed-over middle manager may stay on, but the effect on lower-middle and junior managers is devastating. They will leave in droves. A company can shrug its shoulders to some extent, looking on the exodus as a kind of weeding-out process, but the stark truth is that those who leave are likely to be the ablest and the most promising. A company simply cannot afford to ignore turnover in its young managers or to look for soothing rationalizations to explain it away. It has to discover the truth, even though it hurts, by adopting two basic premises:

1. No manager is lured away from a job situation that satisfies his human needs. Any resignation, therefore, represents an *escape* from a position which, in some way, the manager sees as frustrating and dissatisfying to him.
2. There are always two reasons for a resignation—the announced reason and the true reason. The announced reason is always very socially acceptable and self-enhancing, while the true reason is often unacknowledged by either the leaver or those he leaves.

When a man announces that he is leaving, a company should really dig to find out why. And it should look, not at the features of the new job that attracted him, but at the details of his old job that drove him away. This searching self-examination can be aided by a comparison of the commonly stated reasons for leaving with the true reasons managers leave.

THE ANNOUNCED REASONS

When a manager leaves, he is usually influenced by a desire to let bygones be bygones. Strategy and diplomacy dictate, therefore, that he leave as pleasantly as possible unless the termination is due to a serious interpersonal conflict. A leaving manager usually gives his employer one of three reasons: more money, increased responsibility, or more suitable location.

More money. Money is the most commonly stated reason for resignations, with the figure constituting an amount the losing company cannot match. Often it is unclear whether the announced new salary represents direct compensation, bonuses, or profit sharing. The losing employer usually doesn't inquire.

Analysis has shown that often the departing manager exchanges an increase in salary for a loss of benefits which, when priced out, means that he is moving for less money. He does not admit this even to himself, for it is part of the managerial folklore that a manager leaves a job only because he "owes it to his family" to accept the new job. When a man brings his family into the discussion, no one can argue with him.

Increased responsibility. Usually the additional responsibility a man takes on is represented by a more prestigious title. It is not uncommon for a staff assistant in a large corporation to move to a smaller one but with the title of "vice-president" or "general manager." Again, according to the managerial folklore, a title is more important than responsibility, and managers often seek what they call "a title move."

On close inspection, the fancy title involved in these moves often covers reduced opportunities for growth or even fewer benefits. The departing manager will assure all listeners that in the smaller company he will have greater challenges—challenges which, however, are often matched by greater insecurity. Nevertheless, the individual will represent himself as leaving for a chance to capitalize on his high but largely unappreciated potential. Once again, no one can argue with this position.

Better location. Sometimes the reason for leaving is given as an opportunity to move to a more advantageous geographic location. If the leaver happens to move from a small town to a large city, he will explain that the cultural attractions and the chance to meet men in his field are greater. If he happens to move from a large city to a small town, he will cite the opportunity to meet and mingle socially with corporation executives.

There are many other socially acceptable and irresistible reasons given for leaving, but in nine cases out of ten they are fallacious.

THE TRUE REASONS

Many studies have attempted to uncover the true reasons why managers leave. The most frequently cited are these.

Inadequate promotion program. In a major study of the reasons why 422 managers switched jobs, the reason that emerged as primary was neither money nor security but blocked job advancement. Another survey listed the most frequent reason cited by departing executives as faster development. Managers seem to share a common trait—the willingness to make any number of job changes when they are discouraged by lack of forward progress. Of course, no organization will admit that its policy is not to promote from within; but, as we have pointed out, it takes more than pious platitudes to convince bright executives that promotion from within is a reality.

Poor selection. A largely unappreciated reason for managerial turnover is the inadequacy of the corporate selection and placement program. In the managerial employment process, evaluation focuses almost exclusively on work experience or on technical competence, and such significant and determining factors as attitudes, drive, self-confidence, and aggressiveness are either ignored or only superficially considered. Yet failure to consider these latter variables leads to inadequate placement, and most companies have only one corrective measure for inadequate selection—termination of employment.

Corporate climate. An unstable corporate climate breeds heavy executive turnover. In organizations where there is intense pressure to produce and where human values are largely ignored, a state of insecurity will prevail that generates frequent resignations—particularly among those with great self-confidence and high achievement needs. This situation becomes self-perpetuating because each resignation creates additional insecurity in those who remain, even though this insecurity may not appear on the surface. It can run deep, above all in companies that outwardly pose as benevolent and democratic but are basically power-oriented and autocratic.

Unchallenging job. The job that a young manager is required to do may be far beneath his skill and ability. This is probably the most frequent cause of turnover in the lower managerial ranks. The jobs young managers are asked to do must be relevant to their education, to their social consciences, and to real company needs. To offset the glorified clerical jobs they offer young managers, companies make the mistake of substituting incentives that stress security and stability—incentives that appeal only to a generation whose memory of the 1930 depression is still vivid.

The Case for Managerial Mobility

Why managers leave, then, says a lot about the motivation of managers and the failure to turn them on. But this is not to say that a low turnover rate is necessarily desirable. In terms of the national interest and in terms of individual growth, it is possible to make a good case for managerial mobility.

It would be naive for a corporation to assume that it can meet the needs of an intelligent, achievement-oriented, aggressive person from college graduation until retirement. Regardless of its purpose, an organization's structure must resemble a pyramid, with less higher-level than lower-level positions. If it does its recruitment, selection, and promotion jobs well, a point in its upward arc will be reached where it will have more talent than it can use—unless, of course, the company remains in a state of continuous expansion.

At this precise point it is a sound practice to provide for the outplacement of able managers. The man who is blocked because the path ahead of him is staffed by a supply of able men no older than he should be helped to leave. Such a program can be a powerful recruiting device because it assures the competent young man that he will grow either in the company or out of it.

The nation needs more of this type of mobility, and the larger, well-established companies can provide a real public service by preparing managers for other institutions in society that do not have the resources to develop their own. The worst thing a company can do is hoard its managerial talent, putting a good man on the shelf in order to hold him for inventory.

The emphasis on holding good men within a corporation is due to a misguided notion of loyalty. In the human-resources personnel system, a manager's loyalty is first to the organization purpose, then to his own professional skills, and finally to the contribution he makes to the overall society. For many men, the quickest way up to the top may involve a step sideways into another business, into another industry, or even into government or education. Such movements are all to the good, for there is a great danger to society in freezing managers with unfulfilled talent.

Financial Compensation as a Motivator

Clearly, the biggest deterrent to adequate managerial mobility is the holding power of financial compensation.

Inevitably, any exposition of a model career-progression plan must deal with the matter of compensation, for pay is the most powerful of all work motivators. For a good many years, American management accepted the premise that pay ranked low as an incentive to work. This view received support from certain psychological theories that arranged man's needs hierarchically, appearing to place the satisfaction of basic needs for food, shelter, and clothing well below the needs for understanding and self-actualization.

Pay is, however, a very complicated incentive because it satisfies not only man's biological but his human needs. Not only does it afford him the opportunity to acquire the outward symbols of the good life, but it constitutes an external success rating, a visible index of his accomplishments and his self-worth.

Because salary is so important, the general public takes a keen interest in it. Society has properly accepted the living-wage concept whereby everyone is paid first as a human being. But, when this concept interacts with another, less tenable principle—that all men are essentially equal—radical differences in compensation become unjustifiable. The most tangible product of the interaction of these two principles is the graduated income tax, which may constitute excellent economics and politics but represents very bad psychology. The graduated income tax really expresses a society's deep-seated fear of men with high talent. In a knowledge society, in particular, it makes far greater sense and might yield greater revenues to tax wealth, because such a tax would provide an incentive to the individual to work harder to retain his wealth. Instead, nations prefer to tax talent and energy—which seems very short-sighted.

Consequently, the ever increasing compression of managerial salaries erodes the effect of development and progression programs. An 86-company survey conducted by McKinsey & Company in 1968 examined executive compensation levels in different age groups. It concluded that the rise in starting salaries for management trainees had compressed pay differentials all the way to the top. Since World War II, these starting salaries had increased at twice the rate for executives generally; top executives were receiving a steadily smaller share of the total payroll. The compensation spread between outstanding and average young executives also was relatively narrow because of management's difficulty in evaluating the performance of the younger men. The report concluded that for better motivation of future executives more sophisticated tools for assessing individual performance were essential.[3]

Most managerial compensation plans, therefore, exhibit a pattern of stereotyped, accounting-based thinking that takes no notice of the motivational power of pay. They are based essentially on the notion of time and are tied more to training and experience than to job performance. The modern firm, to a large extent, has become a private welfare state, a development quite contrary to the older American ideal of rugged individualism. Salary increases are considered only after a period of *time* rather than after a period of *accomplishment*. And these increases are calculated within such narrowly defined limits that it is impossible to differentiate clearly and unambiguously between effective and mediocre performance.

In summary, the managerial compensation program must be tied directly to the human needs system, preferably to achievement or power needs rather than, as is most prevalent today, to affiliation and security needs. Companies will have to learn how to give managers the opportunity to earn a good deal of money for their efforts. The motivational program, then, must be built around the progression program and energized by a genuine performance-based compensation plan.

The Managerial Development Program

Supplementing both progression and motivation programs will be a genuine managerial development program that helps a manager to learn and to grow.

The object of a managerial development program is to provide opportunities for a manager to increase his capabilities, his understanding, and his self-confidence by exposure to job-related learning experiences. Development is personal; it is different from training and education, and it is self-initiated. *Training,* which is part of development, refers primarily to the acquisition of such skills as reading, writing, or public speaking. *Education* refers to the cultivation of the whole man as a member of society. *Development* is the realization of one's potential, and it is always the individual's responsibility. Not everyone can attain the status of a well-educated man,

[3] Arch Patton, "What Is Experience Worth?" *Business Horizons,* Vol. 11, No. 5 (Oct. 1968), pp. 31–40.

but everyone can develop his talents to the fullest. An organization, which can develop no one unless he chooses to be developed, creates opportunities for development through on-the-job and off-the-job programs.

On-the-Job Development

Development, being essentially a learning process, is subject to the laws of learning and involves pain, trial and error, and hard work. Development must come principally from on-the-job behavior. Formal coaching and instruction can contribute only 10 or 15 percent to an individual's growth. Mortimer Feinberg, president of BFS Psychological Associates, illustrates the real cost of management development with the following story.

A Long Island electronics-manufacturing company brought out an exciting new product which was developed, manufactured, and made ready for distribution at a unit cost of about $250. The president figured the product was worth $1,100 to his customers, but he was willing to settle for a selling price of $795. Complaining that even at $795 the product would never sell, several young product and sales managers asked for a price of $495. That was ludicrous to the president, who told them so, but they were so insistent that he eventually compromised at $595; that is, $200 less than he had wanted. Much to their surprise, the young marketing managers quickly found eager customers for about a thousand units. Somewhat ashamed, they admitted the new product sold so readily that it would have been bought at any price—certainly at the $795 level the president had originally established. "Well, we sold a thousand units," the president said, "and with each one we left $200 on the table. And $200,000 is a lot of tuition to pay for teaching young men how to price a product. I regret the loss, but I recognize its value. Assuming that these managers have learned their lesson, I am willing to educate them on my money in order to insure the future development of the organization. They are entitled to make mistakes —and, if they make the right mistakes, the mistakes are disastrous. That's the way most men learn."

Other top-level managers agree with this philosophy. As one bank officer said, "There are occasions when it is a good thing to have one of the young men make a bad loan. After he has done so and has sweat blood trying to work through that loan, he will be a much better loan officer." In other words, if a manager is to develop, he *must* learn how to make better decisions, and there is only one way to do this.

Unfortunately, however, many companies are afraid to let their managers make mistakes. Consequently, overprotected young men do not develop, and at the same time it is hard to get decisions in such organizations. There are times, of course, when even the slightest chance of a human error is intolerable—as when a plane is in an airport traffic pattern. But the lengths some companies and public agencies go to in the effort to prevent errors and inhibit learning in their managers is ridiculous.

Let us say that the probability of a manager's making a good decision is .80; that is, out of every 100 decisions he makes, 80 will be sound. To guard against the 20 poor decisions he will make, company policy may require him to secure the concurrence of another manager—who may also have a decision-probability accuracy of .80. Now the probability of an erroneous organization decision is reduced from 20 out of 100 to 4. But the probability of making a good decision is reduced from 80 to 64 and the number of "no decisions" is increased from zero to 32 out of every 100. If two or three more high-quality decision makers are added to the decision structure (a not unusual requirement), the possibility of an erroneous decision is virtually eliminated, but the probability of any decision at all also is reduced drastically and with it goes the chance for genuine managerial development.

Off-the-Job Development

To offset this climate of overprotection and to develop the managers that they need so badly, companies turn to a wide array of off-the-job instructional programs. For, as we stated in the first chapter, American management has placed its money on training as the solution of the managerial crisis and, like the society of which it is a part, has bought the idea of the educability of almost everyone. Training has become virtually a year-round proposition for many managers who are being forced to hit the books again after prolonged absence from the campus.

In pursuit of this training goal, many corporations have opened their own elaborate centers. The Western Electric Company, a wholly owned subsidiary of AT&T, recently dedicated a brand-new $5 million educational center in Hopewell, New Jersey. IBM has for many years maintained a center dedicated to management development at Sands Point, Long Island. General Electric's Management Development Institute at Crotonville, New

York, graduated its first class in 1928, and RCA's Institute is over 60 years old.

Annually, thousands of managers are sent to university programs and to American Management Association seminars and workshops. Other managers are enrolled in correspondence courses, and still others register directly in universities under what are known as tuition-refund programs— that is, their employers have agreed to remunerate them for the tuition charges if they successfully pass their courses.

Essentially, these are often shotgun approaches. The participants have been "sent to school" or have enrolled in courses on their own initiative without an adequate diagnosis of their real training needs. Thus they are subjected to various programs whether or not they can profit from the experience—that is, whether or not it will help them progress in their companies.

For example, a survey of tuition-refund practices made to determine how the courses completed by the students fitted in with their work responsibilities and their overall career development revealed that by and large, these courses were irrelevant. The company officials involved declared that the tuition-refund program was a fringe benefit designed to raise employee morale. As one personnel director put it, "If an employee thinks it is important to him and it keeps him happy on his job, we'll let him take apple culture, ballroom dancing, or piano playing."

The Evaluation Problem

The truth of the matter is that, while enormous amounts of management time and funds are being allocated annually to management training, comparatively little is being put into evaluating the effectiveness of these programs. Yet, if management training is to justify its cost, a program of evaluation must accompany it, offering evidence to support the training rationale and the effort put into it.

The few efforts at evaluation that have been made have used criteria that consisted mainly of behavior-change descriptions by the participants and others. And, while nearly all have suffered from methodological deficiencies, the principal weakness has been that they have offered no real evidence to show that the changes in behavior were due to the training or that it resulted in improved job performance.

A major obstacle to the demonstration of these effects lies in the interaction of the organizational climate and the subject's personality with his posttraining behavior. The literature on managerial effectiveness clearly indicates that performance on the job depends upon situational factors, among which the most important are organizational climate, the personality orientation of the job incumbent, and the task to be performed.

Perfect and absolute evaluation of any program is probably unreasonable but the effort will be well worthwhile and will yield many invaluable by-products in the form of deeper insights into the nature of adult development. It is probable that evaluations of training results will demonstrate that the short-run benefits claimed by most training programs are grossly *over*estimated but that the longer-run benefits may have been *under*estimated.

Need for Performance Evaluation

One basic problem stems from the fact that management development is not always related directly to management progress. And it is essential that the development program be coordinated with the selection program and tailored more specifically to critical role requirements. What is needed to make it more effective and to relate it to management progress is the establishment of a sound performance-evaluation program.

Performance evaluation has been roundly criticized because of the interviewing and appraisal inadequacies of the supervisor, the emotional stress on the person being evaluated, the apparent ineffectiveness of the evaluation procedure in effecting change, and its irrelevancy to the attainment of either individual goals or overall corporate objectives. In effect, critics contend, performance evaluation forces a supervisor to play God, embarrasses the employee, achieves at best inconclusive results, and is needlessly time-consuming.

The fact is, however, that evaluating the performance of a subordinate is central to the act of managing.[4] If the evaluation program is weak, the entire managerial process will be weak. Performance evaluation is the main channel by which supervisor and subordinate improve the latter's contribution to the organization effort. It provides the employee with advice and assistance and an idea of how he is doing, and it offers the supervisor in-

---

[4] For a more extended discussion of this idea see Felix M. Lopez, *Evaluating Employee Performance* (Chicago: Public Personnel Association, 1968), Ch. 12.

valuable information about problems and operations which he needs to make sound decisions.

The objective of performance evaluation is to improve a subordinate's performance in his current job duties. Other gains, such as the acquisition of information on which to base salary and promotion decisions and the personal development of the employee's capacities, accompany the main effect of improved job performance; but these are, in reality, only byproducts of the process. In most cases, however, byproducts unfortunately are substituted for the real objective, which is lost in the confusion.

The nature and the extent of communication between supervisor and supervised with respect to the final evaluation constitute the core of the process. If the interview is conducted poorly, the whole system suffers, and this frequently is the case because supervisors lack training and are very unskilled in this area. There is, too, a subconscious realization that performance evaluation is really a two-way process, that when a manager evaluates a subordinate he also evaluates his own ability as a manager.

The Trend Toward a Results Orientation

In evaluating an employee's performance, employers have traditionally used measures of his personal traits. But it has been contended recently that this process forces the evaluator into the role of a psychologist. The trend, therefore, has been to move toward a results-oriented evaluation, with particular emphasis on the technique known as *management by objectives*.

Management by objectives represents an effort by top management to minimize a tendency for organizational *procedures* to take precedence over organizational *purposes*. The idea is to establish a set of objectives for the corporation, to integrate individual goals with them, and to relate the rewards system to their accomplishment. The underlying assumption is that a manager's performance is properly evaluated by an appraisal of the events that occur as the result of his decisions.

While there seems to be a broad consensus today that this technique represents the surest approach to effective management, its implementation is no easy path. In its most commonly accepted form, management by objectives consists of an orderly sequence of setting goals at the top, communicating the goals to lower-unit managers, developing lower-unit goals that are phased into those set by higher levels, and eventually comparing the results with the goals. The system operates within a network of consultative interviews between supervisor and subordinate in which the subordinate is supposed to receive ample opportunity to establish his own objectives. The whole concept is oriented toward a value system based on the results achieved, and the results must be concrete and measurable.

When properly administered, management by objectives has much to recommend it. It involves the whole organization in a common purpose, it forces top management to think through its objectives, it sets practical work tasks for each individual manager, and it provides a means of insuring that organizational goals are eventually translated into specific assignments. But the experience of most organizations suggests that achieving satisfactory results from management by objectives is quite difficult because accomplishment becomes the measuring rod of managerial success. This idea creates problems of determining what an appropriate criterion of accomplishment may be and what effect that criterion may have on the manager himself. A manager who realizes that he is to be judged on specific achievements, that his career depends upon this judgment, will take steps to cope with it —steps that may be either constructive or destructive to the organization.

A more suitable way of evaluating managerial ability may be to make the *decision* the unit of analysis and evaluation rather than the objective or the result. While a manager may not be held accountable for his results (because many are due to events and circumstances beyond his control), he can be asked to answer for the decisions he does or does not make. Even though a decision leads to disastrous consequences, subsequent analysis may show that, with the information and time available when it was made, it was basically sound. Conversely, a poor decision that results in a happy outcome is still a poor decision. The point is that, over the long run, many sound decisions will lead to optimal organizational results.

In any event, it is difficult to see how a career-progression plan can be administered without a comprehensive, objective program of performance evaluation. Whether it be trait-oriented, results-oriented, or decision-oriented, the evaluation of performance provides information that can be obtained in no other way about a subordinate's effectiveness. The information can then be fed back into the selection and assessment systems to improve and strengthen them.

Individual Crises

In our discussion of the managerial crisis at the beginning of this book, we mentioned the fact that all living organisms encounter crises in their journey from infancy to old age. In the development and progress of his career, a manager also encounters points at which major changes occur.

Career Counseling for Managers

It is precisely at these points of crisis that counseling can be of the greatest value. Indeed, it is difficult to see how an adequate program of motivation or development can proceed without a career-counseling program.

Counseling is the provision of an opportunity for a person with a problem to define it and to explore possible solutions to it in the presence of an understanding person. Normally, we think of counseling as appropriate for young people in their choice of careers or for physically, emotionally, or financially troubled people. A so-called normal, healthy adult is not supposed to need advice and counsel. But nothing could be further from the truth.

Of all the individuals in an organization, managers are most in need of counseling. Because counseling is quite different from coaching, it is not a proper function for a supervisor. For adequate managerial progression and development, an organization must provide a suitable, independent counseling staff.

The Four Crucial Points

Managers face four major crises in their careers. The *first* crisis is exploratory in nature; it involves the determination of a career that fits the human needs of the individual manager. For some, this crisis is encountered and overcome in early college days; but, for many, it occurs in the early stages of employment.

The *second* crisis has to do with establishment in a career. The questions here are "How do I get ahead in my chosen field?" and "How do I prepare myself to excel in it?"

The *third* crisis is reached when a man's career arrives at the plateau stage, when he must face the realization that he is not likely to move any higher. This, the most devastating crisis of all, usually occurs in the early forties, but for some it can be postponed to the mid-fifties.

Finally, there is the *fourth* crisis. This is the onset of decline, the point in a manager's career when he must recognize that it is time for him to turn his work over to younger and now abler men. This crisis, too, can be a traumatic experience in a man's life, involving many personal tragedies.

An organization can do itself a favor by providing competent professional counseling for managers who need advice on how best to handle each of these career crises. Unfortunately, work in this field is now only in a primitive stage. But, as we move into the seventies and eighties, this special field of counseling will become an increasingly important and vital aspect of management development.

* * *

This, then, is the bare outline of managerial development seen as a systematic program of education and counseling. It is a key adjunct to a managerial progression program whose aim is to improve job performance and potential and, by so doing, to enhance the individual and the organization. A corporation that uses managerial development as a complement to its other three programs of procurement, progression, and motivation is well on the road toward the goal of all organizations: individual excellence and continuous self-renewal. And the attainment of these goals is the only solution to the managerial crisis.

Conclusion

And so we return full-circle to the notion with which we began this book—the managerial crisis. We have tried to show that it is not merely a crisis of numbers or of quality, but a crisis in the way in which managers are made. The making of a manager is more than the identification of those with the ability and the motivation to meet the challenges of the next 30 years. It means the creation of a total life-space in which this new manager can grow, contribute, and fulfill himself. It is apparent on all sides that, owing to outmoded notions of managerial identification and development, the managers of most of today's organizations are inadequate to the tasks that lie ahead. They do not know how to manage; they do not know how to decide; and they do not know how to adapt to the changing demands of their environment.

Consequently, in all our major institutions, public and private, there is such an excessive waste of human resources that the young, in particular, have become disillusioned. The task for today's managers is to create the conditions for tomorrow, to prepare their organizations to move into the future. What will be needed is a new concept of the manager, a manager who possesses the courage, the intelligence, and the sensitivity to see the enterprise in total perspective and to deal with the increasing load of non-programable decisions that will confront him in the new environment. This will require a searching look at the way managers are selected, developed, promoted, and motivated.

Present and past methods are no longer useful. At best, they can only be a prologue to the future.

Index

About the Author

Felix M. Lopez is president of IMPART, Inc., the research division of Behavioral Sciences Technology, Inc., a psychological consulting firm in New York City, and a professor at Long Island University's Arthur T. Roth School of Business Administration. Formerly he managed the manpower planning and research division and the selection and placement division of The Port of New York Authority.

Dr. Lopez is the author of *Evaluating Employee Performance, Personnel Interviewing: Theory and Practice,* and *Evaluating Executive Decision Making.* He earned his doctoral degree in personnel psychology at Columbia University.

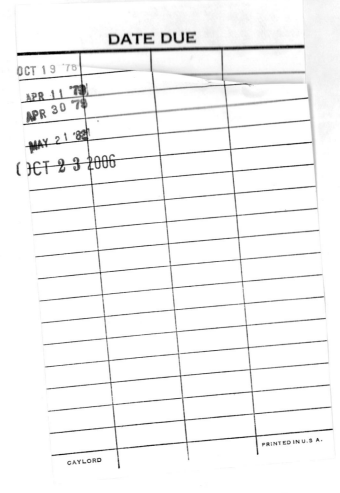

DATE DUE

OCT 19 '78			
APR 11 '79			
APR 30 '79			
MAY 21 '82			
OCT 2 3 2006			